C-4840

THIS IS YOUR **PASSBOOK**® FOR ...

HUMAN RESOURCES SPECIALIST (BENEFITS)

NATIONAL LEARNING CORPORATION®
passbooks.com

COPYRIGHT NOTICE

Copyright © 2020 by

NLC®

National Learning Corporation

212 Michael Drive, Syosset, NY 11791
(516) 921-8888 • www.passbooks.com
E-mail: info@passbooks.com

PUBLISHED IN THE UNITED STATES OF AMERICA

PASSBOOK® SERIES

THE *PASSBOOK® SERIES* has been created to prepare applicants and candidates for the ultimate academic battlefield – the examination room.

At some time in our lives, each and every one of us may be required to take an examination – for validation, matriculation, admission, qualification, registration, certification, or licensure.

Based on the assumption that every applicant or candidate has met the basic formal educational standards, has taken the required number of courses, and read the necessary texts, the *PASSBOOK® SERIES* furnishes the one special preparation which may assure passing with confidence, instead of failing with insecurity. Examination questions – together with answers – are furnished as the basic vehicle for study so that the mysteries of the examination and its compounding difficulties may be eliminated or diminished by a sure method.

This book is meant to help you pass your examination provided that you qualify and are serious in your objective.

The entire field is reviewed through the huge store of content information which is succinctly presented through a provocative and challenging approach – the question-and-answer method.

A climate of success is established by furnishing the correct answers at the end of each test.

You soon learn to recognize types of questions, forms of questions, and patterns of questioning. You may even begin to anticipate expected outcomes.

You perceive that many questions are repeated or adapted so that you can gain acute insights, which may enable you to score many sure points.

You learn how to confront new questions, or types of questions, and to attack them confidently and work out the correct answers.

You note objectives and emphases, and recognize pitfalls and dangers, so that you may make positive educational adjustments.

Moreover, you are kept fully informed in relation to new concepts, methods, practices, and directions in the field.

You discover that you arre actually taking the examination all the time: you are preparing for the examination by "taking" an examination, not by reading extraneous and/or supererogatory textbooks.

In short, this PASSBOOK®, used directedly, should be an important factor in helping you to pass your test.

HUMAN RESOURCES SPECIALIST (BENEFITS)

DUTIES:

Human Resources Specialist II (Benefits) may supervise, train, and schedule work of subordinates; or direct teams engaged in benefit analysis, procedural reengineering, recommending or implementing administrative improvements, including new technologies. They provide direction and assistance to staff in dealing with more complex cases; identify specific issues needing policy clarification; and may be assigned to benchmark items against other employer groups, or to work with counsel's office to evaluate the legal implications of law, rule or regulations on benefits, and the need to seek appropriate revision(s).

Human Resources Specialist II (Benefits Contracts) may function as contract managers for benefit program contracts having smaller annual dollar value. Under general supervision, incumbents perform analysis, participate in the contractor selection process, review and interpret the analytical work of others, serve as liaisons to the insurance carriers, and obtain all necessary reporting data required to appropriately administer the new contract(s) or specific portions of areas of an existing contract.

Human Resources Specialist IV (Benefits) serves as program managers of significant organizational units. They plan, supervise, and coordinate the activities of staff, outsourced vendor/consultant specialists, and interact with representatives of other organizations of jurisdictions with interests in the State employee benefit packages, including public employee unions, associations of interested enrollees, labor/management committees, the Civil Service Commission, the Division of the Budget, the Governor's Office of Employee Relations, and the Office of the State Comptroller.

Human Resources Specialist IV (Benefits Contracts) train and supervise staff engaged in the administration of a wide variety of benefit plans and programs for employees and retirees of state agencies, other participating employers and agencies, and jurisdictions eligible to offer State employee benefit plans to their public employees. They direct and participate in the development of procurement and contract documents and prepare internal and review external reports containing specific analysis pertaining to the utilization, cost and value of existing benefits, as well as proposed benefit changes. Incumbents usually function as contract managers for at least one major benefit plan or program with an annual value of several hundred million dollars.

SUBJECT OF EXAMINATION:

The written test is designed to test for knowledge, skills, and/or abilities in such areas as:

1. **Written expression** - These questions test for the writing skills used in composing memos, reports and correspondence, as well as in reviewing documents produced by others. Both sentence skills and paragraph skills are addressed. The specific points tested include grammar, usage, punctuation, sentence structure, appropriate and correct content, editing, and organizing sentences into well-constructed paragraphs.

2. **Analytic reasoning** - These questions test for the ability to understand information that is provided in a variety of formats and to reason logically. These questions require candidates to perform tasks such as interpreting information, distinguishing between relevant and irrelevant information, determining whether a set of information is complete, and determining whether particular conclusions are correct.

3. **Working effectively with others within and outside your organization** - These questions test for knowledge of the principles used when interacting with individuals and agencies to inform them about topics of concern, clarify agency programs or policies, negotiate x conflicts or resolve complaints, and represent one's agency or program in a professional, effective manner. Questions may also cover working cooperatively with staff of one's own agency or other agencies.

4. **Supervision** - These questions test for knowledge of the principles and practices employed in planning, organizing, and controlling the activities of a work unit toward predetermined objectives. The concepts covered, usually in a situational question format, include such topics as assigning and reviewing work; evaluating performance; maintaining work standards; motivating and developing subordinates; implementing procedural change; increasing efficiency; and dealing with problems of absenteeism, morale, and discipline.

5. **Administrative supervision and management** - These questions test for knowledge of the principles and practices involved in providing supervision to subordinate supervisors and indirect supervision to their unit staff as well as the effective management of work. Questions will cover such areas as assigning and reviewing the work of several units; planning, implementing, and evaluating work initiatives; ensuring the timely and successful completion of unit work; resolving issues around work assignments and staff performance; evaluating the performance of subordinate supervisors; hiring and developing staff; monitoring work performance; implementing change; and dealing with problems of absenteeism, morale, and discipline.

HOW TO TAKE A TEST

I. YOU MUST PASS AN EXAMINATION

A. *WHAT EVERY CANDIDATE SHOULD KNOW*

Examination applicants often ask us for help in preparing for the written test. What can I study in advance? What kinds of questions will be asked? How will the test be given? How will the papers be graded?

As an applicant for a civil service examination, you may be wondering about some of these things. Our purpose here is to suggest effective methods of advance study and to describe civil service examinations.

Your chances for success on this examination can be increased if you know how to prepare. Those "pre-examination jitters" can be reduced if you know what to expect. You can even experience an adventure in good citizenship if you know why civil service exams are given.

B. *WHY ARE CIVIL SERVICE EXAMINATIONS GIVEN?*

Civil service examinations are important to you in two ways. As a citizen, you want public jobs filled by employees who know how to do their work. As a job seeker, you want a fair chance to compete for that job on an equal footing with other candidates. The best-known means of accomplishing this two-fold goal is the competitive examination.

Exams are widely publicized throughout the nation. They may be administered for jobs in federal, state, city, municipal, town or village governments or agencies.

Any citizen may apply, with some limitations, such as the age or residence of applicants. Your experience and education may be reviewed to see whether you meet the requirements for the particular examination. When these requirements exist, they are reasonable and applied consistently to all applicants. Thus, a competitive examination may cause you some uneasiness now, but it is your privilege and safeguard.

C. *HOW ARE CIVIL SERVICE EXAMS DEVELOPED?*

Examinations are carefully written by trained technicians who are specialists in the field known as "psychological measurement," in consultation with recognized authorities in the field of work that the test will cover. These experts recommend the subject matter areas or skills to be tested; only those knowledges or skills important to your success on the job are included. The most reliable books and source materials available are used as references. Together, the experts and technicians judge the difficulty level of the questions.

Test technicians know how to phrase questions so that the problem is clearly stated. Their ethics do not permit "trick" or "catch" questions. Questions may have been tried out on sample groups, or subjected to statistical analysis, to determine their usefulness.

Written tests are often used in combination with performance tests, ratings of training and experience, and oral interviews. All of these measures combine to form the best-known means of finding the right person for the right job.

II. HOW TO PASS THE WRITTEN TEST

A. NATURE OF THE EXAMINATION

To prepare intelligently for civil service examinations, you should know how they differ from school examinations you have taken. In school you were assigned certain definite pages to read or subjects to cover. The examination questions were quite detailed and usually emphasized memory. Civil service exams, on the other hand, try to discover your present ability to perform the duties of a position, plus your potentiality to learn these duties. In other words, a civil service exam attempts to predict how successful you will be. Questions cover such a broad area that they cannot be as minute and detailed as school exam questions.

In the public service similar kinds of work, or positions, are grouped together in one "class." This process is known as *position-classification*. All the positions in a class are paid according to the salary range for that class. One class title covers all of these positions, and they are all tested by the same examination.

B. FOUR BASIC STEPS

1) Study the announcement

How, then, can you know what subjects to study? Our best answer is: "Learn as much as possible about the class of positions for which you've applied." The exam will test the knowledge, skills and abilities needed to do the work.

Your most valuable source of information about the position you want is the official exam announcement. This announcement lists the training and experience qualifications. Check these standards and apply only if you come reasonably close to meeting them.

The brief description of the position in the examination announcement offers some clues to the subjects which will be tested. Think about the job itself. Review the duties in your mind. Can you perform them, or are there some in which you are rusty? Fill in the blank spots in your preparation.

Many jurisdictions preview the written test in the exam announcement by including a section called "Knowledge and Abilities Required," "Scope of the Examination," or some similar heading. Here you will find out specifically what fields will be tested.

2) Review your own background

Once you learn in general what the position is all about, and what you need to know to do the work, ask yourself which subjects you already know fairly well and which need improvement. You may wonder whether to concentrate on improving your strong areas or on building some background in your fields of weakness. When the announcement has specified "some knowledge" or "considerable knowledge," or has used adjectives like "beginning principles of..." or "advanced ... methods," you can get a clue as to the number and difficulty of questions to be asked in any given field. More questions, and hence broader coverage, would be included for those subjects which are more important in the work. Now weigh your strengths and weaknesses against the job requirements and prepare accordingly.

3) Determine the level of the position

Another way to tell how intensively you should prepare is to understand the level of the job for which you are applying. Is it the entering level? In other words, is this the position in which beginners in a field of work are hired? Or is it an intermediate or advanced level? Sometimes this is indicated by such words as "Junior" or "Senior" in the class title. Other jurisdictions use Roman numerals to designate the level – Clerk I, Clerk II, for example. The word "Supervisor" sometimes appears in the title. If the level is not indicated by the title, check the description of duties. Will you be working under very close supervision, or will you have responsibility for independent decisions in this work?

4) Choose appropriate study materials

Now that you know the subjects to be examined and the relative amount of each subject to be covered, you can choose suitable study materials. For beginning level jobs, or even advanced ones, if you have a pronounced weakness in some aspect of your training, read a modern, standard textbook in that field. Be sure it is up to date and has general coverage. Such books are normally available at your library, and the librarian will be glad to help you locate one. For entry-level positions, questions of appropriate difficulty are chosen – neither highly advanced questions, nor those too simple. Such questions require careful thought but not advanced training.

If the position for which you are applying is technical or advanced, you will read more advanced, specialized material. If you are already familiar with the basic principles of your field, elementary textbooks would waste your time. Concentrate on advanced textbooks and technical periodicals. Think through the concepts and review difficult problems in your field.

These are all general sources. You can get more ideas on your own initiative, following these leads. For example, training manuals and publications of the government agency which employs workers in your field can be useful, particularly for technical and professional positions. A letter or visit to the government department involved may result in more specific study suggestions, and certainly will provide you with a more definite idea of the exact nature of the position you are seeking.

III. KINDS OF TESTS

Tests are used for purposes other than measuring knowledge and ability to perform specified duties. For some positions, it is equally important to test ability to make adjustments to new situations or to profit from training. In others, basic mental abilities not dependent on information are essential. Questions which test these things may not appear as pertinent to the duties of the position as those which test for knowledge and information. Yet they are often highly important parts of a fair examination. For very general questions, it is almost impossible to help you direct your study efforts. What we can do is to point out some of the more common of these general abilities needed in public service positions and describe some typical questions.

1) General information

Broad, general information has been found useful for predicting job success in some kinds of work. This is tested in a variety of ways, from vocabulary lists to questions about current events. Basic background in some field of work, such as sociology or economics, may be sampled in a group of questions. Often these are principles which have become familiar to most persons through exposure rather than through formal training. It is difficult to advise you how to study for these questions; being alert to the world around you is our best suggestion.

2) Verbal ability

An example of an ability needed in many positions is verbal or language ability. Verbal ability is, in brief, the ability to use and understand words. Vocabulary and grammar tests are typical measures of this ability. Reading comprehension or paragraph interpretation questions are common in many kinds of civil service tests. You are given a paragraph of written material and asked to find its central meaning.

3) Numerical ability

Number skills can be tested by the familiar arithmetic problem, by checking paired lists of numbers to see which are alike and which are different, or by interpreting charts and graphs. In the latter test, a graph may be printed in the test booklet which you are asked to use as the basis for answering questions.

4) Observation

A popular test for law-enforcement positions is the observation test. A picture is shown to you for several minutes, then taken away. Questions about the picture test your ability to observe both details and larger elements.

5) Following directions

In many positions in the public service, the employee must be able to carry out written instructions dependably and accurately. You may be given a chart with several columns, each column listing a variety of information. The questions require you to carry out directions involving the information given in the chart.

6) Skills and aptitudes

Performance tests effectively measure some manual skills and aptitudes. When the skill is one in which you are trained, such as typing or shorthand, you can practice. These tests are often very much like those given in business school or high school courses. For many of the other skills and aptitudes, however, no short-time preparation can be made. Skills and abilities natural to you or that you have developed throughout your lifetime are being tested.

Many of the general questions just described provide all the data needed to answer the questions and ask you to use your reasoning ability to find the answers. Your best preparation for these tests, as well as for tests of facts and ideas, is to be at your physical and mental best. You, no doubt, have your own methods of getting into an exam-taking mood and keeping "in shape." The next section lists some ideas on this subject.

IV. KINDS OF QUESTIONS

Only rarely is the "essay" question, which you answer in narrative form, used in civil service tests. Civil service tests are usually of the short-answer type. Full instructions for answering these questions will be given to you at the examination. But in case this is your first experience with short-answer questions and separate answer sheets, here is what you need to know:

1) Multiple-choice Questions

Most popular of the short-answer questions is the "multiple choice" or "best answer" question. It can be used, for example, to test for factual knowledge, ability to solve problems or judgment in meeting situations found at work.

A multiple-choice question is normally one of three types—

- It can begin with an incomplete statement followed by several possible endings. You are to find the one ending which *best* completes the statement, although some of the others may not be entirely wrong.
- It can also be a complete statement in the form of a question which is answered by choosing one of the statements listed.
- It can be in the form of a problem – again you select the best answer.

Here is an example of a multiple-choice question with a discussion which should give you some clues as to the method for choosing the right answer:

When an employee has a complaint about his assignment, the action which will *best* help him overcome his difficulty is to
A. discuss his difficulty with his coworkers
B. take the problem to the head of the organization
C. take the problem to the person who gave him the assignment
D. say nothing to anyone about his complaint

In answering this question, you should study each of the choices to find which is best. Consider choice "A" – Certainly an employee may discuss his complaint with fellow employees, but no change or improvement can result, and the complaint remains unresolved. Choice "B" is a poor choice since the head of the organization probably does not know what assignment you have been given, and taking your problem to him is known as "going over the head" of the supervisor. The supervisor, or person who made the assignment, is the person who can clarify it or correct any injustice. Choice "C" is, therefore, correct. To say nothing, as in choice "D," is unwise. Supervisors have and interest in knowing the problems employees are facing, and the employee is seeking a solution to his problem.

2) True/False Questions

The "true/false" or "right/wrong" form of question is sometimes used. Here a complete statement is given. Your job is to decide whether the statement is right or wrong.

SAMPLE: A roaming cell-phone call to a nearby city costs less than a non-roaming call to a distant city.

This statement is wrong, or false, since roaming calls are more expensive.
This is not a complete list of all possible question forms, although most of the others are variations of these common types. You will always get complete directions for

answering questions. Be sure you understand *how* to mark your answers – ask questions until you do.

V. RECORDING YOUR ANSWERS

Computer terminals are used more and more today for many different kinds of exams.

For an examination with very few applicants, you may be told to record your answers in the test booklet itself. Separate answer sheets are much more common. If this separate answer sheet is to be scored by machine – and this is often the case – it is highly important that you mark your answers correctly in order to get credit.

An electronic scoring machine is often used in civil service offices because of the speed with which papers can be scored. Machine-scored answer sheets must be marked with a pencil, which will be given to you. This pencil has a high graphite content which responds to the electronic scoring machine. As a matter of fact, stray dots may register as answers, so do not let your pencil rest on the answer sheet while you are pondering the correct answer. Also, if your pencil lead breaks or is otherwise defective, ask for another.

Since the answer sheet will be dropped in a slot in the scoring machine, be careful not to bend the corners or get the paper crumpled.

The answer sheet normally has five vertical columns of numbers, with 30 numbers to a column. These numbers correspond to the question numbers in your test booklet. After each number, going across the page are four or five pairs of dotted lines. These short dotted lines have small letters or numbers above them. The first two pairs may also have a "T" or "F" above the letters. This indicates that the first two pairs only are to be used if the questions are of the true-false type. If the questions are multiple choice, disregard the "T" and "F" and pay attention only to the small letters or numbers.

Answer your questions in the manner of the sample that follows:

    32. The largest city in the United States is
            A. Washington, D.C.
            B. New York City
            C. Chicago
            D. Detroit
            E. San Francisco

    1) Choose the answer you think is best. (New York City is the largest, so "B" is
        correct.)
    2) Find the row of dotted lines numbered the same as the question you are
        answering. (Find row number 32)
    3) Find the pair of dotted lines corresponding to the answer. (Find the pair of
        lines under the mark "B.")
    4) Make a solid black mark between the dotted lines.

VI. BEFORE THE TEST

Common sense will help you find procedures to follow to get ready for an examination. Too many of us, however, overlook these sensible measures. Indeed, nervousness and fatigue have been found to be the most serious reasons why applicants fail to do their best on civil service tests. Here is a list of reminders:

- Begin your preparation early – Don't wait until the last minute to go scurrying around for books and materials or to find out what the position is all about.
- Prepare continuously – An hour a night for a week is better than an all-night cram session. This has been definitely established. What is more, a night a week for a month will return better dividends than crowding your study into a shorter period of time.
- Locate the place of the exam – You have been sent a notice telling you when and where to report for the examination. If the location is in a different town or otherwise unfamiliar to you, it would be well to inquire the best route and learn something about the building.
- Relax the night before the test – Allow your mind to rest. Do not study at all that night. Plan some mild recreation or diversion; then go to bed early and get a good night's sleep.
- Get up early enough to make a leisurely trip to the place for the test – This way unforeseen events, traffic snarls, unfamiliar buildings, etc. will not upset you.
- Dress comfortably – A written test is not a fashion show. You will be known by number and not by name, so wear something comfortable.
- Leave excess paraphernalia at home – Shopping bags and odd bundles will get in your way. You need bring only the items mentioned in the official notice you received; usually everything you need is provided. Do not bring reference books to the exam. They will only confuse those last minutes and be taken away from you when in the test room.
- Arrive somewhat ahead of time – If because of transportation schedules you must get there very early, bring a newspaper or magazine to take your mind off yourself while waiting.
- Locate the examination room – When you have found the proper room, you will be directed to the seat or part of the room where you will sit. Sometimes you are given a sheet of instructions to read while you are waiting. Do not fill out any forms until you are told to do so; just read them and be prepared.
- Relax and prepare to listen to the instructions
- If you have any physical problem that may keep you from doing your best, be sure to tell the test administrator. If you are sick or in poor health, you really cannot do your best on the exam. You can come back and take the test some other time.

VII. AT THE TEST

The day of the test is here and you have the test booklet in your hand. The temptation to get going is very strong. Caution! There is more to success than knowing the right answers. You must know how to identify your papers and understand variations in the type of short-answer question used in this particular examination. Follow these suggestions for maximum results from your efforts:

1) Cooperate with the monitor

The test administrator has a duty to create a situation in which you can be as much at ease as possible. He will give instructions, tell you when to begin, check to see that you are marking your answer sheet correctly, and so on. He is not there to guard you, although he will see that your competitors do not take unfair advantage. He wants to help you do your best.

2) Listen to all instructions

Don't jump the gun! Wait until you understand all directions. In most civil service tests you get more time than you need to answer the questions. So don't be in a hurry. Read each word of instructions until you clearly understand the meaning. Study the examples, listen to all announcements and follow directions. Ask questions if you do not understand what to do.

3) Identify your papers

Civil service exams are usually identified by number only. You will be assigned a number; you must not put your name on your test papers. Be sure to copy your number correctly. Since more than one exam may be given, copy your exact examination title.

4) Plan your time

Unless you are told that a test is a "speed" or "rate of work" test, speed itself is usually not important. Time enough to answer all the questions will be provided, but this does not mean that you have all day. An overall time limit has been set. Divide the total time (in minutes) by the number of questions to determine the approximate time you have for each question.

5) Do not linger over difficult questions

If you come across a difficult question, mark it with a paper clip (useful to have along) and come back to it when you have been through the booklet. One caution if you do this – be sure to skip a number on your answer sheet as well. Check often to be sure that you have not lost your place and that you are marking in the row numbered the same as the question you are answering.

6) Read the questions

Be sure you know what the question asks! Many capable people are unsuccessful because they failed to *read* the questions correctly.

7) Answer all questions

Unless you have been instructed that a penalty will be deducted for incorrect answers, it is better to guess than to omit a question.

8) Speed tests

It is often better NOT to guess on speed tests. It has been found that on timed tests people are tempted to spend the last few seconds before time is called in marking answers at random – without even reading them – in the hope of picking up a few extra points. To discourage this practice, the instructions may warn you that your score will be "corrected" for guessing. That is, a penalty will be applied. The incorrect answers will be deducted from the correct ones, or some other penalty formula will be used.

9) Review your answers

If you finish before time is called, go back to the questions you guessed or omitted to give them further thought. Review other answers if you have time.

10) Return your test materials

If you are ready to leave before others have finished or time is called, take ALL your materials to the monitor and leave quietly. Never take any test material with you. The monitor can discover whose papers are not complete, and taking a test booklet may be grounds for disqualification.

VIII. EXAMINATION TECHNIQUES

1) Read the general instructions carefully. These are usually printed on the first page of the exam booklet. As a rule, these instructions refer to the timing of the examination; the fact that you should not start work until the signal and must stop work at a signal, etc. If there are any *special* instructions, such as a choice of questions to be answered, make sure that you note this instruction carefully.

2) When you are ready to start work on the examination, that is as soon as the signal has been given, read the instructions to each question booklet, underline any key words or phrases, such as *least, best, outline, describe* and the like. In this way you will tend to answer as requested rather than discover on reviewing your paper that you *listed without describing*, that you selected the *worst* choice rather than the *best* choice, etc.

3) If the examination is of the objective or multiple-choice type – that is, each question will also give a series of possible answers: A, B, C or D, and you are called upon to select the best answer and write the letter next to that answer on your answer paper – it is advisable to start answering each question in turn. There may be anywhere from 50 to 100 such questions in the three or four hours allotted and you can see how much time would be taken if you read through all the questions before beginning to answer any. Furthermore, if you come across a question or group of questions which you know would be difficult to answer, it would undoubtedly affect your handling of all the other questions.

4) If the examination is of the essay type and contains but a few questions, it is a moot point as to whether you should read all the questions before starting to answer any one. Of course, if you are given a choice – say five out of seven and the like – then it is essential to read all the questions so you can eliminate the two that are most difficult. If, however, you are asked to answer all the questions, there may be danger in trying to answer the easiest one first because you may find that you will spend too much time on it. The best technique is to answer the first question, then proceed to the second, etc.

5) Time your answers. Before the exam begins, write down the time it started, then add the time allowed for the examination and write down the time it must be completed, then divide the time available somewhat as follows:

- If 3-1/2 hours are allowed, that would be 210 minutes. If you have 80 objective-type questions, that would be an average of 2-1/2 minutes per question. Allow yourself no more than 2 minutes per question, or a total of 160 minutes, which will permit about 50 minutes to review.
- If for the time allotment of 210 minutes there are 7 essay questions to answer, that would average about 30 minutes a question. Give yourself only 25 minutes per question so that you have about 35 minutes to review.

6) The most important instruction is to *read each question* and make sure you know what is wanted. The second most important instruction is to *time yourself properly* so that you answer every question. The third most important instruction is to *answer every question*. Guess if you have to but include something for each question. Remember that you will receive no credit for a blank and will probably receive some credit if you write something in answer to an essay question. If you guess a letter – say "B" for a multiple-choice question – you may have guessed right. If you leave a blank as an answer to a multiple-choice question, the examiners may respect your feelings but it will not add a point to your score. Some exams may penalize you for wrong answers, so in such cases *only*, you may not want to guess unless you have some basis for your answer.

7) Suggestions
   a. Objective-type questions
      1. Examine the question booklet for proper sequence of pages and questions
      2. Read all instructions carefully
      3. Skip any question which seems too difficult; return to it after all other questions have been answered
      4. Apportion your time properly; do not spend too much time on any single question or group of questions
      5. Note and underline key words – *all, most, fewest, least, best, worst, same, opposite,* etc.
      6. Pay particular attention to negatives
      7. Note unusual option, e.g., unduly long, short, complex, different or similar in content to the body of the question
      8. Observe the use of "hedging" words – *probably, may, most likely,* etc.
      9. Make sure that your answer is put next to the same number as the question
      10. Do not second-guess unless you have good reason to believe the second answer is definitely more correct
      11. Cross out original answer if you decide another answer is more accurate; do not erase until you are ready to hand your paper in
      12. Answer all questions; guess unless instructed otherwise
      13. Leave time for review

   b. Essay questions
      1. Read each question carefully
      2. Determine exactly what is wanted. Underline key words or phrases.
      3. Decide on outline or paragraph answer

4. Include many different points and elements unless asked to develop any one or two points or elements
5. Show impartiality by giving pros and cons unless directed to select one side only
6. Make and write down any assumptions you find necessary to answer the questions
7. Watch your English, grammar, punctuation and choice of words
8. Time your answers; don't crowd material

8) Answering the essay question

Most essay questions can be answered by framing the specific response around several key words or ideas. Here are a few such key words or ideas:

M's: manpower, materials, methods, money, management
P's: purpose, program, policy, plan, procedure, practice, problems, pitfalls, personnel, public relations
   a. Six basic steps in handling problems:
      1. Preliminary plan and background development
      2. Collect information, data and facts
      3. Analyze and interpret information, data and facts
      4. Analyze and develop solutions as well as make recommendations
      5. Prepare report and sell recommendations
      6. Install recommendations and follow up effectiveness

   b. Pitfalls to avoid
      1. *Taking things for granted* – A statement of the situation does not necessarily imply that each of the elements is necessarily true; for example, a complaint may be invalid and biased so that all that can be taken for granted is that a complaint has been registered
      2. *Considering only one side of a situation* – Wherever possible, indicate several alternatives and then point out the reasons you selected the best one
      3. *Failing to indicate follow up* – Whenever your answer indicates action on your part, make certain that you will take proper follow-up action to see how successful your recommendations, procedures or actions turn out to be
      4. *Taking too long in answering any single question* – Remember to time your answers properly

IX. AFTER THE TEST

Scoring procedures differ in detail among civil service jurisdictions although the general principles are the same. Whether the papers are hand-scored or graded by machine we have described, they are nearly always graded by number. That is, the person who marks the paper knows only the number – never the name – of the applicant. Not until all the papers have been graded will they be matched with names. If other tests, such as training and experience or oral interview ratings have been given, scores will be combined. Different parts of the examination usually have different weights. For example, the written test might count 60 percent of the final grade, and a rating of training and experience 40 percent. In many jurisdictions, veterans will have a certain number of points added to their grades.

After the final grade has been determined, the names are placed in grade order and an eligible list is established. There are various methods for resolving ties between those who get the same final grade – probably the most common is to place first the name of the person whose application was received first. Job offers are made from the eligible list in the order the names appear on it. You will be notified of your grade and your rank as soon as all these computations have been made. This will be done as rapidly as possible.

People who are found to meet the requirements in the announcement are called "eligibles." Their names are put on a list of eligible candidates. An eligible's chances of getting a job depend on how high he stands on this list and how fast agencies are filling jobs from the list.

When a job is to be filled from a list of eligibles, the agency asks for the names of people on the list of eligibles for that job. When the civil service commission receives this request, it sends to the agency the names of the three people highest on this list. Or, if the job to be filled has specialized requirements, the office sends the agency the names of the top three persons who meet these requirements from the general list.

The appointing officer makes a choice from among the three people whose names were sent to him. If the selected person accepts the appointment, the names of the others are put back on the list to be considered for future openings.

That is the rule in hiring from all kinds of eligible lists, whether they are for typist, carpenter, chemist, or something else. For every vacancy, the appointing officer has his choice of any one of the top three eligibles on the list. This explains why the person whose name is on top of the list sometimes does not get an appointment when some of the persons lower on the list do. If the appointing officer chooses the second or third eligible, the No. 1 eligible does not get a job at once, but stays on the list until he is appointed or the list is terminated.

X. HOW TO PASS THE INTERVIEW TEST

The examination for which you applied requires an oral interview test. You have already taken the written test and you are now being called for the interview test – the final part of the formal examination.

You may think that it is not possible to prepare for an interview test and that there are no procedures to follow during an interview. Our purpose is to point out some things you can do in advance that will help you and some good rules to follow and pitfalls to avoid while you are being interviewed.

What is an interview supposed to test?

The written examination is designed to test the technical knowledge and competence of the candidate; the oral is designed to evaluate intangible qualities, not readily measured otherwise, and to establish a list showing the relative fitness of each candidate – as measured against his competitors – for the position sought. Scoring is not on the basis of "right" and "wrong," but on a sliding scale of values ranging from "not passable" to "outstanding." As a matter of fact, it is possible to achieve a relatively low score without a single "incorrect" answer because of evident weakness in the qualities being measured.

Occasionally, an examination may consist entirely of an oral test – either an individual or a group oral. In such cases, information is sought concerning the technical knowledges and abilities of the candidate, since there has been no written examination for this purpose. More commonly, however, an oral test is used to supplement a written examination.

Who conducts interviews?

The composition of oral boards varies among different jurisdictions. In nearly all, a representative of the personnel department serves as chairman. One of the members of the board may be a representative of the department in which the candidate would work. In some cases, "outside experts" are used, and, frequently, a businessman or some other representative of the general public is asked to serve. Labor and management or other special groups may be represented. The aim is to secure the services of experts in the appropriate field.

However the board is composed, it is a good idea (and not at all improper or unethical) to ascertain in advance of the interview who the members are and what groups they represent. When you are introduced to them, you will have some idea of their backgrounds and interests, and at least you will not stutter and stammer over their names.

What should be done before the interview?

While knowledge about the board members is useful and takes some of the surprise element out of the interview, there is other preparation which is more substantive. It *is* possible to prepare for an oral interview – in several ways:

1) Keep a copy of your application and review it carefully before the interview

This may be the only document before the oral board, and the starting point of the interview. Know what education and experience you have listed there, and the sequence and dates of all of it. Sometimes the board will ask you to review the highlights of your experience for them; you should not have to hem and haw doing it.

2) Study the class specification and the examination announcement

Usually, the oral board has one or both of these to guide them. The qualities, characteristics or knowledges required by the position sought are stated in these documents. They offer valuable clues as to the nature of the oral interview. For example, if the job involves supervisory responsibilities, the announcement will usually indicate that knowledge of modern supervisory methods and the qualifications of the candidate as a supervisor will be tested. If so, you can expect such questions, frequently in the form of a hypothetical situation which you are expected to solve. NEVER go into an oral without knowledge of the duties and responsibilities of the job you seek.

3) Think through each qualification required

Try to visualize the kind of questions you would ask if you were a board member. How well could you answer them? Try especially to appraise your own knowledge and background in each area, *measured against the job sought*, and identify any areas in which you are weak. Be critical and realistic – do not flatter yourself.

4) Do some general reading in areas in which you feel you may be weak

For example, if the job involves supervision and your past experience has NOT, some general reading in supervisory methods and practices, particularly in the field of human relations, might be useful. Do NOT study agency procedures or detailed manuals. The oral board will be testing your understanding and capacity, not your memory.

5) Get a good night's sleep and watch your general health and mental attitude

You will want a clear head at the interview. Take care of a cold or any other minor ailment, and of course, no hangovers.

What should be done on the day of the interview?

Now comes the day of the interview itself. Give yourself plenty of time to get there. Plan to arrive somewhat ahead of the scheduled time, particularly if your appointment is in the fore part of the day. If a previous candidate fails to appear, the board might be ready for you a bit early. By early afternoon an oral board is almost invariably behind schedule if there are many candidates, and you may have to wait. Take along a book or magazine to read, or your application to review, but leave any extraneous material in the waiting room when you go in for your interview. In any event, relax and compose yourself.

The matter of dress is important. The board is forming impressions about you – from your experience, your manners, your attitude, and your appearance. Give your personal appearance careful attention. Dress your best, but not your flashiest. Choose conservative, appropriate clothing, and be sure it is immaculate. This is a business interview, and your appearance should indicate that you regard it as such. Besides, being well groomed and properly dressed will help boost your confidence.

Sooner or later, someone will call your name and escort you into the interview room. *This is it.* From here on you are on your own. It is too late for any more preparation. But remember, you asked for this opportunity to prove your fitness, and you are here because your request was granted.

What happens when you go in?

The usual sequence of events will be as follows: The clerk (who is often the board stenographer) will introduce you to the chairman of the oral board, who will introduce you to the other members of the board. Acknowledge the introductions before you sit down. Do not be surprised if you find a microphone facing you or a stenotypist sitting by. Oral interviews are usually recorded in the event of an appeal or other review.

Usually the chairman of the board will open the interview by reviewing the highlights of your education and work experience from your application – primarily for the benefit of the other members of the board, as well as to get the material into the record. Do not interrupt or comment unless there is an error or significant misinterpretation; if that is the case, do not hesitate. But do not quibble about insignificant matters. Also, he will usually ask you some question about your education, experience or your present job – partly to get you to start talking and to establish the interviewing "rapport." He may start the actual questioning, or turn it over to one of the other members. Frequently, each member undertakes the questioning on a particular area, one in which he is perhaps most competent, so you can expect each member to participate in the examination. Because time is limited, you may also expect some rather abrupt switches in the direction the questioning takes, so do not be upset by it. Normally, a board member will not pursue a single line of questioning unless he discovers a particular strength or weakness.

After each member has participated, the chairman will usually ask whether any member has any further questions, then will ask you if you have anything you wish to add. Unless you are expecting this question, it may floor you. Worse, it may start you off on an extended, extemporaneous speech. The board is not usually seeking more information. The question is principally to offer you a last opportunity to present further qualifications or to indicate that you have nothing to add. So, if you feel that a significant qualification or characteristic has been overlooked, it is proper to point it out in a sentence or so. Do not compliment the board on the thoroughness of their examination – they have been sketchy, and you know it. If you wish, merely say, "No thank you, I have nothing further to add." This is a point where you can "talk yourself out" of a good impression or fail to present an important bit of information. Remember, *you close the interview yourself.*

The chairman will then say, "That is all, Mr. _____, thank you." Do not be startled; the interview is over, and quicker than you think. Thank him, gather your belongings and take your leave. Save your sigh of relief for the other side of the door.

How to put your best foot forward

Throughout this entire process, you may feel that the board individually and collectively is trying to pierce your defenses, seek out your hidden weaknesses and embarrass and confuse you. Actually, this is not true. They are obliged to make an appraisal of your qualifications for the job you are seeking, and they want to see you in your best light. Remember, they must interview all candidates and a non-cooperative candidate may become a failure in spite of their best efforts to bring out his qualifications. Here are 15 suggestions that will help you:

1) Be natural – Keep your attitude confident, not cocky

If you are not confident that you can do the job, do not expect the board to be. Do not apologize for your weaknesses, try to bring out your strong points. The board is interested in a positive, not negative, presentation. Cockiness will antagonize any board member and make him wonder if you are covering up a weakness by a false show of strength.

2) Get comfortable, but don't lounge or sprawl

Sit erectly but not stiffly. A careless posture may lead the board to conclude that you are careless in other things, or at least that you are not impressed by the importance of the occasion. Either conclusion is natural, even if incorrect. Do not fuss with your clothing, a pencil or an ashtray. Your hands may occasionally be useful to emphasize a point; do not let them become a point of distraction.

3) Do not wisecrack or make small talk

This is a serious situation, and your attitude should show that you consider it as such. Further, the time of the board is limited – they do not want to waste it, and neither should you.

4) Do not exaggerate your experience or abilities

In the first place, from information in the application or other interviews and sources, the board may know more about you than you think. Secondly, you probably will not get away with it. An experienced board is rather adept at spotting such a situation, so do not take the chance.

5) If you know a board member, do not make a point of it, yet do not hide it

Certainly you are not fooling him, and probably not the other members of the board. Do not try to take advantage of your acquaintanceship – it will probably do you little good.

6) Do not dominate the interview

Let the board do that. They will give you the clues – do not assume that you have to do all the talking. Realize that the board has a number of questions to ask you, and do not try to take up all the interview time by showing off your extensive knowledge of the answer to the first one.

7) Be attentive

You only have 20 minutes or so, and you should keep your attention at its sharpest throughout. When a member is addressing a problem or question to you, give him your undivided attention. Address your reply principally to him, but do not exclude the other board members.

8) Do not interrupt

A board member may be stating a problem for you to analyze. He will ask you a question when the time comes. Let him state the problem, and wait for the question.

9) Make sure you understand the question

Do not try to answer until you are sure what the question is. If it is not clear, restate it in your own words or ask the board member to clarify it for you. However, do not haggle about minor elements.

10) Reply promptly but not hastily

A common entry on oral board rating sheets is "candidate responded readily," or "candidate hesitated in replies." Respond as promptly and quickly as you can, but do not jump to a hasty, ill-considered answer.

11) Do not be peremptory in your answers

A brief answer is proper – but do not fire your answer back. That is a losing game from your point of view. The board member can probably ask questions much faster than you can answer them.

12) Do not try to create the answer you think the board member wants

He is interested in what kind of mind you have and how it works – not in playing games. Furthermore, he can usually spot this practice and will actually grade you down on it.

13) Do not switch sides in your reply merely to agree with a board member

Frequently, a member will take a contrary position merely to draw you out and to see if you are willing and able to defend your point of view. Do not start a debate, yet do not surrender a good position. If a position is worth taking, it is worth defending.

14) Do not be afraid to admit an error in judgment if you are shown to be wrong

The board knows that you are forced to reply without any opportunity for careful consideration. Your answer may be demonstrably wrong. If so, admit it and get on with the interview.

15) Do not dwell at length on your present job

The opening question may relate to your present assignment. Answer the question but do not go into an extended discussion. You are being examined for a *new* job, not your present one. As a matter of fact, try to phrase ALL your answers in terms of the job for which you are being examined.

Basis of Rating

Probably you will forget most of these "do's" and "don'ts" when you walk into the oral interview room. Even remembering them all will not ensure you a passing grade. Perhaps you did not have the qualifications in the first place. But remembering them will help you to put your best foot forward, without treading on the toes of the board members.

Rumor and popular opinion to the contrary notwithstanding, an oral board wants you to make the best appearance possible. They know you are under pressure – but they also want to see how you respond to it as a guide to what your reaction would be under the pressures of the job you seek. They will be influenced by the degree of poise you display, the personal traits you show and the manner in which you respond.

ABOUT THIS BOOK

This book contains tests divided into Examination Sections. Go through each test, answering every question in the margin. At the end of each test look at the answer key and check your answers. On the ones you got wrong, look at the right answer choice and learn. Do not fill in the answers first. Do not memorize the questions and answers, but understand the answer and principles involved. On your test, the questions will likely be different from the samples. Questions are changed and new ones added. If you understand these past questions you should have success with any changes that arise. Tests may consist of several types of questions. We have additional books on each subject should more study be advisable or necessary for you. Finally, the more you study, the better prepared you will be. This book is intended to be the last thing you study before you walk into the examination room. Prior study of relevant texts is also recommended. NLC publishes some of these in our Fundamental Series. Knowledge and good sense are important factors in passing your exam. Good luck also helps. So now study this Passbook, absorb the material contained within and take that knowledge into the examination. Then do your best to pass that exam.

———

EXAMINATION SECTION

SAMPLE TEST

DIRECTIONS: Each question or incomplete statement is followed by several suggested answers or completions. Select the one that BEST answers the question or completes the statement. *PRINT THE LETTER OF THE CORRECT ANSWER IN THE SPACE AT THE RIGHT.*

Answer question 1 based on the following passage:

A viable affirmative action program must contain specific procedures designed to achieve equal employment opportunities for specified groups. Appropriate procedures, without necessary determination to carry them out, are useless. Determination, without well-defined procedures, will achieve only partial success.

1. The paragraph best supports the statement that   1._____
   A. well-defined procedures will assure the success of an affirmative action program
   B. a high degree of determination is necessary and sufficient for a highly successful affirmative action program
   C. it is impossible for an agency to develop a viable affirmative action program
   D. an agency may guarantee success of its affirmative action program by developing and implementing well-defined procedures
   E. two important ingredients of a successful affirmative action program are well-defined procedures and sincere resolve to implement those procedures

Answer question 2 based on the following passage:

Claimants who have become unemployed by voluntarily leaving the job, by refusing to accept suitable work, or due to misconduct should be temporarily disqualified from receiving benefits. However, the disqualification period should never be longer than the average period required for a worker to find employment. Unemployment insurance is designed to alleviate hardship due to unemployment. Benefits should definitely be paid if unemployment continues beyond a certain point and the claimant can show that he has made an honest effort to find employment.

2. The paragraph best supports the statement that   2._____
   A. if a claimant cannot find work after a certain period of time, he/she should no longer receive benefits
   B. in cases of willful misconduct, disqualification should continue indefinitely
   C. the reasons for unemployment change as the period of unemployment gets longer
   D. if a claimant cannot find employment after a certain period of time, he/she should be allowed to receive unemployment insurance benefits
   E. if a claimant chooses voluntary unemployment, he/she should receive unemployment insurance benefits immediately

Answer question 3 based on the following passage:

Education in the United States is a state responsibility, a local function and a federal concern. Unlike other social service programs, this arrangement places state governments between the federal government and local governing bodies.

3. The paragraph best supports the statement that 　　　　　3._____
   A. enforcement of federal education policies is left to state discretion
   B. the federal government plays an advisory role only in matters concerning education
   C. federal educational policies are generally implemented by local governments under the direction of the state
   D. no federal funds are used to support local educational programs
   E. federal aid is often used to induce local school systems to implement federal policies

Answer question 4 based on the following passage:

Technological and psychological conditions are changing so rapidly that most agencies and organizations must continually adapt to new situations in order to remain viable.

4. The paragraph best supports the statement that 　　　　　4._____
   A. changes in general conditions determine the effectiveness of an organization
   B. the effectiveness of an organization depends more on technological advances than on psychological changes
   C. organizations must be able to adapt to technological and psychological changes in order to maintain effectiveness
   D. the effectiveness of an organization is equally dependent upon technological advances and psychological changes
   E. the effectiveness of an organization is dependent on its technological and psychological advances

Questions 5 and 6 are based on the following coding directions:

DIRECTIONS: Code the information given in each question, using the keys shown below. Use ONLY the information given to determine the code. The report code should be in the same order shown on the Accident Report Form, from left to right. Select the correct code from the choices given and mark the answer on the space at the right.

- Each accident should be assigned a 7-letter code, representing the following information:
  o First letter: Violation
  o Second letter: Weather condition
  o Third letter: Roadway surface
  o Fourth letter: Roadway condition
  o Fifth letter: Vehicle condition
  o Sixth letter: Alignment
  o Seventh letter: Lighting condition

- In developing the codes for the report, use the following keys:
  - I. Violations
    - A. Exceeding state speed limit
    - B. Exceeding safe speed limit
    - C. Failure to yield
    - D. Following too closely
    - E. Improper turning
    - F. Improper passing
    - G. No violation
  - II. Weather
    - A. Clear
    - B. Cloudy
    - C. Raining
    - D. Fog
    - E. Dust
  - III. Roadway surface
    - A. Concrete
    - B. Blacktop
    - C. Gravel
    - D. Dirt
    - E. Other
  - IV. Roadway condition
    - A. Defective shoulders
    - B. Holes
    - C. Deep ruts
    - D. Bumps
    - E. Loose surface material
    - F. Construction
    - G. Water on road
    - H. No defects
  - V. Vehicle condition
    - A. Defective brakes
    - B. Defective headlights
    - C. Defective signal lights
    - D. Tire failure
    - E. Worn or smooth tires
    - F. Other defects
    - G. No defects
  - VI. Alignment
    - A. Straight – level
    - B. Curve – level
    - C. On grade – straight
    - D. On grade – curve
    - E. Hillcrest – straight
    - F. Hillcrest – curve
  - VII. Lighting
    - A. Daylight
    - B. Dark – no street lights
    - C. Dusk or dawn
    - D. Dark – continuous street light

5. On a straight-level, concrete road, John Doe lost control of his car and skidded into a ditch. The accident occurred at 9:00 a.m. on a clear day. No defects were found in either the car or the roadway. There were no violations. The correct accident report code is

    A. B D C A A F F
    B. D C B E E E E
    C. G A A H G A A
    D. E C D C B C D
    E. None of the above

6. Charlene Baker was ticketed with failure to yield after a collision with another vehicle during daylight hours on a clear spring day. Baker did not stop at a red caution light on a graded curve. Neither the blacktop roadway nor Baker's vehicle showed any evidence of defects. There were injuries, and damage to both cars was slight. The correct report code is

    A. A B B B F F A
    B. F B A B A B A
    C. C A A D B F A
    D. C A B H G D A
    E. None of the above

KEY (CORRECT ANSWERS)

1. E
2. D
3. C
4. C
5. C
6. D

EXAMINATION SECTION
TEST 1

DIRECTIONS: Each question or incomplete statement is followed by several suggested answers or completions. Select the one that BEST answers the question or completes the statement. *PRINT THE LETTER OF THE CORRECT ANSWER IN THE SPACE AT THE RIGHT.*

1. Which of the following is a CORRECT statement concerning health insurance benefits?
   A. Claims and not benefits affect premium rates.
   B. The greater the benefits, the higher the premium.
   C. Each policy has a single type of benefit.
   D. Policyowners who have policies with identical benefits pay the same premiums.

1.____

2. Why are premium computations more complex for health insurance than for life insurance?
   A. Competition among insurers has made it so.
   B. The average claim is much smaller.
   C. There are too many different morbidity tables.
   D. Health insurance involves more than one type of benefit and claims are filed more frequently.

2.____

3. Which of the following is a premium factor with health insurance?
   A. Number of insureds
   B. Claims experience
   C. Size of field force
   D. Number of states in which company is licensed

3.____

4. The purpose of inspection reports is to help
   A. medical examiners review complete medical histories of applicants
   B. the agent check out the family histories of prospects
   C. confirm how many health insurance policies applicants have in force
   D. determine the insurability of some applicants

4.____

5. Which of the following statements regarding Medical Information Bureau (MIB) is TRUE?
   A. It was organized by the American Medical Association at the request of insurers.
   B. MIB is a paramedic center which examines applicants.
   C. A complete file of all applicants of member companies is maintained by the MIB.
   D. Its purpose is to serve as an aid to the underwriting of life and health insurance.

5.____

6. A medical report may be completed by a
    A. solicitor
    B. personal physical of the applicant
    C. medical examiner or paramedic
    D. home office underwriter

6._____

7. The purpose of the agent's report is to
    A. report premium collections to the home office
    B. keep a record of sales interviews conducted each month
    C. furnish additional information about an applicant to home office underwriters
    D. keep a supervisor informed of the agent's progress on a weekly basis

7._____

8. Suppose Harold M., an applicant who is rejected for health insurance, requests medical information about himself from the Medical Information Bureau (MIB). The MIB would honor Harold's request by sending the requested data to
    A. the insurance company
    B. Harold's personal physician
    C. Harold
    D. the insurance agent

8._____

9. The health insurance agent holds a position of
    A. authenticity   B. trust   C. faith   D. favoritism

9._____

10. All of the following may be classified as voluntary service organizations EXCEPT
    A. fraternal benefit societies
    B. health insurance companies
    C. Blue Cross and Blue Shield
    D. Health Maintenance Organizations (HMO)

10._____

11. Major risk factors in health insurance underwriting include the following EXCEPT
    A. physical condition
    B. moral hazard
    C. marital status
    D. occupation

11._____

12. Concerning group medical expense policies, all of the following statements are applicable EXCEPT:
    A. Deductible and coinsurance provisions usually do NOT apply to dental insurance coverage
    B. Major medical coverage may be superimposed on a group hospital plan
    C. Hospital room and board benefit periods generally range from 31 days to 365 days
    D. Surgical expense benefits usually are included

12._____

13. For group insurance, employees may be classified in all of the following ways EXCEPT by
    A. type payroll
    B. duties
    C. length of service
    D. age

13._____

14. All of the following statements apply to Blue Cross and/or Blue Shield 14.____
    EXCEPT:
    A. Both are voluntary, nonprofit organizations
    B. Under a Blue Cross hospital plan, the insured is billed directly for covered
       services received by a member
    C. Both Blue Cross and Blue Shield have contractual arrangements with
       hospitals and participating physicians as to rate or fee schedules
    D. Blue Cross plans are designed primarily to provide hospital benefits

15. All of the following statements about Social Security taxes are true EXCEPT: 15.____
    A. Such taxes are paid each year by employees, employers, and self-
       employed persons
    B. An employee pays a Social Security tax on his or her annual earned
       income up to the amount of a designated wage base
    C. Social Security tax rates are subject to change
    D. Self-employed persons pay a lower tax rate than do employed persons,
       although their tax is figured on the same wage base

16. Concerning the taxation of accident and health insurance benefits, all of the 16.____
    following statements are true EXCEPT:
    A. The benefits of personal medical expense policies are not subject to
       income tax
    B. Five percent of all disability income benefits must be included in taxable
       income
    C. Benefits received as reimbursement for medical expenses deducted in a
       prior year must be included in gross income for tax purposes
    D. benefits received from accident policies are not taxable

17. With regard to conditionally renewable policies, all of the following statements 17.____
    are correct EXCEPT:
    A. Insureds have a conditional right to renew their policies
    B. The company retains the right to refuse renewal on certain conditions as
       stated in the policies
    C. Both medical expense and disability income policies sometimes are
       written as conditionally renewable
    D. The company may reserve the right to raise the premium on an individual
       policy

18. Regarding a company's reserves for health insurance, all of the statements 18.____
    below are true EXCEPT:
    A. Minimum requirements for the reserves are stipulated by federal law
    B. The reserves reflect the insurer's liability for future claims
    C. Part of each policy premium is designated for the reserves
    D. Reserves are invested by the insurer and held until needed to pay claims

19. All of the following statements regarding morbidity are true EXCEPT: 19.____
    A. Morbidity tables are based on large numbers of persons
    B. Morbidity is a major factor in premium calculations for health insurance
    C. Morbidity figures reveal when and how long an individual will be disabled
    D. Morbidity statistics indicate the average number of persons at various age levels who are expected to become disabled each year

20. With health insurance, all of the following are premium factors EXCEPT   20.____
    A. occupation   B. reserves   C. interest   D. expense

21. In health insurance underwriting, risk factors also include the following   21.____
    EXCEPT
    A. age   B. sex
    C. type of residence   D. type of policy requested

22. Insureds typically recognize that all of the following affect the degree of   22.____
    occupational risk EXCEPT
    A. irregular working hours
    B. applicants' high school education
    C. sporadic nature of employment
    D. heavy machinery in the work environment

23. In the classification of risks, all of the following would present occupational   23.____
    hazards in a work environment EXCEPT
    A. heavy machinery   B. strong chemicals
    C. high electrical voltage   D. office equipment

24. All of the following statements apply to deductible provisions in medical   24.____
    expense policies EXCEPT:
    A. Deductible provisions eliminate a large number of small claims
    B. Deductible clauses provide that initial covered medical expenses up to a specified amount must be paid by the insured
    C. Such provisions are not used in group insurance
    D. Such provisions help to maintain the lowest possible premium rates

25. The following statements concerning maternity benefits are correct EXCEPT: 25.____
    A. These benefits typically are handled differently in individual policies than in group insurance
    B. Individual hospital expense policies must include a maternity benefit
    C. A maternity benefit may be based on a specific multiple of the daily hospital room benefit
    D. Hospital benefits provided by employers must be the same for maternity cases as for any illness

KEY (CORRECT ANSWERS)

1.	B	11.	C
2.	D	12.	A
3.	B	13.	D
4.	D	14.	B
5.	D	15.	D
6.	C	16.	B
7.	C	17.	D
8.	B	18.	A
9.	B	19.	C
10.	B	20.	B

21.	C
22.	B
23.	D
24.	C
25.	B

TEST 2

DIRECTIONS: Each question or incomplete statement is followed by several suggested answers or completions. Select the one that BEST answers the question or completes the statement. *PRINT THE LETTER OF THE CORRECT ANSWER IN THE SPACE AT THE RIGHT.*

1. The one of the following which is MOST likely to be an occupational disease is   1.____

   A. cancer   B. cerebral hemorrhage
   C. septicemia   D. arsenic poisoning

2. Statements made by an applicant in an application for health insurance   2.____
   generally are considered to be
   A. irrefutable   B. warranties
   C. testimonial   D. representations

3. A man, age 76, is admitted to a city hospital. He has never worked for a business where   3.____
   he paid F.I.C.A. and has no visible means of support.
   The BEST action for the investigator to take is to have him apply for

   A. Medicare   B. Medicaid
   C. Medicare and Medicaid   D. Blue Cross Senior Care

4. Concerning federal income tax, premiums paid for personal disability income   4.____
   insurance are
   A. fully deductible   B. not deductible
   C. deductible for one-half the amount   D. sometimes deductible

5. As to renewability, which type of policy prevents the company from changing   5.____
   the premium rate or modifying the coverage in any way? _____ renewable.
   A. Guaranteed   B. Conditionally
   C. Non-cancellable and guaranteed D. Optionally

6. For taxable years, how are medical expense insurance premiums to be   6.____
   deducted for income tax purposes?
   A. Ten percent of such premiums may be deducted from adjusted gross
      income.
   B. The premiums are fully deductible from gross income.
   C. When premiums are lumped with other medical expenses, the total
      amount deductible is that which exceeds 5% of the taxpayer's adjusted
      gross income.
   D. Any premium amount that exceeds 3% of adjusted gross income is
      deductible.

7. In general, the Medicaid program will NOT cover   7.____

   A. nursing home care
   B. psychiatric care in a general care institution
   C. cosmetic surgery
   D. tuberculosis care

8. Who are the owners of a mutual company?   8.____
   A. Stockholders   B. Directors
   C. Employees   D. Policyowners

9. Industrial health insurance is offered by which of the following companies? 9.____
   A. Casualty
   B. Home Service (debit)
   C. Life
   D. Mono-line

10. Workers' Compensation covers income losses resulting from 10.____
    A. work-related disabilities
    B. plant closings
    C. any accidental injury
    D. workers being terminated

11. Persons participating in a Health Maintenance Organization (HMO) pay a 11.____
    A. low premium
    B. one-time charge
    C. periodic fee
    D. percentage rate

12. State-sponsored programs that generally provide non-occupational disability coverage are known as 12.____
    A. income security insurance
    B. statutory disability plans
    C. workers' insurance
    D. compensation guaranty programs

13. When some relatively minor extra physical or occupational hazard exists, the applicant may be 13.____
    A. insured for sickness only
    B. charged an extra premium
    C. asked to reapply in one year
    D. rejected as uninsurable

14. In the underwriting of health insurance, a PRIMARY consideration as to occupational risk is the 14.____
    A. past work experience
    B. length of employment
    C. mortality experience
    D. probability of disability

15. Under a change of occupation provision, what happens if the insurer learns that the insured has changed to a more hazardous job? 15.____
    A. The policy benefits will be reduced.
    B. The policy will be canceled.
    C. There will be no change in the insurance coverage.
    D. The policy's premium will be increased.

16. With group health insurance, two MAJOR factors that influence dividends or experience-rating refunds are 16.____
    A. reserves and taxes
    B. competition and size of case
    C. expenses and claim costs
    D. type of employer and number of employees

17. Concerning group health insurance plans, which of the following is a CORRECT statement? 17.____
    A. Experience-rated refunds are guaranteed.
    B. Group health insurance plans generally are non-participating.
    C. Plans issued by mutual companies usually provide for dividends.
    D. A group policy that is experience-rated does not make premium reductions retroactive.

18. Individual health insurance policies usually are written on which basis? 18.____
    A. Distinctive   B. Flexible
    C. Average   D. Nonparticipating

19. In major medical and comprehensive policies, a coinsurance provision 19.____'
    A. helps to satisfy the deductible amount
    B. provides for percentage participation by the insured
    C. has no effect on claims
    D. does not apply until benefits amounts exceed a specific amount

20. Elimination (waiting) periods in disability income policies are designed to 20.____
    A. eliminate claims for long-term disabilities
    B. last generally for one year
    C. help keep premium rates at a profitable level
    D. specify a limited period of time at the start of disability when benefits are not payable

21. Suppose William T. has a policy with a $500 deductible and an 80%-20% 21.____
coinsurance provision. He has a hospital bill for $6,200 of covered expenses. How much of the hospital bill does William have to pay?
    A. $1,640   B. $2,420   C. $1,240   D. $1,320

22. With disability income insurance, an elimination (waiting) period may NOT 22.____
apply when the insured is disabled
    A. while at work   B. by accidental injury
    C. while traveling   D. by sickness

23. Persons of the following ages normally are eligible for Medicare EXCEPT 23.____
    A. 60   B. 62   C. 64   D. 65

24. All of the following statements regarding business overhead expense 24.____
insurance are correct EXCEPT:
    A. The maximum benefit period normally is one or two years
    B. The coverage generally is sold on a group basis
    C. Such policies pay for eligible expenses, such as office rent, utilities, and leased equipment, while the insureds are disabled
    D. premiums are tax deductible, but benefits are treated as taxable income

25. Concerning hospital indemnity policies, all of the following are true EXCEPT: 25.____
    A. They pay a daily, weekly or monthly benefit of a specified amount
    B. To receive benefits, the insured must be a patient in a hospital
    C. Benefits usually are paid directly to the hospital
    D. Claim costs are not affected by increases in medical costs

KEY (CORRECT ANSWERS)

1.	D	11.	C
2.	D	12.	B
3.	C	13.	B
4.	B	14.	D
5.	C	15.	A
6.	C	16.	C
7.	C	17.	C
8.	D	18.	D
9.	B	19.	B
10.	A	20.	D

21.	A
22.	B
23.	A
24.	B
25.	C

TEST 3

DIRECTIONS: Each question or incomplete statement is followed by several suggested answers or completions. Select the one that BEST answers the question or completes the statement. *PRINT THE LETTER OF THE CORRECT ANSWER IN THE SPACE AT THE RIGHT.*

1. Assume that Patrick K., an employee of the ABC Company, paid $2,350 in Social Security taxes based on his earnings for the year. The company would have paid how much additional Social Security taxes based SOLELY on Patrick's earnings for the year?
   A. $1,250   B. $1,825   C. $1,175   D. $2,350

     1.____

2. To be eligible for Social Security disability benefits, an applicant MUST
   A. have a disability which can be expected to result in death or to last six months, or be the result of blindness
   B. be under the age of 60
   C. have a fully insured status
   D. first enroll in a state vocational rehabilitation program

     2.____

3. The waiting period before a person may file a claim for Social Security disability benefits is _____ months.
   A. twelve   B. five   C. three   D. six

     3.____

4. Policies classified as nonoccupational NORMALLY provide coverage for
   A. losses due to sickness or accidents which are not work-related
   B. persons in nonhazardous jobs
   C. losses both on and off the job
   D. sickness but not for accidental injuries

     4.____

5. Investigative reports ordered by insurance companies concerning individual applicants are usually referred to as
   A. inspection reports   B. disclosure summaries
   C. security reports   D. underwriting memoranda

     5.____

6. Which of the following is a CORRECT statement concerning Health Maintenance Organizations (HMO's)?
   A. They place special emphasis on preventive health care.
   B. Participants pay a one-time, fixed fee in advance for health care services.
   C. HMO's generally are owned by life insurance companies.
   D. They primarily provide emergency type treatment for their members.

     6.____

7. Suppose Mary V. signs an application for a major medical policy on November 2. She is asked to take a medical examination and does so on November 5. The policy is issued as requested on November 10 and delivered on November 12, at which time Mary pays the first premium. In that case, Mary's major medical coverage took effect on November
   A. 2   B. 5   C. 10   D. 12

     7.____

8. Assume that Harry P. signs an application for a disability insurance policy
   on June 10, pays the initial premium, and is given a conditional receipt. He
   takes a medical examination, as required, on June 13. The policy is issued as
   requested on June 20 and delivered to Harry on June 26. Harry's disability
   income coverage became effective on June
      A. 10   B. 13   C. 20   D. 26   8.____

9. A guaranteed insurability rider or supplementary agreement may be attached   9.____
   to a(n) _____ policy.
      A. major medical   B. business overhead expense
      C. disability income   D. accident

10. _____ is a term(s) which relates DIRECTLY to the elective indemnity   10.____
    provision.
       A. Assignment   B. Lump-sum payment
       C. Overinsurance   D. Coinsurance

11. Suppose four policyowners, all the same age, purchase identical major   11.____
    medical policies at standard rates. Tom pays his premium monthly, Dick,
    quarterly; Harry, semi-annually; and James, annually. Which policy
    NORMALLY will cost less?
       A. Tom's   B. Dick's   C. Harry's   D. James'

12. All premiums for health insurance (also life insurance) MUST be paid   12.____
       A. in advance   B. at time of application
       C. at the time policies are delivered   D. before a policy is issued

13. A broad statement which generally appears on the first page of a health   13.____
    insurance policy and specifies conditions under which benefits will be paid is
    known as the
       A. assurance clause   B. warranty provision
       C. insuring clause   D. guaranty provision

14. Which of the following is a TRUE statement concerning group insurance?   14.____
       A. A group health insurance plan for a manufacturing plant would have to
          include both plant and office workers.
       B. To qualify, a group must be classified as an association group.
       C. The minimum number of persons to be insured in a group plan is
          specified by federal law.
       D. It is required that a group be a natural group – that is, not be organized
          for the sole purpose of obtaining insurance

15. In the early 70's, the President signed into law legislation designed to stimulate,   15.____
    through federal aid, the establishment of prepaid comprehensive care programs called

       A. Health Maintenance Organizations (HMO's)
       B. Neighborhood Family Care Centers (NFCC's)
       C. Pre-admission Screening Clinics (PASC's)
       D. Professional Standard Review Organizations (PSRO's)

16. When an employer establishes a group health insurance plan, what does each participating employee receive?   16.____
    A. Insurance notice
    B. Certificate of insurance
    C. Letter of confirmation
    D. Coverage form

17. A common feature of group major medical insurance is   17.____
    A. double indemnity
    B. dismemberment benefits
    C. coinsurance
    D. disability income

18. Suppose Marcia K. declines to participate in her employer's group health insurance plan when she has the opportunity. Later she changes her mind and wishes to enroll. The insurance company   18.____
    A. must accept Marcia in the group plan but may charge the employer a separate premium for her coverage
    B. probably will require evidence of insurability and reject Marcia's application if she is a poor risk
    C. will suggest that Marcia wait for the next general enrollment period
    D. has no choice but to accept Marcia's application and enroll her in the plan

19. Under the group insurance conversion privilege, insured members who resign or are terminated by the employer normally have how long to convert their coverage to individual policies WITHOUT evidence of insurability?   19.____
    A. 21 days   B. 90 days   C. 31 days   D. 60 days

20. Assume the ABC Company has 1,000 eligible employees for a contributory group health insurance plan. How many of those employees would have to participate for the plan to be activated?   20.____
    A. 600   B. 750   C. 500   D. 1,000

21. All of the following statements concerning assignment are correct EXCEPT: 21.____
    A. Medical expense policies generally include an assignment provision
    B. Assignment by an insured permits an insurer to pay medical expense benefits
    C. An assignment provision usually is not included with dental insurance
    D. Assignment forms generally stipulate that the insured is responsible for any charges not covered by the insurance

22. Regarding the waiver of premium provision, all of the following statements are true EXCEPT: 22.____
    A. It is generally available with disability income policies
    B. The waiver may apply retroactively to the original date of disability following a waiting period
    C. Such a waiver usually does not apply after the insured reaches age 60
    D. It is frequently included with both individual and group policies

23. All of the following statements are applicable to the insuring clause EXCEPT: 23.____
    A. The clause identifies the insured and the insurer
    B. It defines losses not covered by the policy
    C. The clause usually specifies that benefits are subject to all provisions and terms stated in the policy
    D. It represents the insurer's promise to pay benefits for specific kinds of losses

24. Regarding pre-existing conditions, the following statements are true EXCEPT: 24.____
    A. A pre-existing condition is one that was contracted by the insured at least one year before a policy is issued
    B. Medical expense policies frequently exclude benefits for losses due to such conditions
    C. Specifying exclusions for pre-existing conditions helps an insurer to maintain reasonable premium rates
    D. Disability income policies commonly include a probationary period to help control the risk of pre-existing conditions

25. All of the following statements concerning the conversion privilege for dependents are true EXCEPT: 25.____
    A. Coverage for a dependent child usually ceases when the child marries or reaches a limiting age
    B. Such a provision is generally included in most individual health insurance policies
    C. When a policy is dropped voluntarily, the conversion privilege does not apply
    D. Conversion policies are available to eligible dependents without evidence of insurability

────────────

KEY (CORRECT ANSWERS)

1.	D		11.	D
2.	C		12.	A
3.	B		13.	C
4.	A		14.	D
5.	A		15.	A
6.	A		16.	B
7.	D		17.	C
8.	B		18.	B
9.	C		19.	C
10.	B		20.	B

21.	C
22.	D
23.	B
24.	A
25.	B

EXAMINATION SECTION
TEST 1

DIRECTIONS: Each question or incomplete statement is followed by several suggested answers or completions. Select the one that BEST answers the question or completes the statement. *PRINT THE LETTER OF THE CORRECT ANSWER IN THE SPACE AT THE RIGHT.*

1. The term *first-line supervisor* refers to the lowest level of supervision in an organization. A dilemma faced by the first-line supervisor is that he represents   1.____

     A. management   B. labor
     C. management and labor   D. neither management nor labor

2. Management experts generally consider it advisable to give instructions orally, even though these instructions may later be put in writing for permanent reference. The MAIN reason for this advice is that   2.____

     A. employees sometimes misplace written instructions
     B. explanations can be made in accordance with individual needs
     C. written instructions tend to be unclear and ambiguous
     D. employees resent being given instructions in writing

3. Of the following, the BEST reason why a supervisor should NOT delegate a certain job to a subordinate is that   3.____

     A. he does not have any subordinate who can develop the skills needed to do the job
     B. it is easier and quicker to do it himself
     C. he knows it will be done correctly if he does it himself
     D. he enjoys doing it himself

4. Of the following, the step which the supervisor should take FIRST in handling a complaint from a member of his staff is to   4.____

     A. gather background information relevant to the complaint
     B. establish tentative solutions or answers to the complaint
     C. determine the nature of the complaint as clearly and as fully as possible
     D. make a determination as to whether the complaint is valid

5. Before a supervisor delegates one of the duties which he normally performs to a member of his staff, the FIRST thing he should do is   5.____

     A. determine the long-range purpose of the job
     B. determine exactly what tasks the job involves
     C. decide how long it takes him to do the job
     D. decide to whom he will assign the job

6. When an employee is not sure of the intent of a policy statement, it is usually BEST for him to consult   6.____

     A. a fellow worker   B. a member of the planning staff
     C. his supervisor   D. the manual of procedures

7. The MOST appropriate time for a supervisor to have a discussion with an employee who has violated an agency policy is

   7.____

    A. as soon as possible after the violation has occurred
    B. after a cooling-off period has elapsed
    C. the day after the violation occurred
    D. during the next staff meeting

8. Of the following, the MOST appropriate use of staff conferences is to enable the supervisor to

   8.____

    A. inform staff of the latest administrative policies
    B. obtain the benefits of collective thinking about a problem
    C. let staff know that he is aware of violations of personnel policies
    D. give dissatisfied employees a chance to voice their grievances

9. Of the following, a term used to describe how a supervisor may determine whether he is communicating effectively with his staff is called

   9.____

    A. backlash   B. feedback
    C. implementation   D. delegation

10. False rumors about unpleasant possibilities such as employee cutbacks can do serious damage to morale. Most rumors of this kind in large organizations and public agencies are caused by

   10.____

    A. over-permissiveness and general laxity of supervision
    B. a breakdown in communication between management and employees
    C. employees who distort the facts for their own purposes
    D. newspaper articles planted by special interest groups

11. Of the following, staff meetings are LEAST likely to be productive when

   11.____

    A. only four or five people are present
    B. the chairman conducts the meeting in a formal manner
    C. discussion is kept to a minimum
    D. private discussions are not allowed

12. The one of the following persons who USUALLY would be classified as belonging to middle management is the

   12.____

    A. senior clerk   B. agency head
    C. bureau director   D. deputy commissioner

13. Of the following, the BEST way for a person to develop competence as an interviewer is to

   13.____

    A. attend lectures on interviewing techniques
    B. practice with employees on the job
    C. conduct interviews under the supervision of an experienced instructor
    D. attend a training course in counselling

14. Of the following, the type of employee who would PROBABLY expect to be given the most authority to use independent judgment is the   14.____

    A. chemical engineer   B. clerical worker
    C. bookkeeper   D. registered nurse

15. Assume that you are asked to study and report on employee turnover in several agency units which vary widely as to total number of employees and the number of employees involved in turnover.   15.____
    In order to present an accurate picture of turnover, your report should show, with regard to persons leaving, both actual numbers and

    A. central tendencies   B. percentages
    C. raw data   D. rounded totals

16. Many employees tend to resist a reorganization because they feel that their status and security are threatened. Of the following, the BEST way to make it easier for employees to accept the changes necessitated by reorganization is to   16.____

    A. introduce many changes at the same time
    B. give them a chance to participate in evaluating proposed changes
    C. keep the changes secret until they are put into effect
    D. have staff people who have had little contact with the affected employees initiate the changes

17. The MOST important reason for investigating every accident on the job is to   17.____

    A. find out who was responsible for the accident
    B. determine the organization's legal liability for the accident
    C. correct the conditions or actions which caused the accident
    D. discipline the employee who caused the accident

18. Research studies indicate that an important difference between high-production and low-production supervisors lies in their manner of handling mistakes.   18.____
    When subordinates make mistakes, the high-production supervisor PROBABLY would

    A. concentrate on fixing responsibility and determining the subordinate's excuse for the mistake
    B. take over the assignment himself in order to avoid recurrence of the mistake
    C. look upon the mistake as an opportunity to provide training
    D. give the assignment to a subordinate who is not likely to repeat the mistake

19. The use of statistical controls is generally considered to be one of management's most effective means of determining what is happening at the operating level of an agency.   19.____
    Of the following, statistical controls are LEAST useful for

    A. furthering coordination
    B. measuring morale
    C. setting standards
    D. pinpointing responsibility

20. A basic problem of the supervisor is how to motivate employees. One approach is to   20.____
    internalize motivation by providing opportunities for employees to derive satisfaction from
    the work itself.
    Of the following, internalized motivation would be the LEAST effective approach where
    the employee

    A. enjoys autonomy because of the nature of the job
    B. accepts the organization's objectives
    C. makes the job his central life focus
    D. does a routine or assembly line job

KEY (CORRECT ANSWERS)

1.	C		11.	C
2.	B		12.	C
3.	A		13.	C
4.	C		14.	A
5.	B		15.	B
6.	C		16.	B
7.	A		17.	C
8.	B		18.	C
9.	B		19.	B
10.	B		20.	D

TEST 2

DIRECTIONS: Each question or incomplete statement is followed by several suggested answers or completions. Select the one that BEST answers the question or completes the statement. *PRINT THE LETTER OF THE CORRECT ANSWER IN THE SPACE AT THE RIGHT.*

1. Of the following, the BEST time for a supervisor to give advice about a job-related problem which a subordinate has brought up during an interview is USUALLY after the

    1.____

    A. subordinate has told him all the facts
    B. supervisor has determined the employee's unconscious motives for bringing up the problem
    C. employee has submitted a written report on the problem
    D. supervisor has discussed the problem with his superior

2. Of the following, the situation in which a supervisor would have to make the GREATEST effort in order to communicate effectively with his subordinates would occur when

    2.____

    A. there is a large gap between the supervisor's background and experience and that of his subordinates
    B. the subordinates have already learned about the information through informal channels
    C. the subordinates have completed their education much more recently than the supervisor
    D. the supervisor has been with the organization for a much shorter time than most of his subordinates

3. Of the following, the factor which would be MOST critical in influencing whether subordinates accept or resent a supervisor's authority is the

    3.____

    A. manner in which the supervisor uses his authority
    B. frequency with which the supervisor ignores minor violations of rules
    C. degree of delegation to subordinates by the supervisor
    D. cultural attitudes of individual subordinates toward authority

4. In which one of the following situations would employees be MOST likely to accept temporarily difficult working conditions without excessive complaining?

    4.____

    A. The organization has a strict policy of disciplinary action against uncooperative employees.
    B. Employees do not have the right to take part in *job actions* or strikes.
    C. An atmosphere of mutual trust and good human relations exists between subordinates and managerial personnel.
    D. Relationships between subordinates and managerial personnel are strictly businesslike.

5. Assume that an agency has been reorganized into integrated work teams. Instead of assigning employees performing the same task to a single unit, such as a typing pool, those performing different but interdependent parts of an activity are put into the same work group.
   Of the following, the MOST probable result of such a reorganization would be to

    5.____

    A. permit more efficient work scheduling
    B. achieve greater economy
    C. decrease training costs
    D. improve employee job satisfaction

6. The need for identification with a work group has been found to be one of the most pow-   6.____
erful on-the-job motivations.
Of the following, the employee who is LEAST likely to have a strong attachment to his
work group is one who

    A. is at the very bottom of the organization's promotional ladder
    B. belongs to a small department
    C. works with others of similar background and interests
    D. has worked for the organization for a considerable period of time

7. According to many management experts, the one of the following situations which would   7.____
be the MOST significant indication that employees of an organization are dissatisfied
with their supervisors and feel that they are being treated unfairly is one in which

    A. employees submit a large number of work-related suggestions
    B. many employees are unproductive and seem to be continually loafing on the job
    C. union membership has recently increased
    D. turnover is low in spite of a comparatively good labor market

8. A supervisor who has informal, friendly relationships with his subordinates is conducting   8.____
himself

    A. *appropriately;* good informal relationships set the stage for better communication
between the supervisor and subordinates on work-related problems
    B. *inappropriately;* subordinates who have informal relationships with their supervisor
are not likely to accept his authority
    C. *appropriately;* friendly relationships between the supervisor and his subordinates
will create a true feeling of equality between them
    D. *inappropriately;* subordinates are likely to become suspicious of insincerity and
fearful of being manipulated

9. Specialization is a commonly-used method of increasing productivity and efficiency in a   9.____
large organization. Task specialization means that separate and comparatively simple
parts of a more complex job are performed by different employees.
Of the following, this type of specialization probably would NOT

    A. reduce training costs
    B. permit the use of more specialized equipment
    C. simplify the development of job controls
    D. give most employees a greater sense of accomplishment

10. Some management experts who have studied informal communication patterns in large   10.____
organizations believe that the office grapevine is an effective means of communication.
Of the following, an IMPORTANT function performed by the grapevine is to

    A. permit feedback and spread information faster than most formal communication
systems
    B. give employees important information from reliable sources
    C. permit management to identify rumor-mongers and troublemakers
    D. bring informal leaders to the attention of management

11. Recent studies of morale and productivity tend to show that
    11.____

    A. the correlation between morale and productivity is rather low
    B. high morale is associated with high productivity
    C. low morale is associated with high productivity
    D. low morale is associated with low productivity

12. Research studies have indicated that teamwork among employees is MOST likely to result in higher productivity in a situation where
    12.____

    A. employees accept as legitimate management's demands for higher productivity
    B. management strongly encourages the workers' demands spirit
    C. employees are unified for the purpose of protecting themselves against management's demands
    D. management does not encourage employees to make independent decisions

13. The relationship between boredom on the job and fatigue is CORRECTLY stated as follows:
    13.____

    A. Boredom usually results in increased fatigue
    B. A worker usually becomes bored when he expends a minimum of physical energy
    C. Fatigue usually results in boredom
    D. A worker who is bored does not usually become fatigued

14. The *halo effect* can PROPERLY be suspected of harming supervisor-subordinate relationships when the supervisor
    14.____

    A. does not discriminate between the good and poor work of an employee considered by him to be generally superior
    B. expects his subordinates to treat him in an impersonal and formal manner
    C. hesitates to discipline employees because of an extreme need for them to like him
    D. is unable to gain his employees' confidence because he cannot shed his reputation for being hardboiled and unfair

15. It is generally considered that the best interview is the one in which the interviewer talks less than the person interviewed.
    The one of the following which is an EFFECTIVE device to encourage the other person to talk during the interview is for the interviewer to
    15.____

    A. summarize the feelings the person has expressed, omitting details and incidentals
    B. keep silent and show no indication of his reaction to what the person is saying
    C. clearly show his approval or disapproval of what the person is saying
    D. talk to the person in terms of concepts rather than specifics

16. Studies of groups of workers doing the same job under the same conditions have shown that there are always a few workers who have more accidents than the rest. The one of the following which is LEAST likely to be a finding of such studies is that those who have the MOST accidents PROBABLY are
    16.____

    A. middle-aged
    B. poorly adjusted to work
    C. inexperienced at the job
    D. less efficient than other workers

4 (#2)

17. Work measurement has been defined as *the determination of the proper amount of time*   17.____
and effort required for the effective performance of a specific task.
Of the following, the factor which would be LEAST relevant in studying an operation by
means of work measurement is whether the operation is

    A. repetitive with constant standards of quality
    B. compensated for at a prevailing rate of pay
    C. routine in nature and relatively easy to perform
    D. performed in large volume

18. Of the following, *participative management* can be defined BEST as a method in which   18.____

    A. subordinates have formed groups for the purpose of gaining participation in the
decisions of management
    B. management makes a practice of encouraging subordinates as a group to discuss
and participate in decisions on a wide variety of work-related problems
    C. managerial employees are given varied assignments on a rotating basis
    D. management gives all employees the opportunity to participate in major policy
decisions

19. *Internalized motivation* has been described as a method of motivating employees by   19.____
enabling them to derive satisfaction through doing the job itself. This approach to motivating employees would require management to

    A. assume that most employees like work and enjoy doing a good job
    B. encourage competition among employees for promotions and higher salaries
    C. emphasize improved fringe benefits and conditions of work
    D. consider employee needs to be more important than organizational needs

20. If a supervisor should find that he must issue an order his subordinates will probably   20.____
resist, it is advisable for the supervisor to FIRST

    A. discuss the order with his subordinates and give them an opportunity to ask ques-
tions and make objections
    B. issue the order without comment and discourage discussion and objections by his
subordinates
    C. inform his subordinates that he does not agree with the order he is going to give
them, but must carry out the decisions of higher authority
    D. inform his subordinates that he will take disciplinary action against those who resist
carrying out the order he will present to them

21. When a supervisor finds that his subordinates differ considerably in the amount of atten-   21.____
tion and guidance they require of him, it would be MOST advisable for the supervisor to

    A. adjust his supervisory practices according to individual needs
    B. give an equal amount of attention and guidance to each subordinate in order to be
fair
    C. give less responsibility to subordinates who seek assistance
    D. permit employees who prefer independence to work strictly on their own

26

22. Connecting lines on an organization chart represent liaes of 22._____
    A. management quality controls
    B. work flow
    C. authority and responsibility
    D. fiscal accountability

23. *General supervision* has been defined as a method in which the supervisor makes 23._____
    assignments in broad, general terms and gives considerable autonomy to subordinates,
    in accordance with their knowledge and abilities.
    A supervisor who uses this method is LEAST likely to

    A. do different work from that of subordinates
    B. concentrate on long-range problems
    C. exert excessive pressure on subordinates
    D. devote considerable effort to training subordinates

24. Of the following, the MOST important reason why a supervisor should be cautious about 24._____
    giving subordinates advice about personal problems is that the

    A. subordinate may blame him if the advice turns out to be misleading
    B. supervisor should not discuss personal problems with subordinates on office time
    C. subordinate may lose confidence in his ability to perform on the job
    D. supervisor may not know enough to give helpful advice

25. Professional or technical consultants may be used MOST appropriately by a human ser- 25._____
    vices agency to

    A. direct staff conferences centered around programs
    B. give advice regarding the quality of service or the effectiveness of plans
    C. supervise implementation of programs they have developed
    D. direct the in-service training program

———————

KEY (CORRECT ANSWERS)

1.	A	11.	A
2.	A	12.	A
3.	A	13.	A
4.	C	14.	A
5.	D	15.	A
6.	A	16.	A
7.	B	17.	B
8.	A	18.	B
9.	D	19.	A
10.	A	20.	A

21.	A
22.	C
23.	C
24.	D
25.	B

———

EXAMINATION SECTION
TEST 1

DIRECTIONS: Each question or incomplete statement is followed by several suggested answers or completions. Select the one that BEST answers the question or completes the statement. *PRINT THE LETTER OF THE CORRECT ANSWER IN THE SPACE AT THE RIGHT.*

1. It is GENERALLY accepted that, of the following, the MOST important medium for developing integration and continuity in learning on the job is   1.____

    A. day-to-day experience on the job
    B. the supervisory conference
    C. the staff meeting
    D. the professional seminar

2. Assume that you find that one of your workers is over-identifying with a particular client. Of the following, the MOST appropriate step for you to take FIRST in dealing with this situation is to   2.____

    A. transfer the case to another worker
    B. inform the worker that he cannot give satisfactory service if he overidentifies with a client
    C. interview the client yourself to determine his feelings about his relationship with the worker
    D. arrange a conference with the worker to discuss the reasons for her overidentification with this client

3. The one of the following which is the MOST likely reason why a newly-appointed supervisor would have a tendency to interfere actively in a relationship between one of his workers and a client is that the supervisor   3.____

    A. has unresolved feelings about relinquishing the role of worker, and has not yet accepted his role as supervisor
    B. must give direct assistance in the situation because the worker cannot handle it
    C. is attempting to share with his worker the knowledge and skill which he has developed in direct practice
    D. has not realized that immediate responsibility for work with clients has been delegated to others

4. A worker who has a tendency to resist authority and supervision can be helped MOST effectively if, of the following, the supervisor   4.____

    A. behaves in a strict and impersonal manner so that the worker will accept his authority as a supervisor
    B. modifies the relationship so that he will be less authoritarian and threatening to the worker
    C. gives the worker a simple, matter-of-fact interpretation of the supervisory relationship and has an understanding acceptance of the worker's response
    D. temporarily establishes a peer relationship with the worker in order to overcome his resistance

5. Before interviewing a newly-appointed worker for the first time, of the following, it is DESIRABLE for the supervisor to

    A. learn as much as he can about the worker's background and interests in order to eliminate the routine of asking questions and eliciting answers

    B. review the job information to be covered in order to make it easier to be impersonal and keep to the business at hand

    C. send the worker orientation material about the agency and the job and ask him to study it before the interview

    D. review available information about the worker in order to find an area of shared experience to serve as a *taking off* point for getting acquainted

5.____

6. In interviewing a new worker, of the following, it is IMPORTANT for the supervisor to

    A. give direction to the progress of the interview and maintain a leadership role throughout

    B. allow the worker to take the initiative in order to give him full scope for freedom of expression

    C. maintain a non-directional approach so that the worker will reveal his true attitudes and feelings

    D. avoid interrupting the worker, even though he seems to want to do all the talking

6.____

7. When a new worker, during his first few days, shows such symptoms of insecurity as *stage fright,* helpless immobility, or extreme talkativeness, of the following, it would be MOST helpful for the supervisor to

    A. start the worker out on some activity in which he is relatively secure

    B. ignore the symptoms and allow the worker to *sink or swim* on his own

    C. have a conference with the worker and interpret to him the reasons for his feelings of insecurity

    D. consider the probability that this worker may not be suited for a profession which requires skill in interpersonal relationships

7.____

8. Of the following, the MOST desirable method of minimizing workers' dependence on the supervisor and encouraging self-dependence is to

    A. hold group instead of individual supervisory conferences at regular intervals

    B. schedule individual supervisory conferences only in response to the workers' obvious need for guidance

    C. plan for progressive exposure to other opportunities for learning afforded by the agency and the community

    D. allow workers to learn by trial and error rather than by direct supervisory guidance

8.____

9. Of the following, it would NOT be appropriate for the supervisor to use early supervisory conferences with the new worker as a means of

    A. giving him direct practical help in order to get going on the job

    B. estimating the level of his native abilities, professional skills and experience

    C. getting clues as to his characteristic ways of learning in a new situation

    D. assessing his potential for future supervisory responsibility

9.____

10. Without careful planning by the supervisor for orientation of the new worker, an informal   10._____
system of orientation by co-workers inevitably develops.
Such an informal system of orientation is USUALLY

    A. *beneficial*, because many new workers learn more readily when instructed by their peers
    B. *harmful*, because informal orientation by an undesig-nated co-worker can lead a new worker astray instead of helping him
    C. *beneficial*, because assumption by subordinates of responsibility for orientation will free the supervisor for other urgent work
    D. *harmful*, because such informal orientation by a co-worker will tend to destroy the authority of the supervisor

11. Of the following, the BEST way for a supervisor to assist a subordinate who has unusual   11._____
work pressures is to

    A. relieve him of some of his cases until the pressures subside
    B. help him to decide which cases should be given the most attention during the period of pressure, and how to provide coverage for less urgent cases
    C. inform him that he must learn to tolerate and adjust to such pressures
    D. point out that he should learn to understand the causes of the pressures, which probably resulted from his own deficiencies

12. Many supervisors have a tendency to use case records mainly for the purpose of analy-   12._____
sis of the workers' skill or evaluation of their performance.
Of the following, a PROBABLE result of this practice is that

    A. workers are likely to tie-in recording with supervisory evaluation of their work, without giving proper emphasis to their importance in improving service to clients
    B. the worker is likely to devote an inordinate amount of time to case records at the expense of his clients
    C. the records are likely to be too lengthy and detailed, limiting their value for other important purposes
    D. the records are likely to be of little value for administrative and research purposes

13. A common obstacle to adequate recording in a large social work agency is the fact that   13._____
many workers consider recording to be a time-consuming chore.
In order to obtain the cooperation of staff in keeping proper records, of the following, it
is MOST important for an agency to provide

    A. indisputable evidence of the intelligent use of records as tools in formulating policy and improving service
    B. a system of checks and controls to assure that workers are preparing adequate and timely records
    C. adequate clerical services and mechanical equipment for recording
    D. sufficient time for recording in the organization of every job

14. The one of the following which is NOT a purpose of keeping case records in an agency is   14._____

    A. planning   B. research
    C. training   D. job classification

15. When a supervisor is reviewing the records of a worker, of the following, he should plan   15._____
to read

    A. records of new cases only, following up each interview selectively
    B. the total caseload, in order to determine which aspects of the worker's performance should be examined
    C. those records which the worker has brought to the supervisor's attention because of the need for help
    D. a block of records selected according to the worker's need for help, and some records selected at random

16. The one of the following which is the PRIMARY purpose of the regular staff meeting in an   16._____
agency is

    A. initiation of action in order to get the agency's work done
    B. staff training and development
    C. program and policy determination
    D. communication of new policies and procedures

17. Of the following, group supervision in an agency is intended as a means of   17._____

    A. strengthening the total supervisory process
    B. shifting the focus of supervision from the individual to the group
    C. saving costs in terms of time and manpower
    D. influencing policy through group interaction

18. The supervisor's job brings him closer to such limiting factors in the operation of an   18._____
agency as faulty administrative structure, shortage of funds and lack of facilities, inadequacies in personnel practices, community pressures, and excessive workload.
For the supervisor to make a practice of communicating to his subordinates his feelings of frustration about such limitations in the work setting would be

    A. *appropriate,* because the worker will be more understanding of the supervisor's burdens and frustrations
    B. *inappropriate,* because the climate created will block rather than further the purposes of supervision
    C. *appropriate,* because such communication will create a more democratic climate between the worker and the supervisor
    D. *inappropriate,* because the supervisor must support and condone agency policies and practices in the presence of subordinates

19. A suggestion has been made that the teaching and administrative functions of supervi-   19._____
sion should be separated, so that the supervisor responsible for teaching would not be responsible for evaluation of the same workers.
The one of the following which is the MOST important reason for this point of view is that

    A. elements that confer on the supervisor a position of authority and power unduly threaten the learning situation
    B. teaching skill and administrative ability do aot usually go together
    C. a supervisor who has been responsible for training a worker is likely to be prejudiced in his favor
    D. performance evaluation and total job accountability should be two separate functions

20. In reviewing a worker's cases in preparation for a periodic evaluation, you note that she   20.____
has done a uniformly good job with certain types of cases and poor work with other types
of cases.
Of the following, the BEST approach for you to take in this situation is to

   A. bring this to the worker's attention, find out why she favors certain types of clients,
   and discuss ways in which she can improve her service to all clients
   B. bring this to the worker's attention and suggest that she may need professional
   counselling, as she seems to be blocked in working with certain types of cases
   C. assign to her mainly those cases which she handles best and transfer the types of
   cases which she handles poorly to another worker
   D. accept the fact that a worker cannot be expected to give uniformly good service to
   all clients, and take no further action

KEY (CORRECT ANSWERS)

1.	B		11.	B
2.	D		12.	A
3.	A		13.	A
4.	C		14.	D
5.	D		15.	D
6.	A		16.	A
7.	A		17.	A
8.	C		18.	B
9.	D		19.	A
10.	B		20.	A

TEST 2

DIRECTIONS: Each question or incomplete statement is followed by several suggested answers or completions. Select the one that BEST answers the question or completes the statement. *PRINT THE LETTER OF THE CORRECT ANSWER IN THE SPACE AT THE RIGHT.*

1. Of the following, the choice of method to be used in the supervisory process should be influenced MOST by the   1.____

   A. number and type of cases carried by each worker
   B. emotional maturity of the worker
   C. number of workers supervised and their past experience
   D. subject matter to be learned and the long range goals of supervision

2. In an evaluation conference with a worker, the BEST approach for the supervisor to take is to   2.____

   A. help the worker to identify his strengths as a basis for working on his weaknesses
   B. identify the worker's weaknesses and help him overcome them
   C. allow the worker to identify his weaknesses first and then suggest ways of overcoming them
   D. discuss the worker's weaknesses but emphasize his strengths

3. Assume that a worker is discouraged about the progress of his work and feels that it is futile to attempt to cope with many of his cases.
   Of the following, it would be BEST for the supervisor to   3.____

   A. suggest to the worker that such feelings are inappropriate for a professional worker
   B. tell the worker that he must seek professional help in order to overcome these feelings
   C. reduce the worker's caseload and give him cases that are less complex
   D. review with the worker several of his cases in which there were obvious accomplishments

4. The supervisor is responsible for providing the worker with the following means of support, with the EXCEPTION of   4.____

   A. interest and advice on his personal problems
   B. instruction on community resources
   C. inspiration for carrying out the work of the agency
   D. understanding his strengths and limitations

5. When a worker frequently takes the initiative in asking questions and discussing problems during a supervisory conference, this is PROBABLY an indication that the   5.____

   A. supervisor is not sufficiently interested in the work
   B. conference is a positive learning experience for the worker
   C. worker is hostile and resists supervision
   D. supervisor's position of authority is in question

6. When a supervisor finds that one of his workers cannot accept criticism, of the following, it would be BEST for the supervisor to

    A. have the worker transferred to another supervisor
    B. warn the worker of disciplinary proceedings unless his attitude changes
    C. have the worker suspended after explaining the reason
    D. explore with the worker his attitude toward authority

6.____

7. Of the following, the condition which the inexperienced worker is LEAST likely to be aware of, without the guidance of the supervisor, is

    A. when he is successful in helping a client
    B. when he is not making progress in helping a client
    C. that he has a personal bias toward certain clients
    D. that he feels insecure because of lack of experience

7.____

8. The supervisor should provide an inexperienced worker with controls as well as freedom MAINLY because controls will

    A. enable him to set up his own controls sooner
    B. put him in a situation which is closer to the realities of life
    C. help him to use authority in handling a casework problem
    D. give him a feeling of security and lay the foundation for future self-direction

8.____

9. A result of the use of summarized case recording by the worker is that it

    A. gives the supervisor more responsibility for selecting cases to discuss in conference
    B. makes more time available for other activities
    C. lowers the morale of many workers
    D. decreases discussion of cases by the worker and the supervisor

9.____

10. The distinction between the role of professional workers and the role of auxiliary or sub-professional workers in an agency is based upon the

    A. position within the agency hierarchy
    B. amount of close supervision given
    C. emergent nature of tasks assigned
    D. functions performed

10.____

11. Of the following, the MOST important source of learning for the worker should be

    A. departmental directives and professional literature
    B. his co-workers in the agency
    C. the content of in-service training courses
    D. the clients in his caseload

11.____

12. A client is MOST likely to feel that he is receiving acceptance and understanding if the social worker

    A. gets detailed information about the client's problem
    B. demonstrates that he realistically understands the client's problem
    C. has an intellectual understanding of the client's problem
    D. offers the client assurance of assistance

12.____

13. A client will be MORE encouraged to speak freely about his problems if the worker   13.____

    A. avoids asking too many questions
    B. asks leading rather than pointed questions
    C. suggests possible answers
    D. identifies with the client

14. A client would be MOST likely to be able to accept help in a time of crisis and need if the   14.____
worker

    A. explains agency policy to him
    B. responds immediately to the client's need
    C. explains why help cannot be given immediately
    D. reaches out to help the client establish his rightful claim for assistance

15. It is a generally accepted principle that the worker should interpret for himself what the   15.____
client is saying, but usually should not pass his interpretation on to the client because the
client

    A. will become hostile to the worker
    B. should arrive at his own conclusions at his own pace
    C. must request the interpretation first
    D. usually wants facts, rather than the worker's interpretation

16. In evaluating the client's capacity to cope with his problems, it is MOST important for the   16.____
worker to assess his ability to

    A. form close relationships
    B. ask for help
    C. express his hostility
    D. verbalize his difficulties

17. When a worker finds that he disagrees strongly with an agency policy, it is DESIRABLE   17.____
for him to

    A. share his feelings about the policy with his client
    B. understand fully why he has such strong feelings about the policy
    C. refer cases involving the policy to his supervisor
    D. refuse to give help in cases involving the policy

18. Which of the following practices is BEST for a supervisor to use when assigning work to   18.____
his staff?

    A. Give workers with seniority the most difficult jobs
    B. Assign all unimportant work to the slower workers
    C. Permit each employee to pick the job he prefers
    D. Make assignments based on the workers' abilities

19. In which of the following instances is a supervisor MOST justified in giving commands to people under his supervision?
When

    A. they delay in following instructions which have been given to them clearly
    B. they become relaxed and slow about work, and he wants to speed up their production
    C. he must direct them in an emergency situation
    D. he is instructing them on jobs that are unfamiliar to them

19.____

20. Which of the following supervisory actions or attitudes is MOST likely to result in getting subordinates to try to do as much work as possible for a supervisor?
He

    A. shows that his most important interest is in schedules and production goals
    B. consistently pressures his staff to get the work out
    C. never fails to let them know he is in charge
    D. considers their abilities and needs while requiring that production goals be met

20.____

KEY (CORRECT ANSWERS)

1.	D	11.	D
2.	A	12.	B
3.	D	13.	D
4.	A	14.	D
5.	B	15.	B
6.	D	16.	A
7.	C	17.	B
8.	D	18.	D
9.	B	19.	C
10.	D	20.	D

TEST 3

DIRECTIONS: Each question or incomplete statement is followed by several suggested answers or completions. Select the one that BEST answers the question or completes the statement. *PRINT THE LETTER OF THE CORRECT ANSWER IN THE SPACE AT THE RIGHT.*

1. One of your workers comes to you and complains in an angry manner about your having chosen him for some particular assignment. In your opinion, the subject of the complaint is trivial and unimportant, but it seems to be quite important to your worker.
   The BEST of the following actions for you to take in this situation is to

   A. allow the worker to continue talking until he has calmed down and then explain the reasons for your having chosen him for that particular assignment
   B. warn the worker to moderate his tone of voice at once because he is bordering on insubordination
   C. tell the worker in a friendly tone that he is making a tremendous fuss over an extremely minor matter
   D. point out to the worker that you are his immediate supervisor and that you are running the unit in accordance with official policy

1.____

2. The one of the following which is the LEAST desirable action for an assistant supervisor to take in disciplining a subordinate for an infraction of the rules is to

   A. caution him against repetition of the infraction, even if it is minor
   B. point out his progress in applying the rules at the same time that you reprimand him
   C. be as specific as possible in reprimanding him for rule infractions
   D. allow a cooling-off period to elapse before reprimanding him

2.____

3. A training program for workers assigned to the intake section should include actual practice in simulated interviews under simulated conditions.
   The one of the following educational principles which is the CHIEF justification for this statement is that

   A. the workers will remember what they see better and longer than what they read or hear
   B. the workers will learn more effectively by actually doing the act themselves than they would learn from watching others do it
   C. the conduct of simulated interviews once or twice will enable them to cope with the real situation with little difficulty
   D. a training program must employ methods of a practical nature if the workers are to find anything of lasting value in it

3.____

4. In order for a supervisor to employ the system of democratic leadership in his supervision, it would *generally* be BEST for him to

   A. allow his subordinates to assist in deciding on methods of work performance and job assignments but only in those areas where decisions have not been made on higher administrative levels

4.____

    B.   allow his subordinates to decide how to do the required work, interposing his authority when work is not completed on schedule or is improperly completed

    C.   attempt to make assignments of work to individuals only of the type which they enjoy doing

    D.   maintain control over job assignment and work production, but allow the subordinates to select methods of work and internal conditions of work at democratically conducted staff conferences

5.   In a unit in which supervision has been considered quite effective, it has become necessary to press for above-normal production for a limited period to achieve a required goal. The one of the following which is a LEAST likely result of this pressure is that   5._____

    A.   there will be more *griping* by employees

    B.   some workers will do both more and better work than has been normal for them

    C.   there will be an enhanced feeling of group unity

    D.   there will be increased absenteeism

6.   For a supervisor to encourage competitive feelings among his staff is   6._____

    A.   *advisable,* chiefly because the workers will perform more efficiently when they have proper motivation

    B.   *inadvisable,* chiefly because the workers will not perform well under the pressure of competition

    C.   *advisable,* chiefly because the workers will have a greater incentive to perform their job properly

    D.   *inadvisable,* chiefly because the workers may focus their attention on areas where they excel and neglect other essential aspects of the job

7.   In selecting jobs to be assigned to a new worker, the supervisor should assign those jobs which   7._____

    A.   give the worker the greatest variety of experience

    B.   offer the worker the greatest opportunity to achieve concrete results

    C.   present the worker with the greatest stimulation because of their interesting nature

    D.   require the least amount of contact with outside agencies

8.   A supervisor should avoid a detailed discussion of a worker-client interview with a new worker before the worker has fully recorded the interview CHIEFLY because such a discussion might   8._____

    A.   cover matters which are already fully covered and explained in the written record

    B.   make the worker forget some important detail learned during the interview

    C.   color the recording according to the worker's reaction to his supervisor's opinions

    D.   minimize the worker's feeling of having reached a decision independently

9.   Some supervisors encourage their workers to submit a list of their questions about specific jobs or their comments about problems they wish to discuss in advance of the worker-supervisor conference. This practice is   9._____

    A.   *desirable,* chiefly because it helps to stimulate and focus the worker's thinking about his caseload

    B.   *undesirable,* chiefly because it will stifle the worker's free expression of his problems and attitudes

C. *desirable,* chiefly because it will allow the conference to move along more smoothly and quickly

D. *undesirable,* chiefly because it will restrict the scope of the conference and the variety of jobs discussed

10. An alert supervisor hears a worker apparently giving the wrong information to a client and immediately reprimands him severely.
For the supervisor to reprimand the worker at this point is poor CHIEFLY because

10.____

A. instruction must precede correct performance
B. oral reprimands are less effective than written reprimands
C. the worker was given no opportunity to explain his reasons for what he did
D. more effective training can be obtained by discussing the errors with a group of workers

11. The one of the following circumstances when it would generally be MOST proper for a supervisor to do a job himself rather than to train a subordinate to do the job is when it is

11.____

A. a job which the supervisor enjoys doing and does well
B. not a very time-consuming job but an important one
C. difficult to train another to do the job, yet is not difficult for the supervisor to do
D. unlikely that this or any similar job will have to be done again at any future time

12. Effective training of subordinates requires that the supervisor understand certain facts about learning and forgetting processes.
Among these is the fact that people GENERALLY

12.____

A. forget what they learned at a much greater rate during the first day than during subsequent periods
B. both learn and forget at a relatively constant rate and this rate is dependent upon their general intellectual capacity
C. learn at a relatively constant rate except for periods of assimilation when the quantity of retained learning decreases while information is becoming firmly fixed in the mind
D. learn very slowly at first when introduced to a new topic, after which there is a great increase in the rate of learning

13. It has been suggested that a subordinate who likes his supervisor will tend to do better work than one who does not.
According to the MOST widely held current theories of supervision, this suggestion is a

13.____

A. *bad* one, since personal relationships tend to interfere with proper professional relationships
B. *bad* one, since the strongest motivating factors are fear and uncertainty
C. *good* one, since liking one's supervisor is a motivating factor for good work performance
D. *good* one, since liking one's supervisor is the most important factor in employee performance

14. One factor which might be given consideration in deciding upon the optimum span of   14.____
    control of a supervisor over his immediate subordinates is the position of the supervisor
    in the hierarchy of the organization.
    It is *generally* considered PROPER that the number of subordinates immediately
    supervised by a higher, upper echelon supervisor _____ the number supervised by
    lower level supervisors.

    A. is unrelated to and tends to form no pattern with
    B. should be about the same as
    C. should be larger than
    D. should be smaller than

15. The one of the following instances when it is MOST important for an upper level supervi-   15.____
    sor to follow the chain of command is when he is

    A. communicating decisions   B. communicating information
    C. receiving suggestions   D. seeking information

16. At the end of his probationary period, a supervisor should be considered potentially valu-   16.____
    able in his position if he shows

    A. awareness of his areas of strength and weakness, identification with the adminis-
        tration of the department, and ability to learn under supervision
    B. skill in work, supervision, and administration, and a friendly, democratic approach
        to the staff
    C. knowledge of departmental policies and procedures and ability to carry them out,
        ability to use authority, and ability to direct the work of the staff
    D. an identification with the department, acceptance of responsibility, and ability to
        give help to the individuals who are to be supervised

17. Good supervision is selective because   17.____

    A. it is not necessary to direct all the activities of the person
    B. a supervisor would never have time to know the whole caseload of a worker
    C. workers resent too much help from a supervisor
    D. too much reading is a waste of valuable time

18. An important administrative problem is how precisely to define the limits of authority that   18.____
    is delegated to subordinate supervisors.
    Such definition of limits of authority should be

    A. as precise as possible and practicable in all areas
    B. as precise as possible and practicable in areas of function, but should allow con-
        siderable flexibility in the area of personnel management
    C. as precise as possible and practicable in the area
    D. of personnel management, but should allow considerable flexibility in the areas of
        function
    E. in general terms so as to allow considerable flexibility both in the areas of function
        and in the areas of personnel management

19. Experts in the field of personnel relations feel that it is generally a bad practice for subor- 19.____
dinate employees to become aware of pending or contemplated changes in policy or
organizational set-up via the *grapevine* CHIEFLY because

    A. evidence that one or more responsible officials have proved untrustworthy will
undermine confidence in the agency
    B. the information disseminated by this method is seldom entirely accurate and gen-
erally spreads needless unrest among the subordinate staff
    C. the subordinate staff may conclude that the administration feels the staff cannot be
trusted with the true information
    D. the subordinate staff may conclude that the administration lacks the courage to
make an unpopular announcement through official channels

20. Supervision is subject to many interpretations, depending on the area in which it func- 20.____
tions.
Of the following, the statement which represents the MOST appropriate meaning of
supervision as it is known in social work practice is that it

    A. is a leadership process for the development of new leaders
    B. is an educational and administrative process aimed at teaching personnel the goal
of improved service to the client
    C. is an activity aimed chiefly at insuring that workers will adhere to all agency direc-
tives
    D. provides the opportunity for administration to secure staff reaction to agency poli-
cies

21. A supervisor may utilize various methods in the supervisory process. 21.____
The one of the following upon which sound supervisory practice rests in the selection
of supervisory techniques is

    A. an estimate of the worker arrived at through current and past evaluation of perfor-
mance as well as through worker's participation
    B. the previous supervisor's evaluation and recommendation
    C. the worker's expression of his personal preference for certain types of experience
    D. the amount of time available to supervisor and supervisee

22. It is the practice of some supervisors, when they believe that it would be desirable for a 22.____
subordinate to take a particular action in a case, to inform the subordinate of this in the
form of a suggestion rather than in the form of a direct order.
In general, this method of getting a subordinate to take the desired action is

    A. *inadvisable;* it may create in the mind of the subordinate the impression that the
supervisor is uncertain about the efficacy of her plan and is trying to avoid what-
ever responsibility she may have in resolving the case
    B. *advisable;* it provides the subordinate with the maximum opportunity to use her
own judgment in handling the case
    C. *inadvisable;* it provides the subordinate with no clear-cut direction and, therefore, is
likely to leave her with a feeling of uncertainty and frustration
    D. *advisable;* it presents the supervisor's view in a manner which will be most likely to
evoke the subordinate's cooperation

23. A veteran supervisor noticed that one of her workers of average ability had begun developing some bad work habits, becoming especially careless in her recordkeeping. After reprimand from the supervisor, the investigator corrected her errors and has been doing satisfactory work since then.
For the supervisor to keep referring to this period of poor work during her weekly conferences with this employee would *generally* be considered poor personnel practice CHIEFLY because

    A. praise rather than criticism is generally the best method to use in improving the work of an unsatisfactory worker
    B. the supervisor cannot know whether the employee's errors will follow an established pattern
    C. the fault which evoked the original negative criticism no longer exists
    D. this would tend to frustrate the worker by making her strive overly hard to reach a level of productivity which is beyond her ability to achieve

23.____

24. Assume that you are now a supervisor in a specific unit. Two experienced investigators in your unit, both of whom do above average work, have for some time not gotten along with each other for personal reasons. Their attitude toward one another has suddenly become hostile and noisy disagreement has taken place in the office.
The BEST action for you to take FIRST in this situation is to

    A. transfer one of the two investigators to another unit where contact with the other investigator will be unnecessary
    B. discuss the problem with the two investigators together, insisting that they confide in you and tell you the cause of their mutual antagonism
    C. confer with the two investigators separately, pointing out to each the need to adopt an adult professional attitude with respect to their on-the-job relations
    D. advise the two investigators that should the situation grow worse, disciplinary action will be considered

24.____

25. It has long been recognized that relationships exist between worker morale and working conditions. The one of the following which BEST clarifies these existing relationships is that morale is

    A. affected for better or for worse in direct relationship to the magnitude of the changes in working conditions for better or worse
    B. better when working conditions are better
    C. little affected by working conditions so long as the working conditions do not approach the intolerable
    D. more affected by the degree of interest shown in providing good working conditions than by the actual conditions and may, perversely, be highest when working conditions are worst

25.____

KEY (CORRECT ANSWERS)

1.	A		11.	D
2.	D		12.	A
3.	B		13.	C
4.	A		14.	D
5.	D		15.	A
6.	D		16.	D
7.	B		17.	A
8.	C		18.	A
9.	A		19.	B
10.	C		20.	B

21.	A
22.	D
23.	C
24.	C
25.	D

SUPERVISION, ADMINISTRATION, MANAGEMENT AND ORGANIZATION

EXAMINATION SECTION
TEST 1

DIRECTIONS: Each question or incomplete statement is followed by several suggested answers or completions. Select the one that BEST answers the question or completes the statement. *PRINT THE LETTER OF THE CORRECT ANSWER IN THE SPACE AT THE RIGHT.*

1. One of the responsibilities of the supervisor is to provide top administration with information about clients and their problems that will help in the evaluation of existing policies and indicate the need for modifications.
   In order to fulfill this responsibility, it would be MOST essential for the supervisor to

   A. routinely forward all regularly prepared and recurrent reports from his subordinates to his immediate superior
   B. regularly review agency rules, regulations and policies to make sure that he has sufficient knowledge to make appropriate analyses
   C. note repeated instances of failure of staff to correctly administer a policy and schedule staff conferences for corrective training
   D. analyze reports on cases submitted by subordinates, in order to select relevant trend material to be forwarded to his superiors

1.____

2. You find that your division has a serious problem because of unusually long delays in filing reports and overdue approvals to private agencies under contract for services.
   The MOST appropriate step to take FIRST in this situation would be to

   A. request additional staff to work on reports and approvals
   B. order staff to work overtime until the backlog is eliminated
   C. impress staff with the importance of expeditious handling of reports and approvals
   D. analyze present procedures for handling reports and approvals

2.____

3. When a supervisor finds that he must communicate orally information that is significant enough to affect the entire staff, it would be MOST important to

   A. distribute a written summary of the information to his staff before discussing it orally
   B. tell his subordinate supervisors to discuss this information at individual conferences with their subordinates
   C. call a follow-up meeting of absentees as soon as they return
   D. restate and summarize the information in order to make sure that everyone understands its meaning and implications

3.____

4. Of the following, the BEST way for a supervisor to assist a subordinate who has unusually heavy work pressures is to

   A. point out that such pressures go with the job and must be tolerated
   B. suggest to him that the pressures probably result from poor handling of his workload
   C. help him to be selective in deciding on priorities during the period of pressure
   D. ask him to work overtime until the period of pressure is over

4.____

5. Leadership is a basic responsibility of the supervisor. The one of the following which would be the LEAST appropriate way to fulfill this role is for the supervisor to

    A. help staff to work up to their capacities in every possible way
    B. encourage independent judgment and actions by staff members
    C. allow staff to participate in decisions within policy limits
    D. take over certain tasks in which he is more competent than his subordinates

5.____

6. Assume that you have assigned a very difficult administrative task to one of your best subordinate supervisors, but he is reluctant to take it on because he fears that he will fail in it. It is your judgment, however, that he is quite capable of performing this task.
The one of the following which is the MOST desirable way for you to handle this situation is to

    A. reassure him that he has enough skill to perform the task and that he will not be penalized if he fails
    B. reassign the task to another supervisor who is more achievement-oriented and more confident of his skills
    C. minimize the importance of the task so that he will feel it is safe for him to attempt it
    D. stress the importance of the task and the dependence of the other staff members on his succeeding in it

6.____

7. Assume that a member of your professional staff deliberately misinterprets a new state directive because he fears that its enforcement will have an adverse effect on clients. Although you consider him to be a good supervisor and basically agree with him, you should direct him to comply.
Of the following, the MOST desirable way for you to handle this situation would be to

    A. avoid a confrontation with him by transferring responsibility for carrying out the directive to another member of your staff
    B. explain to him that you are in a better position than he to assess the implications of the new directive
    C. discuss with him the basic reasons for his misinterpretation and explain why he must comply with the directive
    D. allow him to interpret the directive in his own way as long as he assumes full responsibility for his actions

7.____

8. Of the following, the MAIN reason it is important for an administrator in a large organization to properly coordinate the work delegated to subordinates is that such coordination

    A. makes it unnecessary to hold frequent staff meetings and conferences with key staff members
    B. reduces the necessity for regular evaluation of procedures and programs, production and performance of personnel
    C. results in greater economy and stricter accountability for the organization's resources
    D. facilitates integration of the contributions of the numerous staff members who are responsible for specific parts of the total workload

8.____

9. The one of the following which would NOT be an appropriate reason for the formulation   9.____
of an entirely NEW policy is that it would

    A. serve as a positive affirmation of the agency's function and how it is to be carried
out
    B. give focus and direction to the work of the staff, particularly in decision-making
    C. inform the public of the precise conditions under which services will be rendered
    D. provide procedures which constitute uniform methods of carrying out operations

10. Of the following, it is MOST difficult to formulate policy in an organization where   10.____

    A. work assignments are narrowly specialized by units
    B. staff members have varied backgrounds and a wide range of competency
    C. units implementing the same policy are in the same geographic location
    D. staff is experienced and fully trained

11. For a supervisor to feel that he is responsible for influencing the attitudes of his staff   11.____
members is GENERALLY considered

    A. *undesirable;* attitudes of adults are emotional factors which usually cannot be
changed
    B. *desirable;* certain attitudes can be obstructive and should be modified in order to
provide effective service to clients
    C. *undesirable;* the supervisor should be nonjudgmental and accepting of widely dif-
ferent attitudes and social patterns of staff members
    D. *desirable;* influencing attitudes is a teaching responsibility which the supervisor
shares with the training specialist

12. The one of the following which is NOT generally a function of the higher-level supervisor   12.____
is

    A. projecting the budget and obtaining financial resources
    B. providing conditions conducive to optimum employee production
    C. maintaining records and reports as a basis for accountability and evaluation
    D. evaluating program achievements and personnel effectiveness in accordance with
goals and standards

13. As a supervisor in a recently decentralized services center offering multiple services, you   13.____
are given responsibility for an orientation program for professional staff on the recent
reorganization of the Department.
Of the following, the MOST appropriate step to take FIRST would be to

    A. organize a series of workshops for subordinate supervisors
    B. arrange a tour of the new geographic area of service
    C. review supervisors' reports, statistical data and other relevant material
    D. develop a resource manual for staff on the reorganized center

14. Experts generally agree that the content of training sessions should be closely related to   14.____
workers' practice.
Of the following, the BEST method of achieving this aim is for the training conference
leader to

    A. encourage group discussion of problems that concern staff in their practice
    B. develop closer working relationships with top administration

C.   coordinate with central office to obtain feedback on problems that concern staff
D.   observe workers in order to develop a pattern of problems for class discussion

15. The one of the following which is generally the MOST useful teaching tool for profes-   15.____
sional staff development is

A.   visual aids and tape recordings
B.   professional literature
C.   agency case material
D.   lectures by experts

16. The one of the following which is NOT a good reason for using group conferences as a   16.____
method of supervision is to

A.   give workers a feeling of mutual support through sharing common problems
B.   save time by eliminating the need for individual conferences
C.   encourage discussion of certain problems that are not as likely to come up in indi-
vidual conferences
D.   provide an opportunity for developing positive identification with the department
and its programs

17. The supervisor, in his role as teacher, applies his teaching in line with his understanding   17.____
of people and realizes that teaching is a highly individualized process, based on understanding of the worker as a person and as a learner. This statement implies, MOST
NEARLY, that the supervisor must help the worker to

A.   overcome his biases
B.   develop his own ways of working
C.   gain confidence in his ability
D.   develop the will to work

18. Of the following, the circumstance under which it would be MOST appropriate to divide a   18.____
training conference for professional staff into small workshops is when

A.   some of the trainees are not aware of the effect of their attitudes and behavior on
others
B.   the trainees need to look at human relations problems from different perspectives
C.   the trainees are faced with several substantially different types of problems in their
job assignments
D.   the trainees need to know how to function in many different capacities

19. Of the following, the MAIN reason why it is important to systemically evaluate a specific   19.____
training program while it is in progress is to

A.   collect data that will serve as a valid basis for improving the agency's overall training program and maintaining control over its components
B.   insure that instruction by training specialists is conducted in a manner consistent
with the planned design of the training program
C.   identify areas in which additional or remedial training for the training specialists can
be planned and implemented
D.   provide data which are usable in effecting revisions of specific components of the
training program

20. Staff development has been defined as an educational process which seeks to provide agency staff with knowledge about specific job responsibilities and to effect changes in staff attitudes and behavior patterns. Assume that you are assigned to define the educational objectives of a specific training program.
    In accordance with the above concept, the MOST helpful formulation would be a statement of the

    A. purpose and goals of each training session
    B. generalized patterns of behavior to be developed in the trainees
    C. content material to be presented in the training sessions
    D. kind of behavior to be developed in the trainees and the situations in which this behavior will be applied

20.____

21. In teaching personnel under your supervision how to gather and analyze facts before attempting to solve a problem, the one of the following training methods which would be MOST effective is

    A. case study
    B. role playing
    C. programmed learning
    D. planned experience'

21.____

22. The importance of analyzing functions traditionally included in the position of caseworker, with a view toward identifying and separating those activities to be performed by the most highly skilled personnel, has been widely discussed.
    Of the following, an IMPORTANT *secondary* gain which can result from such differential use of staff is that

    A. supporting job assignments can be given to persons unable to meet the demands of casework, to the satisfaction of all concerned
    B. documentation will be provided on workers who are not suited for all the duties now part of the caseworker's job
    C. caseworkers with a high level of competence in working with people can be rewarded through promotion or merit increases
    D. incompetent workers can be identified and categorized, as a basis for transfer or separation from the service

22.____

23. Of the following, a serious DISADVANTAGE of a performance evaluation system based on standardized evaluation factors is that such a system tends to

    A. exacerbate the anxieties of those supervisors who are apprehensive about determining what happens to another person
    B. subject the supervisor to psychological stress by emphasizing the incompatibility of his dual role as both judge and counselor
    C. create organizational conflict by encouraging personnel who wish to enhance their standing to become too aggressive in the performance of their duties
    D. lead many staff members to concentrate on measuring up in terms of the evaluation factors and to disregard other aspects of their work

23.____

24. Which of the following would contribute MOST to the achievement of conformity of staff activities and goals to the intent of agency policies and procedures?

    A. Effective communications and organizational discipline
    B. Changing nature of the underlying principles and desired purpose of the policies and procedures

24.____

C. Formulation of specific criteria for implementing the policies and procedures
D. Continuous monitoring of the essential effectiveness of agency operations

25. Job enlargement, a management device used by large organizations to counteract the adverse effects of specialization on employee performance, is LEAST likely to improve employee motivation if it is accomplished by   25.____

A. lengthening the job cycle and adding a large number of similar tasks
B. allowing the employee to use a greater variety of skills
C. increasing the scope and complexity of the employee's job
D. giving the employee more opportunities to make decisions

KEY (CORRECT ANSWERS)

1.	D	11.	B
2.	D	12.	A
3.	D	13.	A
4.	C	14.	A
5.	D	15.	C
6.	A	16.	B
7.	C	17.	B
8.	D	18.	C
9.	D	19.	A
10.	B	20.	D

21.	A
22.	A
23.	D
24.	A
25.	A

TEST 2

DIRECTIONS: Each question or incomplete statement is followed by several suggested answers or completions. Select the one that BEST answers the question or completes the statement. *PRINT THE LETTER OF THE CORRECT ANSWER IN THE SPACE AT THE RIGHT.*

1. When a supervisor requires approval for case action on a higher level, the process used is known as   1._____

   A. administrative clearance
   C. administrative consultation
   B. going outside channels
   D. delegation of authority

2. In delegating authority to his subordinates, the one of the following to which a GOOD supervisor should give PRIMARY consideration is the   2._____

   A. results expected of them
   B. amount of power to be delegated
   C. amount of responsibility to be delegated
   D. their skill in the performance of present tasks

3. Of the following, the type of decision which could be SAFELY delegated to LOWER-LEVEL staff without undermining basic supervisory responsibility is one which   3._____

   A. involves a commitment that can be fulfilled only over a long period of time
   B. has fairly uncertain goals and premises
   C. has the possibility of modification built into it
   D. may generate considerable resistance from those affected by it

4. Of the following, the MOST valuable contribution made by the informal organization in a large public service agency is that such an organization   4._____

   A. has goals and values which are usually consistent with and reinforce those of the formal organization
   B. is more flexible than the formal organization and more adaptable to changing conditions
   C. has a communications system which often contributes to the efficiency of the formal organization
   D. represents a sound basis on which to build the formal organizational structure

5. Of the following, the condition under which it would be MOST useful for an agency to develop detailed procedures is when   5._____

   A. subordinate supervisory personnel need a structure to help them develop greater independence
   B. employees have little experience or knowledge of how to perform certain assigned tasks
   C. coordination of agency activities is largely dependent upon personal contact
   D. agency activities must continually adjust to changes in local circumstances

6. Assume that a certain administrator has the management philosophy that his agency's responsibility is to routinize existing operations, meet each day's problems as they arise, and resolve problems with a minimum of residual effect upon himself or his agency. The possibility that this official would be able to administer his agency without running into serious difficulties would be MORE likely during a period of   6._____

   A. economic change
   C. economic crisis
   B. social change
   D. social and economic stability

7. Some large organizations have adopted the practice of allowing each employee to estab-   7._____
   lish his own performance goals, and then later evaluate himself in an individual conference with his immediate supervisor.
   Of the following, a DRAWBACK of this approach is that the employee

   A. may set his goals too low and rate himself too highly
   B. cannot control those variables which may improve his performance
   C. has no guidelines for improving his performance
   D. usually finds it more difficult to criticize himself than to accept criticism from others

8. Decentralization of services cannot completely eliminate the requirement of central office   8._____
   approval for certain case actions. The MOST valid reason for complaint about this
   requirement is that

   A. unavoidable delay created by referral to central office may cause serious problems
       for the client
   B. it may lower morale of supervisors who are not given the authority to take final
       action on urgent cases
   C. the concept of role responsibility is minimized
   D. the objective of delegated responsibility tends to be negated

9. Which of the following would be the MOST useful administrative tool for the purpose of   9._____
   showing the sequence of operations and staff involved? A(n)

   A. organization chart   B. flow chart
   C. manual of operating procedures D. statistical review

10. The prevailing pattern of organization in large public agencies consists of a limited span   10._____
    of control and organization by function or, at lower levels, process.
    Of the following, the PRINCIPAL effect which this pattern of organization has on the
    management of work is that it

    A. reduces the management burden in significant ways
    B. creates a time lag between the perception of a problem and action on it
    C. makes it difficult to direct and observe employee performance
    D. facilitates the development of employees with managerial ability

11. The one of the following which would be the MOST appropriate way to reduce tensions   11._____
    between line and staff personnel in public service agencies is to

    A. provide in-service training that will increase the sensitivity of line and staff person-
        nel to their respective roles
    B. assign to staff personnel the role of providing assistance only when requested by
        line personnel
    C. separate staff from line personnel and provide staff with its own independent
        reward structure
    D. give line and staff personnel equal status in making decisions

12. In determining the appropriate span of control for subordinate supervisors, which of the   12._____
    following principles should be followed? The more

    A. complex the work, the broader the effective span of control
    B. similar the jobs being supervised, the more narrow the effective span of control

C.   interdependent the jobs being supervised, the more narrow the effective span of control
D.   unpredictable the work, the broader the effective span of control

13.   A method sometimes used in public service agencies to improve upward communication is to require subordinate supervisory staff to submit to top management monthly narrative reports of any problems which they deem important for consideration.
Of the following, a major DISADVANTAGE of this method is that it may

   A.   enable subordinate supervisors to avoid thinking about their problems by simply referring such matters to their superiors
   B.   obscure important issues so that they are not given appropriate attention
   C.   create a need for numerous staff conferences in order to handle all of the reported problems
   D.   encourage some subordinate supervisors to focus on irrelevant matters and compete with each other in the length and content of their reports

13.____

14.   The use of a committee as an approach to the problem of coordinating interdepartmental activities can present difficulties if the committee functions PRIMARILY as a(n)

   A.   means of achieving personal objectives and goals
   B.   instrument for coordinating activities that flow across departmental lines
   C.   device for involving subordinate personnel in the decision-making process
   D.   means of giving representation to competing interest groups

14.____

15.   A study was recently made of the attitudes and perceptions of a sample of workers who had experienced a major organizational change and redefinition of their jobs as a result of separation of certain functions.
Questionnaires administered to these workers indicated that a disproportionate number of workers in the larger agencies were dissatisfied with the reorganization and their new assignments.
Of the following, the MOST plausible reason for this dissatisfaction is that workers in larger agencies are

   A.   less likely to be known to management and to be personally disciplined if they expressed dissatisfaction with their new roles
   B.   less likely to have the opportunity to participate in planning a reorganization and to be given consideration for the assignments they preferred
   C.   given a shorter lead period to implement the changes and therefore had insufficient time to plan the reorganization and carry it out efficiently
   D.   usually made up of more older members who have had routinized their work according to habit and find it more difficult to adjust to change

15.____

16.   An article which recently appeared in a professional journal presents a proposal for participatory leadership, in which the goal of supervision would be development of subordinates' self-reliance, with the premise that each staff member is held accountable for his own performance.
The one of the following which would NOT be a desirable outcome of this type of supervision is the

   A.   necessity for subordinates to critically examine their performance
   B.   development by some subordinates of skills not possessed by the supervisor

16.____

C. establishment of a quality control unit for sample checking and identification of errors
D. relaxation of demands made on the supervisor

17. The "management by objectives" concept is a major development in the administration of services organizations. The purpose of this approach is to establish a system for   17.____

A. reduction of waiting time
B. planning and controlling work output
C. consolidation of organizational units
D. work measurement

18. Assume that you encounter a serious administrative problem in implementing a new pro-   18.____
gram. After consulting with the members of your staff individually, you come up with several alternate solutions.
Of the following, the procedure which would be MOST appropriate for evaluating the relative merits of each solution would be to

A. try all of them on a limited experimental basis
B. break the problem down into its component parts and analyze the effect of each solution on each component in terms of costs and benefits
C. break the problem down into its component parts, eliminate all intangibles, and measure the effect of the tangible aspects of each solution on each component in terms of costs and benefits
D. bring the matter before your weekly staff conference, discuss the relative merits of each alternate solution, and then choose the one favored by the majority of the conference

19. When establishing planning objectives for a service program under your supervision, the   19.____
one of the following principles which should be followed is that objectives

A. are rarely verifiable if they are qualitative
B. should be few in number and of equal importance
C. should cover as many of the activities of the program as possible
D. should be set in the light of assumptions about future funding

20. Assume that you have been assigned responsibility for coordinating various aspects of a   20.____
program in a community services center. Which of the following administrative concepts would NOT be applicable to this assignment?

A. Functional job analysis   B. Peer group supervision
C. Differential use of staff   D. Systems design

21. Good administrative practice includes the use of outside consultants as an effective tech-   21.____
nique in achieving agency objectives. However, the one of the following which would NOT be an appropriate role for the consultant is

A. provision of technical or professional expertise not otherwise available in the agency
B. administrative direction of a new program activity
C. facilitating coordination and communication among agency staff
D. objective measurement of the effectiveness of agency services

22. Of the following, the MOST common fault of research projects attempting to measure the effectiveness of social programs has been their

    A. questionable methodology
    B. inaccurate findings
    C. unrealistic expectations
    D. lack of objectivity

22.____

23. One of the most difficult tasks of supervision in a modern public agency is teaching workers to cope with the hostile reactions of clients. In order to help the disconcerted worker analyze and understand a client's hostile behavior, the supervisor should FIRST

    A. encourage the worker to identify with the client's frustrations and deprivations
    B. give the worker a chance to express and accept his feelings about the client
    C. ask the worker to review his knowledge of the client and his circumstances
    D. explain to the worker that the client's anger is not directed at the worker personally

23.____

24. Determination of the level of participation, or how much of the public should participate in a given project, is a vital step in community organization.
In order to make this determination, the FIRST action that should be taken is to

    A. develop the participants
    B. fix the goals of the project
    C. evaluate community interest in the project
    D. enlist the cooperation of community leaders

24.____

25. The one of the following which would be the MOST critical factor for SUCCESSFUL operation of a decentralized system of programs and services is

    A. periodic review and evaluation of services delivered at the community level
    B. transfer of decision-making authority to the community level wherever feasible
    C. participation of indigenous non-professionals in service delivery
    D. formulation of quantitative plans for dealing with community problems wherever feasible

25.____

KEY (CORRECT ANSWERS)

1.	A		11.	A
2.	A		12.	C
3.	C		13.	D
4.	C		14.	A
5.	B		15.	B
6.	D		16.	D
7.	A		17.	B
8.	A		18.	C
9.	B		19.	D
10.	B		20.	B

21.	B
22.	C
23.	B
24.	B
25.	B

———

TEST 3

DIRECTIONS: Each question or incomplete statement is followed by several suggested answers or completions. Select the one that BEST answers the question or completes the statement. *PRINT THE LETTER OF THE CORRECT ANSWER IN THE SPACE AT THE RIGHT.*

1. Douglas McGregor's theory of human motivation classifies worker behavior into two distinct categories: Theory X and Theory Y. Theory X, the traditional view, states that the average man dislikes to work and will avoid work if he can, unless coerced. Theory Y holds essentially the opposite view. The executive can apply both of these theories to worker behavior BEST if he

    1.____

    A. follows an "open-door" policy only with respect to his immediate subordinates
    B. recognizes his subordinates' mental and social needs as well as agency needs
    C. recognizes that executive responsibility is primarily limited to fulfillment of agency productivity goals
    D. directs his subordinate managers to follow a policy of close supervision

2. In interpersonal communications it is of paramount importance to determine whether or not what has been said has been understood by others. One of the MOST important sources of such information is known as

    2.____

    A. the halo effect   B. evaluation
    C. feedback   D. quantitative analysis

3. The grapevine most often provides a USEFUL service by

    3.____

    A. correcting some of the deficiencies of the formal communication system
    B. rapidly conveying a true picture of events
    C. involving staff in current organizational changes
    D. interfering with the operation of the formal communication system

4. People who are in favor of a leadership style in which the subordinates help make decisions, contend that it produces favorable effects in a work unit. According to these people, which of the following is NOT likely to be an effect of such "participative management"?

    4.____

    A. Reduced turnover
    B. Accelerated learning of duties
    C. Greater acceptance of change
    D. Reduced acceptance of the work unit's goals

5. Employees of a public service agency will be MOST likely to develop meaningful goals for both the agency and the employee and become committed to attaining them if supervisors

    5.____

    A. allow them unilaterally to set their own goals
    B. provide them with a clear understanding of the premises underlying the agency's goals
    C. encourage them to concentrate on setting only short-range goals for themselves
    D. periodically review the agency's goals in order to suggest changes in accordance with current conditions

6. The insights of Chester Barnard have influenced the development of management   6.____
   thought in significant ways. He is MOST closely identified with a position that has
   become known as the

   A. acceptance theory of authority
   B. principle of the manager's or executive's span of control
   C. "Theory X" and "Theory Y" dichotomy
   D. unity of command principle

7. If a manager believes that man is primarily motivated by economic incentives and,above   7.____
   all,seeks security, he MOST usually should operate on the assumption that his subordinates

   A. need to be closely directed and have relatively little ambition
   B. are more responsive to the social forces of their peer group than to the incentives
      of management
   C. are capable of learning not only to accept but to seek responsibility
   D. are capable of responding favorably to many different kinds of managerial strate-
      gies

8. Of the following, the MOST important reason why it is in the interest of public service   8.____
   agencies to involve subordinate personnel in setting goals is that the more committed
   employees are to the goals of their agency the

   A. *more* likely they are to develop a desire for the agency's achievement of success
   B. *more* likely they are to prefer difficult rather than easy tasks
   C. *more* likely they are to perceive their individual performance as a reliable indicator
      of the agency's performance
   D. *less* likely they are to choose unreasonably difficult goals

9. As a result of gaining more recent knowledge about motivation, modern executives have   9.____
   had to rethink their notions about what motivates their subordinate managers. Which of
   the following factors is GENERALLY considered MOST important in modern motivation
   theory?

   A. Fringe benefits
   B. Working conditions
   C. Recognition of good work performance
   D. Education and experience required for the job

10. Of the following, the MAIN reason why cooperative interrelationships among personnel   10.____
    are more likely than competitive interrelationships to promote efficiency in the operation
    of a public service agency is that cooperation

    A. allows for a greater degree of specialization by function
    B. increases the opportunities for employees to check on each others' work
    C. provides a feeling of identification with the organization and enhances the desire
       for accomplishment
    D. improves the capacity of employees to acquire knowledge and learn new skills

11. Four statements are given below. Three of them describe approaches which are desir-   11.____
able in developing a program of employee motivation. The one which does NOT describe
such an approach is:

  A. "Establish attainable goals to give employees a sense of achievement."
  B. "Largely discount the self-interest motive because it is impractical to consider it."
  C. "Allow for the participation of persons included in the plans."
  D. "Base plans on group considerations as well as individual considerations."

12. It is GENERALLY acknowledged that certain conditions should exist to insure that a sub-   12.____
ordinate will decide to accept a communication as being authoritative. Which of the following is LEAST valid as a condition which should exist?

  A. The subordinate understands the communication
  B. At the time of the subordinate's decision, he views the communication as consis-
tent with the organization's purpose and his personal interest
  C. At the time of the subordinate's decision, he views the communication as more
consistent with his personal purpose than with the organization's interests
  D. The subordinate is mentally and physically able to comply with the communication

13. In exploring the effects that employee participation has on putting changes in work meth-   13.____
ods into effect, certain relationships have been established between participation and
productivity. It has MOST generally been found that HIGHEST productivity occurs in
groups that are given

  A. participation in the process of change only through representatives of their group
  B. no participation in the change process
  C. full participation in the change process
  D. intermittent participation in the process of change

14. Of the following statements, the one which represents a trend LEAST likely to occur in   14.____
the area of employee-management relations is that:

  A. Employees will exert more influence on decisions affecting their interests.
  B. Technological change will have a stronger impact on organizations' human
resources.
  C. Labor will judge management according to company profits.
  D. Government will play a larger role in balancing the interests of the parties in labor-
management affairs.

15. Members of an organization must satisfy several fundamental psychological needs in   15.____
order to be happy and productive. The broadest and MOST basic needs are

  A. achievement, recognition and acceptance
  B. competition, recognition and accomplishment
  C. salary increments and recognition
  D. acceptance of competition and economic reward

16. Morale has been defined as the capacity of a group of people to pull together steadily for   16.____
a common purpose. Morale thus defined is MOST generally dependent on which one of
the following conditions?

  A. Job security
  B. Group and individual self-confidence
  C. Organizational efficiency
  D. Physical health of the individuals

17. Assume that consideration is being given to forming a committee for the purpose of get-   17.____
ting a. new program under way which requires the coordination of several organizational
units. Which one of the following would be a MAJOR weakness of using the "committee"
approach in this situation?

    A. Its inappropriateness for decision-making
    B. The necessity to include line and staff employees
    C. The difficulty of achieving proper representation
    D. Its independence from the formal organization

18. Which of the following techniques is NOT used as an approach to encourage communi-   18.____
cation between individuals at the same level?

    A. The informal organization   B. The chain of command
    C. Committee meetings   D. Distribution of written reports

19. In everyday actual operations, downward communications MOST often concern   19.____

    A. specific directives about job performance
    B. information about worker performance
    C. information about the rationale of the job
    D. information to indoctrinate the organization's staff on goals to be achieved

20. Communication has been thought of for a long time as a vital process in a formal organi-   20.____
zation system. Of the following, the MOST accurate statement that can be made concerning this process is that

    A. decision-making depends on communication and organizational structure
    B. communication does not interact but is interdependent with organizational struc-
ture and decision-making
    C. effective decision-making is dependent on organizational structure but not on com-
munication
    D. communication is dependent on the decision-making process but not on organiza-
tional structure

21. In coaching a subordinate manager in the use of the type of management in which sub-   21.____
ordinate employees participate, an executive would be MOST accurate in emphasizing
that participative management

    A. uses consultative as opposed to democratic techniques
    B. uses democratic as opposed to consultative techniques
    C. requires the involvement of subordinates while reserving for the superior the right
to make decisions
    D. requires involving subordinates and giving them the right to make most decisions

22. In most work situations, employees tend to form informal groups and relationships. The   22.____
BEST way for a supervisor interested in high productivity to deal with such groups and
relationships is to

    A. take them into account as much as possible when making work assignments and
schedules
    B. ignore them, since such relationships and groups usually have no effect on work
productivity

C. attempt to destroy such groups and relationships since they are usually counter-productive
D. ignore them, even though they are usually counterproductive, since nothing can be done about them

23. Assume that in an office an entirely new method has been introduced in the handling of applications for service and related information. Employees USUALLY approach such a sudden change in their work routine with an attitude of   23._____

   A. *apprehension,* chiefly because such a change makes them uncertain of their position
   B. *indifference,* chiefly because most people don't care what they are doing, as long as they are paid
   C. *approval,* chiefly because such a change provides a welcome change of pace in their work
   D. *acceptance,* mainly because most people prefer changes to the same routines

24. In what order should the following steps be taken when revising office procedure?   24._____
         I. To develop the improved method as determined by time and motion studies and effective workplace layout
        II. To find out how the task is now performed
       III. To apply the new method
        IV. To analyze the current method
   The CORRECT order is:

   A. IV, II, I, III   B. II, I, III, IV
   C. I, II, IV, III   D. II, IV, I, III

25. In contrast to broad spans of control, narrow spans of control are MOST likely to   25._____

   A. provide opportunity for more personal contact between superior and subordinate
   B. encourage decentralization
   C. stress individual initiative
   D. foster group or team effort

KEY (CORRECT ANSWERS)

1.	B	11.	B
2.	C	12.	C
3.	A	13.	C
4.	D	14.	C
5.	B	15.	A
6.	A	16.	B
7.	A	17.	A
8.	A	18.	B
9.	C	19.	A
10.	C	20.	A

21.	C
22.	A
23.	A
24.	D
25.	A

EXAMINATION SECTION
TEST 1

DIRECTIONS: Each question or incomplete statement is followed by several suggested answers or completions. Select the one that BEST answers the question or completes the statement. *PRINT THE LETTER OF THE CORRECT ANSWER IN THE SPACE AT THE RIGHT.*

1. A supervisor notices that one of his more competent subordinates has recently been showing less interest in his work. The work performed by this employee has also fallen off and he seems to want to do no more than the minimum acceptable amount of work. When his supervisor questions the subordinate about his decreased interest and his mediocre work performance, the subordinate replies: *Sure, I've lost interest in my work. I don't see any reason why I should do more than I have to. When I do a good job, nobody notices it. But, let me fall down on one minor job and the whole place knows about it! So why should I put myself out on this job?*
If the subordinate's contentions are true, it would be correct to assume that the

    A. subordinate has not received adequate training
    B. subordinate's workload should be decreased
    C. supervisor must share responsibility for this employee's reaction
    D. supervisor has not been properly enforcing work standards

1.____

2. *How many subordinates should report directly to each supervisor? While there is agreement that there are limits to the number of subordinates that a manager can supervise well, this limit is determined by a number of important factors.*
Which of the following factors is most likely to increase the number of subordinates that can be effectively supervised by one supervisor in a particular unit?

    A. The unit has a great variety of activities
    B. A staff assistant handles the supervisor's routine duties
    C. The unit has a relatively inexperienced staff
    D. The office layout is being rearranged to make room for more employees

2.____

3. Mary Smith, an Administrative Assistant, heads the Inspection Records Unit of Department Y. She is a dedicated supervisor who not only strives to maintain an efficient operation, but she also tries to improve the competence of each individual member of her staff. She keeps these considerations in mind when assigning work to her staff. Her bureau chief asks her to compile some data based on information contained in her records. She feels that any member of her staff should be able to do this job. The one of the following members of her staff who would probably be given LEAST consideration for this assignment is

    A. Jane Abel, a capable Supervising Clerk with considerable experience in the unit
    B. Kenneth Brown, a Senior Clerk recently transferred to the unit who has not had an opportunity to demonstrate his capabilities
    C. Laura Chance, a Clerk who spends full time on a single routine assignment
    D. Michael Dunn, a Clerk who works on several minor jobs but still has the lightest workload

3.____

4. *There are very few aspects of a supervisor's job that do not involve communication, either in writing or orally.*
Which of the following statements regarding oral and written orders is NOT correct?

4.____

A. Oral orders usually permit more immediate feedback than do written orders.
B. Written orders, rather than oral orders, should generally be given when the subordinate will be held strictly accountable.
C. Oral orders are usually preferable when the order contains lengthy detailed instructions.
D. Written orders, rather than oral orders, should usually be given to a subordinate who is slow to understand or is forgetful.

5. Assume that you are the head of a large clerical unit in Department R. Your department's personnel office has appointed a Clerk, Roberta Rowe, to fill a vacancy in your unit. Before bringing this appointee to your office, the personnel office has given Roberta the standard orientation on salary, fringe benefits, working conditions, attendance and the department's personnel rules. In addition, he has supplied her with literature covering these areas. Of the following, the action that you should take FIRST after Roberta has been brought to your office is to

A. give her an opportunity to read the literature furnished by the personnel office so that she can ask you questions about it
B. escort her to the desk she will use and assign her to work with an experienced employee who will act as her trainer
C. explain the duties and responsibilities of her job and its relationship with the jobs being performed by the other employees of the unit
D. summon the employee who is currently doing the work that will be performed by Roberta and have him explain and demonstrate how to perform the required tasks

6. Your superior informs you that the employee turnover rate in your office is well above the norm and must be reduced. Which one of the following initial steps would be LEAST appropriate in attempting to overcome this problem?

A. Decide to be more lenient about performance standards and about employee requests for time off, so that your office will gain a reputation as an easy place to work
B. Discuss the problem with a few of your key people whose judgment you trust to see if they can shed some light on the underlying causes of the problem
C. Review the records of employees who have left during the past year to see if there is a pattern that will help you understand the problem
D. Carefully review your training procedures to see whether they can be improved

7. In issuing instructions to a subordinate on a job assignment, the supervisor should ordinarily explain why the assignment is being made. Omission of such an explanation is best justified when the

A. subordinate is restricted in the amount of discretion he can exercise in carrying out the assignment
B. assignment is one that will be unpopular with the subordinate
C. subordinate understands the reason as a result of previous similar assignments
D. assignment is given to an employee who is in need of further training

8. When a supervisor allows sufficient time for training and makes an appropriate effort in the training of his subordinates, his chief goal is to

A. increase the dependence of one subordinate upon another in their everyday work activities
B. spend more time with his subordinates in order to become more involved in their work
C. increase the capability and independence of his subordinates in carrying out their work
D. increase his frequency of contact with his subordinates in order to better evaluate their performance

9. In preparing an evaluation of a subordinate's performance, which one of the following items is usually irrelevant?

A. Remarks about tardiness or absenteeism
B. Mention of any unusual contributions or accomplishments
C. A summary of the employee's previous job experience
D. An assessment of the employee's attitude toward the job

10. The ability to delegate responsibility while maintaining adequate controls is one key to a supervisor's success. Which one of the following methods of control would minimize the amount of responsibility assumed by the subordinate?

A. Asking for a monthly status report in writing
B. Asking to receive copies of important correspondence so that you can be aware of potential problems
C. Scheduling periodic project status conferences with your subordinate
D. Requiring that your subordinate confer with you before making decisions on a project

11. You wish to assign an important project to a subordinate who you think has good potential. Which one of the following approaches would be most effective in successfully completing the project while developing the subordinate's abilities?

A. Describe the project to the subordinate in general terms and emphasize that it must be completed as quickly as possible
B. Outline the project in detail to the subordinate and emphasize that its successful completion could lead to career advancement
C. Develop a detailed project outline and timetable, discuss the details and timing with him and assign the subordinate to carry out the plan on his own
D. Discuss the project objectives and suggested approaches with the subordinate, and ask the subordinate to develop a detailed project outline and timetable of your approval

12. Research studies reveal that an important difference between high-production and low-production supervisors lies not in their interest in eliminating mistakes, but in their manner of handling mistakes. High-production supervisors are most likely to look upon mistakes as primarily

A. an opportunity to provide training
B. a byproduct of subordinate negligence
C. an opportunity to fix blame in a situation
D. a result of their own incompetence

13. Supervisors should try to establish what has been called *positive discipline*, an atmo-   13.____
sphere in which subordinates willingly abide by rules which they consider fair. When a
supervisor notices a subordinate violating an important rule, his FIRST course of action
should be to

    A. stop the subordinate and tell him what he is doing wrong
    B. wait a day or two before approaching the employee involved
    C. call a meeting of all subordinates to discuss the rule
    D. forget the matter in the hope that it will not happen again

14. The working climate is the feeling, degree of freedom, the tone and the mood of the   14.____
working environment. Which of the following contributes most to determining the working
climate in a unit or group?

    A. The rules set for rest periods
    B. The example set by the supervisor
    C. The rules set for morning check-in
    D. The wages paid to the employees

15. John Polk is a bright, ingenious clerk with a lot of initiative. He has made many good sug-   15.____
gestions to his supervisor in the Training Division of Department T, where he is
employed. However, last week one of his bright ideas literally *blew up*. In setting up some
electronic equipment in the training classroom, he crossed some wires resulting in a
damaged tape recorder and a classroom so filled with smoke that the training class had
to be held in another room. When Mr. Brown, his supervisor, learned of this occurrence,
he immediately summoned John to his private office. There Mr. Brown spent five minutes
bawling John out, calling him an overzealous, overgrown kid, and sent him back to his job
without letting John speak once. Of the following, the action of Mr. Brown that most
deserves approval is that he

    A. took disciplinary action immediately without regard for past performance
    B. kept the disciplinary interview to a brief period
    C. concentrated his criticism on the root cause of the occurrence
    D. held the disciplinary interview in his private office .

16. Typically, when the technique of *supervision by results* is practiced, higher management   16.____
sets down, either implicitly or explicitly, certain performance standards or goals that the
subordinate is expected to meet. So long as these standards are met, management
interferes very little. The most likely result of the use of this technique is that it will

    A. lead to ambiguity in terms of goals
    B. be successful only to the extent that close direct supervision is practiced
    C. make it possible to evaluate both employee and supervisory effectiveness
    D. allow for complete autonomy on the subordinate's part

17. Assume that you, an Administrative Assistant, are the supervisor of a large clerical unit   17.____
performing routine clerical operations. One of your clerks consistently produces much
less work than other members of your staff performing similar tasks. Of the following, the
action you should take FIRST is to

    A. ask the clerk if he wants to be transferred to another unit

B. reprimand the clerk for his poor performance and warn him that further disciplinary action will be taken if his work does not improve
C. quietly ask the clerk's co-workers whether they know why his performance is poor
D. discuss this matter with the clerk to work out plans for improving his performance

18. When making written evaluations and reviews of the performance of subordinates, it is usually advisable to

18.____

A. avoid informing the employee of the evaluation if it is critical because it may create hard feelings
B. avoid informing the employee of the evaluation whether critical or favorable because it is tension-producing
C. permit the employee to see the evaluation but not to discuss it with him because the supervisor cannot be certain where the discussion might lead
D. discuss the evaluation openly with the employee because it helps the employee understand what is expected of him

19. There are a number of well-known and respected human relations principles that successful supervisors have been using for years in building good relationships with their employees. Which of the following does NOT illustrate such a principle?

19.____

A. Give clear and complete instructions
B. Let each person know how he is getting along
C. Keep an open-door policy
D. Make all relationships personal ones

20. Assume that it is your responsibility as an Administrative Assistant to maintain certain personnel records that are continually being updated. You have three senior clerks assigned specifically to this task. Recently you have noticed that the volume of work has increased substantially, and the processing of personnel records by the clerks is backlogged. Your supervisor is now receiving complaints due to the processing delay. Of the following, the best course of action for you to take FIRST is to

20.____

A. have a meeting with the clerks, advise them of the problem, and ask that they do their work faster; then confirm your meeting in writing for the record
B. request that an additional position be authorized for your unit
C. review the procedures being used for processing the work, and try to determine if you can improve the flow of work
D. get the system moving faster by spending some of your own time processing the backlog

21. Assume that you are in charge of a payroll unit consisting of four clerks. It is Friday, November 14. You have just arrived in the office after a conference. Your staff is preparing a payroll that must be forwarded the following Monday. Which of the following new items on your desk should you attend to FIRST?

21.____

A. A telephone message regarding very important information needed for the statistical summary of salaries paid for the month of November
B. A memorandum regarding a new procedure that should be followed in preparing the payroll
C. A telephone message from an employee who is threatening to endorse his paycheck *Under Protest* because he is dissatisfied with the amount

D. A memorandum from your supervisor reminding you to submit the probationary period report on a new employee

22. You are an Administrative Assistant in charge of a unit that orders and issues supplies. On a particular day you are faced with the following four situations. Which one should you take care of FIRST?

    A. One of your employees who is in the process of taking the quarterly inventory of supplies has telephoned and asked that you return his call as soon as possible
    B. A representative of a company that is noted for producing excellent office supplies will soon arrive with samples for you to distribute to the various offices in your agency
    C. A large order of supplies which was delivered this morning has been checked and counted and a deliveryman is waiting for you to sign the receipt
    D. A clerk from the purchase division asks you to search for a bill you failed to send to them which is urgently needed in order for them to complete a report due this morning

22.____

23. As an Administrative Assistant, assume that it is necessary for you to give an unpleasant assignment to one of your subordinates. You expect this employee to raise some objections to this assignment. The most appropriate of the following actions for you to take FIRST is to issue the assignment

    A. orally, with the further statement that you will not listen to any complaints
    B. in writing, to forestall any complaints by the employee
    C. orally, permitting the employee to express his feelings
    D. in writing, with a note that any comments should be submitted in writing

23.____

24. Assume that you are an Administrative Assistant supervising the Duplicating and Reproduction Unit of Department B. One of your responsibilities is to prepare a daily schedule showing when and on which of your unit's four duplicating machines jobs are to be run off. Of the following, the factor that should be given LEAST consideration in preparing the schedule is the

    A. priority of each of the jobs to be run off
    B. production speed of the different machines that will be used
    C. staff available to operate the machines
    D. date on which the job order was received

24.____

25. *Cycling is an arrangement where papers are processed throughout a period according to an orderly plan rather than as a group all at one time. This technique has been used for a long time by public utilities in their cycle billing.* Of the following practices, the one that best illustrates this technique is that in which

    A. paychecks for per annum employees are issued bi-weekly and those for per diem employees are issued weekly
    B. field inspectors report in person to their offices one day a week, on Fridays, when they do all their paperwork and also pick up their paychecks
    C. the dates for issuing relief checks to clients vary depending on the last digit of the clients' social security numbers
    D. the last day for filing and paying income taxes is the same for Federal, State and City income taxes

25.____

26. The employees in your division have recently been given an excellent up-to-date office manual, but you find that a good number of employees are not following the procedures outlined in it. Which one of the following would be most likely to ensure that employees begin using the manual effectively?

    A. Require each employee to keep a copy of the manual in plain sight on his desk
    B. Issue warnings periodically to those employees who deviate most from procedures prescribed in the manual
    C. Tell an employee to check his manual when he does not follow the proper procedures
    D. Suggest to the employees that the manual be studied thoroughly

26._____

27. The one of the following factors which should be considered FIRST in the design of office forms is the

    A. information to be included in the form
    B. sequence of the information
    C. purpose of the form
    D. persons who will be using the form

27._____

28. *Window envelopes are being used to an increasing extent by government and private industry.* The one of the following that is NOT an advantage of window envelopes is that they

    A. cut down on addressing costs
    B. eliminate the need to attach envelopes to letters being sent forward for signature by a superior
    C. are less costly to buy than regular envelopes
    D. reduce the risk of having letters placed in wrong envelopes

28._____

29. Your bureau head asks you to prepare the office layouts for several of his units being moved to a higher floor in your office building. Of the following possibilities, the one that you should AVOID in preparing the layouts is to

    A. place the desks of the first-line supervisors near those of the staffs they supervise
    B. place the desks of employees whose work is most closely related near one another
    C. arrange the desks so that employees do not face one another
    D. locate desks with many outside visitors farthest from the office entrance

29._____

30. Which one of the following conditions would be LEAST important in considering a change of the layout in a particular office?

    A. Installation of a new office machine
    B. Assignment of five additional employees to your office
    C. Poor flow of work
    D. Employees' personal preferences of desk location

30._____

31. Suppose Mr. Bloom, an Administrative Assistant, is dictating a letter to a stenographer. His dictation begins with the name of the addressee and continues to the body of the letter. However, Mr. Bloom does not dictate the address of the recipient of the letter. He expects the stenographer to locate it. The use of this practice by Mr. Bloom is

    A. acceptable, especially if he gives the stenographer the letter to which he is responding

31._____

B. acceptable, especially if the letter is lengthy and detailed
C. unacceptable, because it is not part of a stenographer's duties to search for information
D. unacceptable, because he should not rely on the accuracy of the stenographer

32. Assume that there are no rules, directives or instructions concerning the filing of materials in your office or the retention of such files. A system is now being followed of placing in *inactive files any materials that are more than one year old. Of the following, the most appropriate thing to do with material that has been in an inactive* file in your office for more than one year is to

A. inspect the contents of the files to decide how to dispose of them
B. transfer the material to a remote location, where it can be obtained if necessary
C. keep the material intact for a minimum of another three years
D. destroy the material which has not been needed for at least a year

33. Suppose you, an Administrative Assistant, have just returned to your desk after engaging in an all-morning conference. Joe Burns, a Clerk, informs you that Clara McClough, an administrator in another agency, telephoned during the morning and that, although she requested to speak with you, he was able to give her the desired information. Of the following, the most appropriate action for you to take in regard to Mr. Burns' action is to

A. thank him for assisting Ms. McClough in your absence
B. explain to him the proper telephone practice to use in the future
C. reprimand him for not properly channeling Ms. McClough's call
D. issue a memo to all clerical employees regarding proper telephone practices

34. *When interviewing subordinates with problems, supervisors frequently find that asking direct questions of the employee results only in evasive responses. The supervisor may therefore resort to the non-directive interview technique. In this technique the supervisor avoids pointed questions; he leads the employee to continue talking freely uninfluenced by the supervisor's preconceived notions. This technique often enables the employee to bring his problem into sharp focus and to reach a solution to his problem.*
Suppose that you are a supervisor interviewing a subordinate about his recent poor attendance record. On calling his attention to his excessive lateness record, he replies:
I just don't seem to be able to get up in the morning. Frankly, I've lost interest in this job. I don't care about it. When I get up in the morning, I have to skip breakfast and I'm still late. I don't care about this job.
If you are using the *non-directive* technique in this interview, the most appropriate of the following responses for you to make is

A. *You don't care about this job?*
B. *Don't you think you are letting your department down?*
C. *Are you having trouble at home?*
D. *Don't you realize your actions are childish?*

35. An employee in a work group made the following comment to a co-worker: *It's great to be a lowly employee instead of an Administrative Assistant because you can work without thinking. The Administrative Assistant is getting paid to plan, schedule and think. Let him see to it that you have a productive day.*
Which one of the following statements about this quotation best reflects an understanding of good personnel management techniques and the role of the supervising Administrative Assistant?

A. The employee is wrong in attitude and in his perception of the role of the Administrative Assistant

B. The employee is correct in attitude but is wrong in his perception of the role of the Administrative Assistant

C. The employee is correct in attitude and in his perception of the role of the Administrative Assistant

D. The employee is wrong in attitude but is right in his perception of the role of the Administrative Assistant

---

KEY (CORRECT ANSWERS)

1.	C	11.	D	26.	C
2.	B	12.	A	27.	C
3.	A	13.	A	28.	C
4.	C	14.	B	29.	D
5.	C	15.	D	30.	D
6.	A	16.	C/D	31.	A
7.	C	17.	D	32.	A/B
8.	C	18.	D	33.	A
9.	C	19.	D	34.	A
10.	D	20.	C	35.	D
		21.	B		
		22.	C		
		23.	C		
		24.	D		
		25.	C		

TEST 2

DIRECTIONS: Each question or incomplete statement is followed by several suggested answers or completions. Select the one that BEST answers the question or completes the statement. *PRINT THE LETTER OF THE CORRECT ANSWER IN THE SPACE AT THE RIGHT.*

Questions 1 through 5 are to be answered solely on the basis of the following passage:

General supervision, in contrast to close supervision, involves a high degree of delegation of authority and requires some indirect means to ensure that employee behavior conforms to management needs. Not everyone works well under general supervision, however. General supervision works best where subordinates desire responsibility. General supervision also works well where individuals in work groups have strong feelings about the quality of the finished work products. Strong identification with management goals is another trait of persons who work well under general supervision. There are substantial differences in the amount of responsibility people are willing to accept on the job. One person may flourish under supervision that another might find extremely restrictive.

Psychological research provides evidence that the nature of a person's personality affects his attitude toward supervision. There are some employees with a low need for achievement and high fear of failure who shy away from challenges and responsibilities. Many seek self-expression off the job and ask only to be allowed to daydream on it. There are others who have become so accustomed to the authoritarian approach in their culture, family and previous work experience that they regard general supervision as no supervision at all. They abuse the privileges it bestows on them and refuse to accept the responsibilities it demands.

Different groups develop different attitudes toward work. Most college graduates, for example, expect a great deal of responsibility and freedom. People with limited education, on the other hand, often have trouble accepting the concept that people should make decisions for themselves, particularly decisions concerning work. Therefore, the extent to which general supervision will be effective varies greatly with the subordinates involved.

1. According to the above passage, which one of the following is a necessary part of management policy regarding general supervision?   1.____

    A. Most employees should formulate their own work goals
    B. Deserving employees should be rewarded periodically
    C. Some controls on employee work patterns should be established
    D. Responsibility among employees should generally be equalized

2. It can be inferred from the above passage that an employee who avoids responsibilities and challenges is most likely to   2.____

    A. gain independence under general supervision
    B. work better under close supervision than under general supervision
    C. abuse the liberal guidelines of general supervision
    D. become more restricted and cautious under general supervision

3. Based on the above passage, employees who succeed under general supervision are most likely to   3.____

    A. have a strong identification with people and their problems
    B. accept work obligations without fear
    C. seek self-expression off the job
    D. value the intellectual aspects of life

4. Of the following, the best title for the passage is   4.____

    A. Benefits and Disadvantages of General Supervision
    B. Production Levels of Employees Under General Supervision
    C. Employee Attitudes Toward Work and the Work Environment
    D. Employee Background and Personality as a Factor in Utilizing General Supervision

5. It can be inferred from the above passage that the one of the following employees who is   5.____
    most likely to work best under general supervision is one who

    A. is a part-time graduate student
    B. was raised by very strict parents
    C. has little self-confidence
    D. has been closely supervised in past jobs

Questions 6 through 10 are to be answered solely on the basis of the information in the
following passage:

The concept of *program management* was first developed in order to handle some of the
complex projects undertaken by the U.S. Department of Defense in the 1950's. Program
management is an administrative system combining planning and control techniques to guide
and coordinate all the activities which contribute to one overall program or project. It has been
used by the federal government to manage space exploration and other programs involving
many contributing organizations. It is also used by state and local governments and by some
large firms to provide administrative integration of work from a number of sources, be they
individuals, departments or outside companies.

One of the specific administrative techniques for program management is Program Evaluation Review Technique (PERT). PERT begins with the assembling of a list of all the activities needed to accomplish an overall task. The next step consists of arranging these activities
in a sequential network showing both how much time each activity will take and which activities must be completed before others can begin. The time required for each activity is estimated by simple statistical techniques by the persons who will be responsible for the work,
and the time required to complete the entire string of activities along each sequential path
through the network is then calculated. There may be dozens or hundreds of these paths, so
the calculation is usually done by computer. The longest path is then labeled the *critical path*
because no matter how quickly events not on this path are completed, the events along the
longest path must be finished before the project can be terminated. The overall starting and
completion dates are then pinpointed, and target dates are established for each task. Actual
progress can later be checked by comparison to the network plan.

6. Judging from the information in the above passage, which one of the following projects is   6.____
    most suitable for handling by a program management technique?

    A. Review and improvement of the filing system used by a city office
    B. Computerization of accounting data already on file in an office
    C. Planning and construction of an urban renewal project
    D. Announcing a change in city tax regulations to thousands of business firms

7. The passage indicates that program management methods are now in wide use by vari-   7.____
    ous kinds of organizations. Which one of the following organizations would you LEAST
    expect to make much use of such methods today?

A. An automobile manufacturer
B. A company in the aerospace business
C. The government of a large city
D. A library reference department

8. In making use of the PERT technique, the first step is to determine   8._____

   A. every activity that must take place in order to complete the project
   B. a target date for completion of the project
   C. the estimated time required to complete each activity which is related to the whole
   D. which activities will make up the longest path on the chart

9. Who estimates the time required to complete a particular activity in a PERT program?   9._____

   A. The people responsible for the particular activity
   B. The statistician assigned to the program
   C. The organization that has commissioned the project
   D. The operator who programs the computer

10. Which one of the following titles best describes the contents of the passage?   10._____

    A. *The Need For Computers in Today's Projects*
    B. *One Technique For Program Management*
    C. *Local Governments Can Now Use Space-Age Techniques*
    D. *Why Planning Is Necessary For Complex Projects*

11. An Administrative Assistant has been criticized for the low productivity in the group which   11._____
    he supervises. Which of the following best reflects an understanding of supervisory
    responsibilities in the area of productivity? An Administrative Assistant should be held
    responsible for

    A. his own individual productivity and the productivity of the group he supervises,
       because he is in a position where he maintains or increases production through
       others
    B. his own personal productivity only, because the supervisor is not likely to have any
       effect on the productivity of subordinates
    C. his own individual productivity but only for a drop in the productivity of the group he
       supervises, since subordinates will receive credit for increased productivity individ-
       ually
    D. his own personal productivity only, because this is how he would be evaluated if he
       were not a supervisor

12. A supervisor has held a meeting in his office with an employee about the employee's   12._____
    grievance. The grievance concerned the sharp way in which the supervisor reprimanded
    the employee for an error the employee made in the performance of a task assigned to
    him. The problem was not resolved. Which one of the following statements about this
    meeting best reflects an understanding of good supervisory techniques?

    A. It is awkward for a supervisor to handle a grievance involving himself. The supervi-
       sor should not have held the meeting.
    B. It would have been better if the supervisor had held the meeting at the employee's
       workplace, even though there would have been frequent distractions, because the
       employee would have been more relaxed.

C. The resolution of a problem is not the only sign of a successful meeting. The achievement of communication was worthwhile.
D. The supervisor should have been forceful. There is nothing wrong with raising your voice to an employee every once in a while.

13. John Hayden, the owner of a single-family house, complains that he submitted an application for reduction of assessment that obviously was not acted upon before his final assessment notice was sent to him. The timely receipt of the application has been verified in a departmental log book. As the supervisor of the clerical unit through which this application was processed and where this delay occurred, you should be LEAST concerned with   13.____

    A. what happened   B. who is responsible
    C. why it happened   D. what can be learned from it

14. The one of the following that applies most appropriately to the role of the first-line supervisor is that usually he is   14.____

    A. called upon to help determine agency policy
    B. involved in long-range agency planning
    C. responsible for determining some aspects of basic organization structure
    D. a participant in developing procedures and methods

15. Sally Jones, an Administrative Assistant, gives clear and precise instructions to Robert Warren, a Senior Clerk. In these instructions, Ms. Jones clearly delegates authority to Mr. Warren to undertake a well-defined task. In this situation Ms. Jones should expect Mr. Warren to   15.____

    A. come to her to check out details as he progresses with the task
    B. come to her only with exceptional problems
    C. ask her permission if he wishes to use his delegated authority
    D. use his authority to redefine the task and its related activities

16. Planning involves establishing departmental goals and programs and determining ways of reaching them. The main advantage of such planning is that   16.____

    A. there will be no need for adjustments once a plan is put into operation
    B. it ensures that everyone is working on schedule
    C. it provides the framework for an effective operation
    D. unexpected work problems are easily overcome

17. As a result of reorganization, the jobs in a large clerical unit were broken down into highly specialized tasks. Each specialized task was then assigned to a particular employee to perform. This action will probably lead to an increase in   17.____

    A. flexibility   B. job satisfaction
    C. need for coordination   D. employee initiative

18. Your office carries on a large volume of correspondence concerned with the purchase of supplies and equipment for city offices. You use form letters to deal with many common situations. In which one of the following situations would use of a form letter be LEAST appropriate?   18.____

A. Informing suppliers of a change in city regulations concerning purchase contracts
B. Telling a new supplier the standard procedures to be followed in billing
C. Acknowledging receipt of a complaint and saying that the complaint will be investigated
D. Answering a city councilman's request for additional information on a particular regulation affecting suppliers

19. Assume that you are an Administrative Assistant heading a large clerical unit. Because of the great demands being made on your time, you have designated Tom Smith, a Supervising Clerk, to be your assistant and to assume some of your duties. Of the following duties performed by you, the most appropriate one to assign to Tom Smith is to   19._____

A. conduct the on-the-job training of new employees
B. prepare the performance appraisal reports on your staff members
C. represent your unit in dealings with the heads of other units
D. handle matters that require exception to general policy

20. In establishing rules for his subordinates, a superior should be primarily concerned with   20._____

A. creating sufficient flexibility to allow for exceptions
B. making employees aware of the reasons for the rules and the penalties for infractions
C. establishing the strength of his own position in relation to his subordinates
D. having his subordinates know that such rules will be imposed in a personal manner

21. The practice of conducting staff training sessions on a periodic basis is generally considered   21._____

A. poor; it takes employees away from their work assignments
B. poor; all staff training should be done on an individual basis
C. good; it permits the regular introduction of new methods and techniques
D. good; it ensures a high employee productivity rate

22. Suppose, as an Administrative Assistant, you have just announced at a staff meeting with your subordinates that a radical reorganization of work will take place next week. Your subordinates at the meeting appear to be excited, tense and worried. Of the following, the best action for you to take at that time is to   22._____

A. schedule private conferences with each subordinate to obtain his reaction to the meeting
B. close the meeting and tell your subordinates to return immediately to their work assignments
C. give your subordinates some time to ask questions and discuss your announcement
D. insist that your subordinates do not discuss your announcement among themselves or with other members of the agency

23. Suppose that as an Administrative Assistant you were recently placed in charge of the Duplicating and Stock Unit of Department Y. From your observation of the operations of your unit during your first week as its head, you get the impression that there are inefficiencies in its operations causing low productivity. To obtain an increase in its productivity, the FIRST of the following actions you should take is to   23._____

A. seek the advice of your immediate superior on how he would tackle this problem
B. develop plans to correct any unsatisfactory conditions arising from other than man-power deficiencies
C. identify the problems causing low productivity
D. discuss your productivity problem with other unit heads to find out how they han-dled similar problems

24. Assume that you are an Administrative Assistant recently placed in charge of a large clerical unit. At a meeting, the head of another unit tells you, *My practice is to give a worker more than he can finish. In that way you can be sure that you are getting the most out of him.* For you to adopt this practice would be   24._____

    A. advisable, since your actions would be consistent with those practiced in your agency
    B. inadvisable, since such a practice is apt to create frustration and lower staff morals
    C. advisable, since a high goal stimulates people to strive to attain it
    D. inadvisable, since management may, in turn, set too high a productivity goal for the unit

25. Suppose that you are the supervisor of a unit in which there is an increasing amount of friction among several of your staff members. One of the reasons for this friction is that the work of some of these staff members cannot be completed until other staff members complete related work. Of the following, the most appropriate action for you to take is to   25._____

    A. summon these employees to a meeting to discuss the responsibilities each has and to devise better methods of coordination
    B. have a private talk with each employee involved and make each understand that there must be more cooperation among the employees
    C. arrange for interviews with each of the employees involved to determine what his problems are
    D. shift the assignments of these employees so that each will be doing a job different from his current one

26. An office supervisor has a number of responsibilities with regard to his subordinates. Which one of the following functions should NOT be regarded as a basic responsibility of the office supervisor?   26._____

    A. Telling employees how to solve personal problems that may be interfering with their work
    B. Training new employees to do the work assigned to them
    C. Evaluating employees' performance periodically and discussing the evaluation with each employee
    D. Bringing employee grievances to the attention of higher-level administrators and seeking satisfactory resolutions

27. One of your most productive subordinates frequently demonstrates a poor attitude toward his job. He seems unsure of himself, and he annoys his co-workers because he is continually belittling himself and the work that he is doing. In trying to help him overcome this problem, which of the following approaches is LEAST likely to be effective?   27._____

A. Compliment him on his work and assign him some additional responsibilities, telling him that he is being given these responsibilities because of his demonstrated
ability

B. Discuss with him the problem of his attitude, and warn him that you will have to
report it on his next performance evaluation

C. Assign him a particularly important and difficult project, stressing your confidence
in his ability to complete it successfully

D. Discuss with him the problem of his attitude, and ask him for suggestions as to how
you can help him overcome it

28. You come to realize that a personality conflict between you and one of your subordinates   28.____
is adversely affecting his performance. Which one of the following would be the most
appropriate FIRST step to take?

    A. Report the problem to your superior and request assistance. His experience may
be helpful in resolving this problem.

    B. Discuss the situation with several of the subordinate's co-workers to see if they can
suggest any remedy.

    C. Suggest to the subordinate that he get professional counseling or therapy.

    D. Discuss the situation candidly with the subordinate, with the objective of resolving
the problem between yourselves.

29. Assume that you are an Administrative Assistant supervising the Payroll Records Sec-   29.____
tion in Department G. Your section has been requested to prepare and submit to the
department's budget officer a detailed report giving a breakdown of labor costs under
various departmental programs and sub-programs. You have assigned this task to a
Supervising Clerk, giving him full authority for seeing that this job is performed satisfacto-
rily. You have given him a written statement of the job to be done and explained the purpose and use of this report. The next step that you should take in connection with this
delegated task is to

    A. assist the Supervising Clerk in the step-by-step performance of the job

    B. assure the Supervising Clerk that you will be understanding of mistakes if made at
the beginning

    C. require him to receive your approval for interim reports submitted at key points
before he can proceed further with his task

    D. give him a target date for the completion of this report

30. Assume that you are an Administrative Assistant heading a unit staffed with six clerical   30.____
employees. One Clerk, John Snell, is a probationary employee appointed four months
ago. During the first three months, John learned his job quickly, performed his work accurately and diligently, and was cooperative and enthusiastic in his attitude. However, during the past few weeks his enthusiasm seems dampened, he is beginning to make
mistakes and at times appears bored. Of the following, the most appropriate action for
you to take is to

    A. check with John's co-workers to find out whether they can explain John's change in
attitude and work habits

    B. wait a few more weeks before taking any action, so that John will have an opportu-
nity to make the needed changes on his own initiative

    C. talk to John about the change in his work performance and his decreased enthusi-
asm

D. change John's assignment since this may be the basic cause of John's change in attitude and performance

31. The supervisor of a clerical unit, on returning from a meeting, finds that one of his subordinates is performing work not assigned by him. The subordinate explains that the group supervisor had come into the office while the unit supervisor was out and directed the employee to work on an urgent assignment. This is the first time the group supervisor had bypassed the unit supervisor. Of the following, the most appropriate action for the unit supervisor to take is to 31.____

A. explain to the group supervisor that bypassing the unit supervisor is an undesirable practice
B. have the subordinate stop work on the assignment until the entire matter can be clarified with the group supervisor
C. raise the matter of bypassing a supervisor at the next staff conference held by the group supervisor
D. forget about the incident

32. Assume that you are an Administrative Assistant in charge of the Mail and Records Unit of Department K. On returning from a meeting, you notice that Jane Smith is not at her regular work location. You learn that another employee, Ruth Reed, had become faint, and that Jane took Ruth outdoors for some fresh air. It is a long-standing rule in your unit that no employee is to leave the building during office hours except on official business or with the unit head's approval. Only a few weeks ago, John Duncan was reprimanded by you for going out at 10:00 a.m. for a cup of coffee. With respect to Jane Smith's violation of this rule, the most appropriate of the following actions for you to take is to 32.____

A. issue a reprimand to Jane Smith, with an explanation that all employees must be treated in exactly the same way
B. tell Jane that you should reprimand her, but you will not do so in this instance
C. overlook this rule violation in view of the extenuating circumstances
D. issue the reprimand with no further explanation, treating her in the same manner that you treated John Duncan

33. Assume that you are an Administrative Assistant recently assigned as supervisor of Department X's Mail and Special Services Unit. In addition to processing your department's mail, your clerical employees are often sent on errands in the city. You have learned that, while on such official errands, these clerks sometimes take care of their own personal matters or those of their co-workers. The previous supervisor had tolerated this practice even though it violated a departmental personnel rule. The most appropriate of the following actions for you to take is to 33.____

A. continue to tolerate this practice so long as it does not interfere with the work of your unit
B. take no action until you have proof that an employee has violated this rule; then give a mild reprimand
C. wait until an employee has committed a gross violation of this rule; then bring him up on charges
D. discuss this rule with your staff and caution them that its violation might necessitate disciplinary action

34. *Supervisors who exercise 'close supervision' over their subordinates usually check up on their employees frequently, give them frequent instructions and, in general, limit their freedom to do their work in their own way. Those who exercise 'general supervision' usually set forth the objectives of a job, tell their subordinates what they want accomplished, fix the limits within which the subordinates can work and let the employees (if they are capable) decide how the job is to be done.* Which one of the following conditions would contribute LEAST to the success of the *general supervision* approach in an organizational unit?   34.____

    A. Employees in the unit welcome increased responsibilities
    B. Work assignments in the unit are often challenging
    C. Work procedures must conform with those of other units
    D. Staff members support the objectives of the unit

35. Assume that you are an Administrative Assistant assigned as supervisor of the Clerical Services Unit of a large agency's Labor Relations Division. A member of your staff comes to you with a criticism of a policy followed by the Labor Relations Division. You also have similar views regarding this policy. Of the following, the most appropriate action for you to take in response to his criticism is to   35.____

    A. agree with him, but tell him that nothing can be done about it at your level
    B. suggest to him that it is not wise for him to express criticism of policy
    C. tell the employee that he should direct his criticism to the head of your agency if he wants quick action
    D. ask the employee if he has suggestions for revising the policy

---

KEY (CORRECT ANSWERS)

1.	C	11.	A	26.	A
2.	B	12.	C	27.	B
3.	B	13.	B	28.	D
4.	D	14.	D	29.	D
5.	A	15.	B	30.	C
6.	C	16.	C	31.	D
7.	D	17.	C	32.	C
8.	A	18.	D	33.	D
9.	A	19.	A	34.	C
10.	B	20.	B	35.	D
		21.	C		
		22.	C		
		23.	C		
		24.	B		
		25.	A		

TEST 3

DIRECTIONS: Each question or incomplete statement is followed by several suggested answers or completions. Select the one that BEST answers the question or completes the statement. *PRINT THE LETTER OF THE CORRECT ANSWER IN THE SPACE AT THE RIGHT.*

1. At the request of your bureau head you have designed a simple visitor's referral form. The form will be cut from 8-1/2" x 11" stock.
Which of the following should be the dimensions of the form if you want to be sure that there is no waste of paper?

   A. 2-3/4" x 4-1/4"   B. 3-1/4" x 4-3/4"
   C. 3-3/4" x 4-3/4"   D. 4-1/2" x 5-1/2"

1.____

2. An office contains six file cabinets, each containing three drawers. One of your responsibilities as a new Administrative Assistant is to see that there is sufficient filing space. At the present time, 1/4 of the file space contains forms, 2/9 contains personnel records, 1/3 contains reports, and 1/7 of the remaining space contains budget records.
If each drawer may contain more than one type of record, how much drawer space is now *empty*?

   A. 0 drawers   B. 13/14 of a drawer
   C. 3 drawers   D. 3-1/2 drawers

2.____

3. Assume that there were 21 working days in March. The five clerks in your unit had the following number of absences in March:
   Clerk H - 2 absences
   Clerk J - 1 absence
   Clerk K - 6 absences
   Clerk L - 0 absences
   Clerk M - 10 absences

   To the nearest day, what was the *average* attendance in March for the five clerks in your unit?

   A. 4   B. 17   C. 18   D. 21

3.____

Questions 4-12

DIRECTIONS: Questions 4 through 12 each consist of a sentence which may or may not be an example of good English usage. Consider grammar, punctuation, spelling, capitalization, verbosity, awkwardness, etc. Examine each sentence, and then choose the correct statement about it from the four choices below it. If the English usage in the sentence is better as given than with any of the changes suggested in options B, C or D, choose option A.

4. The stenographers who are secretaries to commissioners have more varied duties than the stenographic pool.

   A. This is an example of effective writing.
   B. In this sentence there would be a comma after *commissioners* in order to break up the sentence into clauses.
   C. In this sentence the words *stenographers in* should be inserted after the word *than*.
   D. In this sentence the word *commissioners* is misspelled.

4.____

5. A person who becomes an administrative assistant will be called upon to provide leader-   5._____
ship, to insure proper quantity and quality of production, and many administrative chores
must be performed.

    A.   This sentence is an example of effective writing.
    B.   The sentence should be divided into three separate sentences, each describing a
        duty.
    C.   The words *many administrative chores must be performed* should be changed to
        to perform many administrative chores.
    D.   The words *to provide leadership* should be changed to *to be a leader.*

6. A complete report has been submitted by our branch office, giving details about this   6._____
transaction.

    A.   This sentence is an example of effective writing.
    B.   The phrase *giving details about this transaction* should be placed between the
        words *report* and *has.*
    C.   A semi-colon should replace the comma after the word *office* to indicate indepen-
        dent clauses.
    D.   A colon should replace the comma after the word *office* since the second clause
        provides further explanation.

7. The report was delayed because of the fact that the writer lost his rough draft two days   7._____
before the deadline.

    A.   This sentence is an example of effective writing.
    B.   In this sentence the words *of the fact that* are unnecessary and should be deleted.
    C.   In this sentence the words *because of the fact that* should be shortened to *due to.*
    D.   In this sentence the word *before* should be replaced by *prior to.*

8. Included in this offer are a six months' guarantee, a complete set of instructions, and one   8._____
free inspection of the equipment.

    A.   This sentence is an example of effective writing.
    B.   The word *is* should be substituted for the word *are.*
    C.   The word *months* should have been spelled *month's.*
    D.   The word *months* should be spelled *months.*

9. Certain employees come to the attention of their employers. Especially those with poor   9._____
work records and excessive absences.

    A.   This sentence is an example of effective writing.
    B.   The period after the word *employers* should be changed to a comma, and the first
        letter of the word *Especially* should be changed to a small *e.*
    C.   The period after the word *employers* should be changed to a semicolon, and the
        first letter of the word *Especially* should be changed to a small *e.*
    D.   The period after the word *employers* should be changed to a colon.

10. The applicant had decided to decline the appointment by the time he was called for the   10._____
interview.

A. This sentence is an example of effective writing.
B. In this sentence the word *had* should be deleted.
C. In this sentence the phrase *was called* should be replaced by *had been called*.
D. In this sentence the phrase *had decided to decline* should be replaced by *declined*.

11. There are two elevaters, each accommodating ten people.   11.____

    A. This sentence is correct.
    B. In this sentence the word *elevaters* should be spelled *elevators*.
    C. In this sentence the word *each* should be replaced by the word *both*.
    D. In this sentence the word *accommodating* should be spelled *accomodating*.

12. With the aid of a special device, it was possible to alter the letterhead on the department's stationary.   12.____

    A. This sentence is correct.
    B. The word *aid* should be spelled *aide*.
    C. The word *device* should be spelled *devise*.
    D. The word *stationary* should be spelled *stationery*.

13. Examine the following sentence and then choose from the options below the correct word to be inserted in the blank space.   13.____
Everybody in both offices _____ involved in the project.

    A. are   B. feel   C. is

Questions 14-18

DIRECTIONS: Answer questions 14 through 18 SOLELY on the basis of the information in the following passage.

A new way of looking at job performance promises to be a major advance in measuring and increasing a person's true effectiveness in business. The fact that individuals differ enormously in their judgment of when a piece of work is actually finished is significant. It is believed that more than half of all people in the business world are defective in the *sense of closure,* that is they do not know the proper time to throw the switch that turns off their effort in one direction and diverts it to a new job. Only a minority of workers at any level have the required judgment and the feeling of responsibility to work on a job to the point of maximum effectiveness. The vast majority let go of each task far short of the completion point.

Very often, a defective sense of closure exists in an entire staff. When that occurs, it usually stems from a long-standing laxness on the part of higher management. A low degree of responsibility has been accepted and it has come to be standard. Combating this requires implementation of a few basic policies. Firstly, it is important to make each responsibility completely clear and to set certain guideposts as to what constitutes complete performance. Secondly, excuses for delays and failures should not be dealt with too sympathetically, but interest should be shown in the encountered obstacles. Lastly, a checklist should be used periodically to determine whether new levels of expectancy and new closure values have been set.

14. According to the above passage, a *majority of* people in the business world   14.____

    A. do not complete their work on time

B. cannot properly determine when a particular job is completed
C. make lame excuses for not completing a job on time
D. can adequately judge their own effectiveness at work

15. It can be *inferred from* the above passage that when a poor sense of closure is observed   15._____
among all the employees in a unit, the responsibility for raising the performance level
belongs to

A. non-supervisory employees
B. the staff as a whole
C. management
D. first-line supervisors

16. It is *implied by* the above passage that, by the establishment of work guideposts, employ-   16._____
ees may develop a

A. better understanding of expected performances
B. greater interest in their work relationships
C. defective sense of closure
D. lower level of performance

17. It can be inferred from the above passage that an individual's idea of whether a job is fin-   17._____
ished is *most closely* associated with his

A. loyalty to management
B. desire to overcome obstacles
C. ability to recognize his own defects
D. sense of responsibility

18. Of the following, the BEST heading for the above passage is   18._____

A. Management's Role in a Large Bureaucracy
B. Knowing When a Job is Finished
C. The Checklist, a Supervisor's Tool for Effectiveness
D. Supervisory Techniques

Questions 19-25

DIRECTIONS: Answer questions 19 through 25 assuming that you are in charge of public
information for an office which issues reports and answers questions from
other offices and from the public on changes in land use. The charts below
represent comparative land use in four neighborhoods. The area of each
neighborhood is expressed in city blocks. Assume that all city blocks are the
same size.

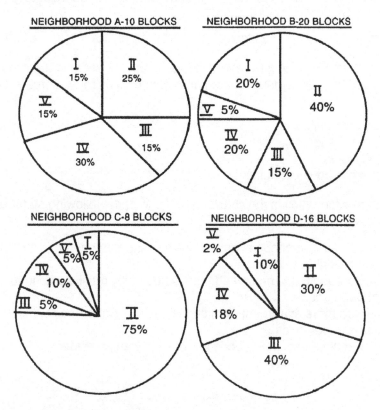

NEIGHBORHOOD A-10 BLOCKS

NEIGHBORHOOD B-20 BLOCKS

NEIGHBORHOOD C-8 BLOCKS

NEIGHBORHOOD D-16 BLOCKS

KEY: I - One- and two-family houses
      II - Apartment buildings
      III - Office buildings
      IV - Retail stores
      V - Factories and warehouses

19. In how many of these neighborhoods does residential use (categories I and II together)
    account for *more than 50%* of the land use?

    A. 1   B. 2   C. 3   D. 4

    19.____

20. How many of the neighborhoods have an area of land occupied by apartment buildings
    which is *greater than* the area of land occupied by apartment buildings in Neighborhood
    C?

    A. none   B. 1   C. 2   D. 3

    20.____

21. Which neighborhood has the LARGEST land area occupied by factories and ware-
    houses?

    A. A   B. B   C. C   D. D

    21.____

22. In which neighborhood is the LARGEST percentage of the land devoted to *both* office
    buildings and retail stores?

    A. A   B. B   C. C   D. D

    22.____

85

23. What is the difference, to the nearest city block, between the amount of land devoted to one- and two-family houses in Neighborhood A and the amount devoted to similar use in Neighborhood C?

23.____

    A. 1 block   B. 2 blocks   C. 5 blocks   D. 10 blocks

24. Which one of the following types of buildings occupies the same amount of land area in Neighborhood B as the amount of land area occupied by retail stores in Neighborhood A?

24.____

    A. Apartment buildings
    B. Office buildings
    C. Retail stores
    D. Factories and warehouses

25. Based on the information in the charts, which one of the following statements must be TRUE?

25.____

    A. Factories and warehouses are gradually disappearing from all the neighborhoods except Neighborhood A.
    B. Neighborhood B has more land area occupied by retail stores than any of the other neighborhoods.
    C. There are more apartment dwellers living in Neighborhood C than in any of the other neighborhoods.
    D. All four of these neighborhoods are predominantly residential.

―――――

KEY (CORRECT ANSWERS)

1.	A		11.	B
2.	C		12.	D
3.	B		13.	C
4.	C		14.	B
5.	C		15.	C
6.	B		16.	A
7.	B		17.	D
8.	A		18.	B
9.	B		19.	B
10.	A		20.	B

21.	A
22.	D
23.	A
24.	B
25.	B

―――――

EXAMINATION SECTION
TEST 1

DIRECTIONS: Each question or incomplete statement is followed by several suggested answers or completions. Select the one that *BEST* answers the question or completes the statement. *PRINT THE LETTER OF THE CORRECT ANSWER IN THE SPACE AT THE RIGHT.*

1. It is often desirable for an administrator to consult, during the planning process, the persons to be affected by those plans.
   Of the following, the MAJOR justification for such consultation is that it recognizes the

   A. fact that participating in horizontal planning is almost always more effective than participating in vertical planning
   B. principle of participation and the need for a sense of belonging as a means of decreasing resistance and developing support
   C. principle that lower-level administrators normally are more likely than higher-level administrators to emphasize longer-range goals
   D. fact that final responsibility for the approval of plans should be placed in committees not individuals

   1.____

2. In evaluating performance and, if necessary, correcting what is being done to assure attainment of results according to plan, it is GENERALLY best for the administrator to do which one of the following?

   A. Make a continual effort to increase the number of written control reports prepared.
   B. Thoroughly investigate in equal detail all possible deviations indicated by comparison of performance to expectation.
   C. Decentralize, within an operating unit or division, the responsibility for correcting deviations.
   D. Concentrate on the exceptions, or outstanding variations, from the expected results or standards

   2.____

3. Generally, changes in the ways in which the supervisors and employees in an organization do things are MORE likely to be welcomed by them when the changes

   A. threaten the security of the supervisors than when they do not
   B. are inaugurated after prior change has been assimilated than when they are inaugurated before other major changes have been assimilated
   C. follow a series of failures in changes when they follow a series of successful changes
   D. are dictated by personal order rather than when they result from an application of previously established impersonal principles

   3.____

4. For sound organizational relationships, of the following, it is generally MOST desirable that

   A. authority and responsibility be segregated from each other, in order to facilitate control
   B. the authority of a manager should be commensurate with his responsibility, and vice versa

   4.____

C. authority be defined as the obligation of an individual to carry out assigned activities to the best of his or her ability

D. clear recognition be given to the fact that delegation of authority benefits only the manager who delegates it

5. In utilizing a checklist of questions for general managerial planning, which one of the following generally isthe FIRST question to be asked and answered? 5.____

    A. Where will it take place?
    B. How will it be done?
    C. Why must it be done?
    D. Who will do it?

6. Of the following, it is *USUALLY* best to set administrative objectives so that they are 6.____

    A. at a level that is unattainable, so that administrators will continually be strongly motivated
    B. at a level that is attainable, but requires some stretching and reaching by administrators trying to attain them
    C. stated in qualitative rather than quantitative terms whenever a choice between the two is possible
    D. stated in a general and unstructured manner, to permit each administrator maximum freedom in interpreting them

7. In selecting from among administrative alternatives, three general bases for decision are open to the manager experience, experimentation, and research and analysis. 7.____
Of the following, the best argument AGAINST primary reliance upon experimentation as the methods of evaluating administrative alternatives is that experimentation is

    A. generally the most expensive of the three techniques
    B. almost always legally prohibited in procedural matters
    C. possible only in areas
    D. where results may be easily duplicated by other experimenters at any time
    E. an approach that requires information on scientific method seldom available to administrators

8. The administrator who utilizes the techniques of operations research, linear programming, and simulation in making an administrative decision should MOST appropriately be considered to be using the techniques of _____ analysis. 8.____

    A. intuitive   B. quantitative
    C. nonmathematical   D. qualitative

9. When an additional organizational level is added within a department, that department has MOST directly manifested 9.____

    A. horizontal growth   B. horizontal shrinkage
    C. vertical growth   D. vertical shrinkage

10. Of the following, the one which GENERALLY is the most intangible planning factor is 10.____

    A. budget dollars allocated to a function
    B. square feet of space for office use
    C. number of personnel in various clerical titles
    D. emotional impact of a proposed personnel policy among employees

11. Departmentation by function is the same as, or most similar to, departmentation by . 11.____

    A. equipment   B. clientele
    C. territory   D. activity

12. Such verifiable factors as turnover, absenteeism, or volume of grievances would gener- 12.____
ally BEST assist in measuring the effectiveness of a program to improve

    A. forms control   B. employee morale
    C. linear programming   D. executive creativit

13. An organization increases the number of subordinates reporting to a manager up to the 13.____
point where incremental savings in costs, better communication and morale, and other
factors equal incremental losses in effectiveness of control, direction, and similar factors.
This action MOST specifically employs the technique of

    A. role playing
    B. queuing theory
    C. marginal analysis
    D. capital standards analysis

14. The term *computer hardware* is MOST likely to refer to 14.____

    A. machines and equipment
    B. programmed instruction texts and compiler decks
    C. training manuals
    D. documentation supporting usage of computing machines

15. Determining what is being accomplished, that is, evaluating the performance and, if nec- 15.____
essary, applying corrective measures so that performance takes place according to plans
is MOST appropriately called management

    A. actuating   B. planning
    C. controlling   D. motivating

16. Of the following, the BEST overall technique for choosing from among several alternative 16.____
public programs proposed to try to achieve the same broad objective generally is

    A. random-sample analysis
    B. input analysis
    C. cost-effectiveness analysis
    D. output analysis

17. When the success of a plan in achieving specific program objectives is measured against 17.____
that plan's costs, the measure obtained is most directly that of the plan's

    A. pervasiveness   B. control potential
    C. primacy   D. efficiency

18. Generally, the degree to which an organization's planning will be coordinated varies
MOST directly with the degree to which

    A. the individuals charged with executing plans are better compensated than those
charged with developing and evaluating plans
    B. the individuals charged with planning understand and agree to utilize consistent
planning premises
    C. a large number of position classification titles have been established for those indi-
viduals charged with organizational planning functions
    D. subordinate unit objectives are allowed to control the overall objectives of the
departments of which such subordinate units are a part

18.____

19. The responsibility for specific types of decisions generally is BEST delegated to

    A. the highest organizational level at which there is an individual possessing the abil-
ity, desire, impartiality and access to relevant information needed to make these
decisions
    B. the lowest organizational level at which there is an individual possessing the ability,
desire, impartiality and access to relevant information needed to make these decisions
    C. a group of executives, rather than a single executive, if these decisions deal with an
emergency
    D. The organizational level midway between that which will have to carry out these
decisions and that which will have to authorize the resources for their implementation

19.____

20. The process of managing by objectives is MOST likely to lead to a situation in which the

    A. goal accomplishment objectives of managers tend to have a longer time span as
one goes lower down the line in an organization
    B. establishment of quantitative goals for staff positions is generally easier than the
establishment of quantitative goals for line positions
    C. development of objectives requires the manager to think of the way he will accom-
plish given results, and of the organization, personnel and resources that he will
need
    D. superiors normally develop and finally approve detailed goals for subordinates
without any prior consultation with either those subordinates or with the top-level
executives responsible for the longer-run objectives of the organization

20.____

21. As used with respect to decision making, the application of scientific method to the study
of alternatives in a problem situation, with a view to providing a quantitative basis for
arriving at an optimum solution in terms of the goals sought is MOST appropriately called

    A. simple number departmentation
    B. geographic decentralization
    C. operations research
    D. trait rating

21.____

22. Assume that a bureau head proposes that final responsibility and authority for all planning within the bureau is to be delegated to one employee who is to be paid at the level of
an assistant division head in that bureau.
Of the following, the MOST appropriate comment about this proposal is that it is

22.____

A. *improper;* mainly because planning does not call for someone at such a high level
B. *improper;* mainly because responsibility for a basic management function such as planning may not properly be delegated as proposed
C. *proper;* mainly because ultimate responsibility for all bureau planning is best placed as proposed
D. *proper;* mainly because every well-managed bureau should have a full-time planning officer

23. Of the following, the MOST important reason that participation has motivating effects is generally that it gives to the individual participating   23.____

    A. a recognition of his desire to feel important and to contribute to achievement of worthwhile goals
    B. an opportunity to participate in work that is beyond the scope of the class specification for his title
    C. a secure knowledge that his organization's top leadership is as efficient as possible considering all major circumstances
    D. the additional information which is likely to be crucial to his promotion

24. Of the following, the MOST essential characteristic of an effective employee suggestion system is that   24.____

    A. suggestions be submitted upward through the chain of command
    B. suggestions be acted upon promptly so that employees may be promptly informed of what happens to their submitted suggestions
    C. suggesters be required to sign their names on the material sent to the actual evaluators for evaluation
    D. suggesters receive at least 25% of the agency's savings during the first two years after their suggestions have been accepted and put into effect by the agency

25. Two organizations have the same basic objectives and the same total number of employees. The span of authority of each intermediate manager is narrower in one organization than it is in the other organization. It is MOST likely that the organization in which each intermediate manager has a narrower span of authority will have   25.____

    A. fewer intermediate managers
    B. more organizational levels
    C. most managers reporting to a larger number of immediate supervisors
    D. more characteristics of a *flat* organizational structure

KEY (CORRECT ANSWERS)

1.	B		11.	D
2.	D		12.	B
3.	B		13.	C
4.	B		14.	A
5.	C		15.	C
6.	B		16.	C
7.	A		17.	D
8.	B		18.	B
9.	C		19.	B
10.	D		20.	C

21.	C
22.	B
23.	A
24.	B
25.	B

———

TEST 2

DIRECTIONS: Each question or incomplete statement is followed by several suggested answers or completions. Select the one that *BEST* answers the question or completes the statement. *PRINT THE LETTER OF THE CORRECT ANSWER IN THE SPACE AT THE RIGHT.*

1. Which one of the following BEST expresses the essence of the merit idea or system in public employment?

    A. A person's worth to the organization–the merit of his attributes and capacities–is the governing factor in his selection, assignment, pay, recognition, advancement and retention.

    B. Written tests of the objective type are the only fair way to select on a merit basis from among candidates for open-competitive appointment to positions within the merit system.

    C. Employees who have qualified for civil service positions shall have life-time tenure during good behavior in those positions regardless of changes in public programs.

    D. Periodic examinations with set date limits within which all persons desiring to demonstrate their merit may apply, shall be publicly advertised and held for all promotional titles.

1.____

2. Of the following, the promotion selection policy generally considered MOST antithetical to the merit concept is the promotion selection policy which

    A. is based solely on objective tests of competence

    B. is based solely on seniority

    C. may require a manager to lose his best employee to another part of the organization

    D. permits operating managers collectively to play a significant role in promotion decisions

2.____

3. Of the following, the problems encountered by government establishments which are MOST likely to make extensive delegation of authority difficult to effectuate tend to be problems of

    A. accountability and insuring uniform administration

    B. line and staff relationships within field offices

    C. generally employee opposition to such delegation of authority and to the subsequent record-keeping activities

    D. use of the management-by-objectives approach

3.____

4. The major decisions as to which jobs shall be created and who shall carry which responsibilities should GENERALLY be made by

    A. budgetary advisers

    B. line managers

    C. classification specialists

    D. peer-level rating committees

4.____

5. The ultimate controlling factor in structuring positions in the public service, MOST generally, should be the

5.____

A. possibility of providing upgrading for highly productive employees
B. collective bargaining demands initially made by established public employee unions
C. positive motivational effects upon productivity resulting from an inverted pyramid job structure
D. effectivenss of the structuring in serving the mission of the organization

6. Of the following, the most usual reason for UNSATISFACTORY line-staff relationships is   6.____

A. inept use of the abilities of staff personnel by line management
B. the higher salaries paid to line officials
C. excessive consultation between line officials and staff officials at the same organizational level
D. a feeling among the staff members thatv only lower-level line members appreciate their work

7. Generally, an employee receiving new information from a fellow employee is MOST likely to   7.____

A. forget the new information if it is consistent with his existing beliefs much more easily than he forgets the new information if it is inconsistent with his existing beliefs
B. accept the validity of the new information if it is consistent with his existing beliefs more readily than he accepts the validity of the new information if it is inconsistent with his existing beliefs
C. have a less accurate memory of the new information if it is consistent with his existing beliefs than he has of the new information if it is inconsistent with his existing beliefs.
D. ignore the new information if it is consistent with his existing beliefs more often than he ignores the new information if it is inconsistent with his existing beliefs

8. Virtually all of us use this principle in our human communications -- perhaps without realizing it. In casual conversations, we are alert for cues to whether we are understood (e.g., attentive nods from the other person). Similarly, an instructor is always interested in reactions among those to whom he is giving instruction. The effective administrator is equally conscious of the need to determine his subordinates' reactions to what he is trying to communicate.
The principle referred to in the above selection is MOST appropriately called   8.____

A. cognitive dissonance   B. feedback
C. negative reinforcement   D. noise transmission

9. Of the following, the PRINCIPAL function of an *ombudsman* generally is to   9.____

A. review departmental requests for new data processing equipment so as to reduce duplication
B. receive and investigate complaints from citizens who are displeased with the actions or non-actions of administrative officials and try to effectuate warranted remedies
C. review proposed departmental reorganizations in order to advise the chief executive whether or not they are in accordance with the latest principles of proper management structuring
D. presiding over courts of the judiciary convened to try *sitting* judges

10. Of the following, the MOST valid reason for recruiting an intermediate-level administrator from outside an agency, rather than from within the agency, normally is to   10.____

    A. improve the public image of the agency as a desirable place in which to be employed

    B. reduce the number of potential administrators who must be evaluated prior to filling the position

    C. minimize the morale problems arising from frequent internal staff upgradings

    D. obtain fresh ideas and a fresh viewpoint on agency problems

11. A group of positions that are sufficiently similar in nature and level of duties, responsibilities, and qualifications required to warrant similar treatment for purposes of recruitment, examination, and pay, is MOST appropriately called a(n)   11.____

    A. grade   B. pay range

    C. class   D. occupational group

12. Governmental personnel testing, MOST generally, has done which one of the following?   12.____

    A. Shown greater precision in testing for creativity and courage than in testing for intelligence and achievement

    B. Developed more useful tests of intelligence, aptitude and achievement than of creativity, courage, and commitment

    C. Failed in the attempt to develop any testing mechanisms in the areas of aptitude or achievement to the point where they are of any use in eliminating extraneous, prejudicial factors in the selection process

    D. Made more use of previous employment records in selecting novices from the outside for junior positions than it has in selecting persons from the outside to fill more senior positions

13. Of the following, the MAJOR objective of government managers in most job restructuring generally should be to   13.____

    A. reduce the percentage that lower-level employees in the government service constitute of the total

    B. reduce the percentage range of the salaries paid within each classified title

    C. concentrate as much of the higher-skill duties in as few of the jobs as possible

    D. package duties into job combinations that are the same as the job combinations traditionally used by lower-paying private employers in the surrounding geographical area

14. Which one of the following statements is MOST generally supported by modern industrial and behavioral research?   14.____

    A. High productivity and high quality each show a substantial negative correlation with high morale.

    B. Where professional employees participate in defining how much and what caliber of their service should be considered acceptable, they generally will set both types of goals substantially below those which management alone would have set.

    C. Professional employees get greater satisfaction out of work that challenges them to exert their capacities fully.

    D. The participative approach to management relieves the manager of the need to be a decision-maker.

15. The term *PPBS* relates MOST directly to one of the systems principally designed to do which one of the following?

    A. Reduce the number of mistakes resulting in spoilage and wasted effort to zero
    B. Obtain greater cost effectiveness
    C. Assure that all operations are performed at the highest quality level that is techni-cally attainable at the present time
    D. Assure that all output units are fully verified prior to being sent out

15.____

16. Assume that you are working with a computer programmer to solve a complex problem. Together, you have defined your problem in everyday English clearly enough to proceed. In the next step, you both start breaking down the information in the definition so that you both can decide on the operations needed for programming the problem. This next step of getting from the definition *to* the problem to the point where you can begin laying out the steps actually to be taken in solving the problem is MOST appropriately called

    A. completing the documentation
    B. implementing the solution
    C. identifying the problem statement
    D. analyzing the problem

16.____

17. Assume that during the fiscal year 2006-2007, a bureau produced 20% more work units than it produced in the fiscal year 2005-2006. Also, assume that during the fiscal year 2006-2007 that bureau's staff was 20% SMALLER than it was in the fiscal year 2005-2006.
On the basis of this information, it would be most proper to conclude that the number of work units produced per staff member in that bureau in the fiscal year 2006-2007 exceeded the number of work units produced per staff member in that bureau in the fiscal year 2005-2006 by which one of the following percentages?

    A. 20%   B. 25%   C. 40%   D. 50%

17.____

18. Assume that during the following five fiscal years (FY), a bureau has received the follow-ing appropriations:
    FY 1997-1998 - $200,000: FY 1998-1999 - $240,000
    FY 1999-2000 - $280,000: FY 2000-2001 - $390,000
    FY 2001-2002 - $505,000
The bureau's appropriation for which one of the following fiscal years showed the LARGEST percentage of increase over the bureau's appropriation for the immediately previous fiscal year?

    A. FY 1998-1999   B. FY 1999-2000
    C. FY 2000-2001   D. FY 2001-2002

18.____

19. A bureau has a very large number of clerical personnel engaged in very similar duties, and only a limited portion can be absent at any one time if the workload is to be handled properly.
Which one of the following would generally be the bureau head's BEST approach toward scheduling the annual leave time (vacations, etc.) to be taken by the employees of that bureau? The bureau head

19.____

A. personally receives from each employee his preferred schedule of annual leave time, personally decides on when the employee can most conveniently be spared from the Viewpoint of the office workload, and issues his decisions to all concerned in the form of a binding memorandum.

B. advises his subordinate supervisors and employees of the parameters and constraints in time and numbers upon annual leave. The employees and subordinate supervisors prepare a proposed annual leave schedule within those limitations and submit it to the bureau head for approval or modification, and for promulgation.

C. initially asks his subordinate supervisors to prepare a proposed annual leave schedule for employees with a minimum of consultation with the employees. He then circulates this schedule to the employees over his signature as a proposed schedule and invites reaction directly to him.

D. asks employee or union representatives to prepare a proposed schedule with all leave to be taken spread evenly over the entire vacation period. He personally reviews and accepts or modifies this proposal.

20. An agency head desires to have an estimate of the *potential* of a middle-level administrative employee for development for higher-level administrative positions. He also desires to try to minimize possible errors or capriciousness which might creep into that estimate. Of the following, it would generally be MOST desirable to have the estimate   20._____

A. result from the pooled judgment of three or more past or present substantial-level supervisors of the subject employee and of persons with lateral or service contracts with the subject employee

B. made solely by substantial-level executives outside the past or present direct line of supervision above the subject employee

C. result from the pooled judgment of substantial level personnel staff members rather than line executives

D. made solely by the present immediate line supervisor of the subject employee

21. Which one of the following generally BEST characterizes the basic nature of budget making and budget administration from a managerial viewpoint?   21._____

A. Budget administration is control, while budget making is planning.
B. Budget administration is planning, while budget making is control.
C. Both budget making and budget administration are only control functions; neither is a planning function.
D. Both budget making and budget administration are only planning functions; neither is a control function.

22. In preparing his annual budget request for a large bureau with both substantial continuing and anticipated new activities, the bureau head must consider various factors (e.g., retaining credibility and obtaining required funds). Of the following, the BEST long-range budgeting strategy would NORMALLY be for the bureau head to request   22._____

A. twice what is actually needed on the assumption that higher authorities will generally cut the requested amount in half

B. ten per cent less than he actually estimates to be needed and to submit a supplementary request later for that ten per cent

C. what is needed for the continuing activities plus twenty-five per cent to allow some slack funds

D.   what he estimates is needed to continue existing essential programs and to fund needed new activities

23.   If we total all of the occasions in which all governmental positions are filled with new faces (persons who did not occupy those specific positions previously), we generally would find that a GREATER number will result from

A.   new accessions from the outside than from movement of personnel within the organization
B.   movement of personnel within the organization than from new accessions from the outside
C.   promotion of staff personnel to higher staff jobs than from promotion of line personnel to higher line jobs
D.   filling of Exempt and Non-Competitive Class positions than from filling of Competitive Class positions

23._____

24.   Listed immediately below are four measures to be utilized to try to achieve a major personnel goal:
   (1)   Diversifying tasks in any one unit as much as feasible
   (2)   Delegating authority to each layer in the hierarchy to the maximum extent cosistent with the clarity of policy guides, training of staff, and the effectiveness of post-audit procedures
   (3)   Assigning whole integrals of functions to individuals or units instead of splitting them into fine specializations with separate employees or groups concentrating on each
   (4)   Permitting workers to follow through on tasks or projects from start to finish rather than carry out single segments of the process
The major personnel goal which all of the above measures, taken together, may BEST be expected to serve is

A.   increasing job simplification
B.   promoting E.E.O. affirmative action
C.   making and keeping jobs as meaningful as they can practically be
D.   increasing the number of promotional levels available so as to maximize advancement opportunities as much as possible

24._____

25.   Which one of the following is generally the BEST criterion for determining the classification title to which a position should be allocated?
The

A.   personal qualifications possessed by the present or expected appointee to the position
B.   consequences of the work of the position or the responsibility it carries
C.   number of work units required to be produced or completed in the position
D.   consequences of inadequate overall governmental pay scales upon recruitment of outstanding personnel

25._____

KEY (CORRECT ANSWERS)

1.	A		11.	C
2.	B		12.	B
3.	A		13.	C
4.	B		14.	C
5.	D		15.	B
6.	A		16.	D
7.	B		17.	D
8.	B		18.	C
9.	B		19.	B
10.	D		20.	A

21.	A
22.	D
23.	B
24.	C
25.	B

Evaluating Conclusions in Light of Known Facts

EXAMINATION SECTION
TEST 1

DIRECTIONS: Each question or incomplete statement is followed by several suggested answers or completions. Select the one that BEST answers the question or completes the statement. *PRINT THE LETTER OF THE CORRECT ANSWER IN THE SPACE AT THE RIGHT.*

Questions 1-9.

DIRECTIONS: In questions 1-9, you will read a set of facts and a conclusion drawn from them. The conclusion may be valid or invalid, based on the facts—it's your task to determine the validity of the conclusion.

For each question, select the letter before the statement that BEST expresses the relationship between the given facts and the conclusion that has been drawn from them. Your choices are:
A. The facts prove the conclusion
B. The facts disprove the conclusion; or
C. The facts neither prove nor disprove the conclusion.

1. FACTS: If the supervisor retires, James, the assistant supervisor, will not be transferred to another department. James will be promoted to supervisor if he is not transferred. The supervisor retired.

   CONCLUSION: James will be promoted to supervisor.

   A. The facts prove the conclusion.
   B. The facts disprove the conclusion.
   C. The facts neither prove nor disprove the conclusion.

1.____

2. FACTS: In the town of Luray, every player on the softball team works at Luray National Bank. In addition, every player on the Luray softball team wears glasses.

   CONCLUSION: At least some of the people who work at Luray National Bank wear glasses.

   A. The facts prove the conclusion.
   B. The facts disprove the conclusion.
   C. The facts neither prove nor disprove the conclusion.

2.____

3. FACTS: The only time Henry and June go out to dinner is on an evening when they have childbirth classes. Their childbirth classes meet on Tuesdays and Thursdays.

   CONCLUSION: Henry and June never go out to dinner on Friday or Saturday.

   A. The facts prove the conclusion.
   B. The facts disprove the conclusion.
   C. The facts neither prove nor disprove the conclusion.

3.____

4. FACTS: Every player on the field hockey team has at least one bruise. Everyone on the field hockey team also has scarred knees.

CONCLUSION: Most people with both bruises and scarred knees are field hockey players.

   A. The facts prove the conclusion.
   B. The facts disprove the conclusion.
   C. The facts neither prove nor disprove the conclusion.

4.____

5. FACTS: In the chess tournament, Lance will win his match against Jane if Jane wins her match against Mathias. If Lance wins his match against Jane, Christine will not win her match against Jane.

CONCLUSION: Christine will not win her match against Jane if Jane wins her match against Mathias.

   A. The facts prove the conclusion.
   B. The facts disprove the conclusion.
   C. The facts neither prove nor disprove the conclusion.

5.____

6. FACTS: No green lights on the machine are indicators for the belt drive status. Not all of the lights on the machine's upper panel are green. Some lights on the machine's lower panel are green.

CONCLUSION: The green lights on the machine's lower panel may be indicators for the belt drive status.

   A. The facts prove the conclusion.
   B. The facts disprove the conclusion.
   C. The facts neither prove nor disprove the conclusion.

6.____

7. FACTS: At a small, one-room country school, there are eight students: Amy, Ben, Carla, Dan, Elliot, Francine, Greg, and Hannah. Each student is in either the 6th, 7th, or 8th grade. Either two or three students are in each grade. Amy, Dan, and Francine are all in different grades. Ben and Elliot are both in the 7th grade. Hannah and Carl are in the same grade.

CONCLUSION: Exactly three students are in the 7th grade.

   A. The facts prove the conclusion.
   B. The facts disprove the conclusion.
   C. The facts neither prove nor disprove the conclusion.

7.____

8. FACTS: Two married couples are having lunch together. Two of the four people are German and two are Russian, but in each couple the nationality of a spouse is not necessarily the same as the other's. One person in the group is a teacher, the other a lawyer, one an engineer, and the other a writer. The teacher is a Russian man. The writer is Russian, and her husband is an engineer. One of the people, Mr. Stern, is German.

CONCLUSION: Mr. Stern's wife is a writer.

8.____

A. The facts prove the conclusion.
B. The facts disprove the conclusion.
C. The facts neither prove nor disprove the conclusion.

9. FACTS: The flume ride at the county fair is open only to children who are at least 36   9._____
    inches tall. Lisa is 30 inches tall. John is shorter than Henry, but more than 10 inches
    taller than Lisa.

    CONCLUSION: Lisa is the only one who can't ride the flume ride.

    A. The facts prove the conclusion.
    B. The facts disprove the conclusion.
    C. The facts neither prove nor disprove the conclusion.

Questions 10-17.

DIRECTIONS: Questions 10-17 are based on the following reading passage. It is not your
              knowledge of the particular topic that is being tested, but your ability to reason
              based on what you have read. The passage is likely to detail several proposed
              courses of action and factors affecting these proposals. The reading passage
              is followed by a conclusion or outcome based on the facts in the passage, or a
              description of a decision taken regarding the situation. The conclusion is fol-
              lowed by a number of statements that have a possible connection to the con-
              clusion. For each statement, you are to determine whether:

              A. The statement proves the conclusion.
              B. The statement supports the conclusion but does not prove it.
              C. The statement disproves the conclusion.
              D. The statement weakens the conclusion but does not disprove it.
              E. The statement has no relevance to the conclusion.

Remember that the conclusion after the passage is to be accepted as the outcome of
what actually happened, and that you are being asked to evaluate the impact each statement would have had on the conclusion.

PASSAGE:

The Grand Army of Foreign Wars, a national veteran's organization, is struggling to
maintain its National Home, where the widowed spouses and orphans of deceased members
are housed together in a small village-like community. The Home is open to spouses and children who are bereaved for any reason, regardless of whether the member's death was
related to military service, but a new global conflict has led to a dramatic surge in the number
of members' deaths: many veterans who re-enlisted for the conflict have been killed in action.

The Grand Army of Foreign Wars is considering several options for handling the
increased number of applications for housing at the National Home, which has been traditionally supported by membership dues. At its national convention, it will choose only one of the
following:

The first idea is a one-time $50 tax on all members, above and beyond the dues they pay
already. Since the organization has more than a million members, this tax should be sufficient

for the construction and maintenance of new housing for applicants on the existing grounds of the National Home. The idea is opposed, however, by some older members who live on fixed incomes. These members object in principle to the taxation of Grand Army members. The Grand Army has never imposed a tax on its members.

The second idea is to launch a national fund-raising drive and public relations campaign that will attract donations for the National Home. Several national celebrities are members of the organization, and other celebrities could be attracted to the cause. Many Grand Army members are wary of this approach, however: in the past, the net receipts of some fund-raising efforts have been relatively insignificant, given the costs of staging them.

A third approach, suggested by many of the younger members, is to have new applicants share some of the costs of construction and maintenance. The spouses and children would pay an up-front "enrollment" fee, based on a sliding scale proportionate to their income and assets, and then a monthly fee adjusted similarly to contribute to maintenance costs. Many older members are strongly opposed to this idea, as it is in direct contradiction to the principles on which the organization was founded more than a century ago.

The fourth option is simply to maintain the status quo, focus the organization's efforts on supporting the families who already live at the National Home, and wait to accept new applicants based on attrition.

CONCLUSION: At its annual national convention, the Grand Army of Foreign Wars votes to impose a one-time tax of $10 on each member for the purpose of expanding and supporting the National Home to welcome a larger number of applicants. The tax is considered to be the solution most likely to produce the funds needed to accommodate the growing number of applicants.

10. Actuarial studies have shown that because the Grand Army's membership consists mostly of older veterans from earlier wars, the organization's membership will suffer a precipitous decline in numbers in about five years.

    10._____

    A.
    B.
    C.
    D.
    E.

11. After passage of the funding measure, a splinter group of older members appeals for the "sliding scale" provision to be applied to the tax, so that some members may be allowed to contribute less based on their income.

    11._____

    A.
    B.
    C.
    D.
    E.

12. The original charter of the Grand Army of Foreign Wars specifically states that the organization will not levy any taxes or duties on its members beyond its modest annual dues. It takes a super-majority of attending delegates at the national convention to make alterations to the charter.

    12.____

    A.
    B.
    C.
    D.
    E.

13. Six months before Grand Army of Foreign Wars'national convention, the Internal Revenue Service rules that because it is an organization that engages in political lobbying, the Grand Army must no longer enjoy its own federal tax-exempt status.

    13.____

    A.
    B.
    C.
    D.
    E.

14. Two months before the national convention, Dirk Rockwell, arguably the country's most famous film actor, announces in a nationally televised interview that he has been saddened to learn of the plight of the National Home, and that he is going to make it his own personal crusade to see that it is able to house and support a greater number of widowed spouses and orphans in the future.

    14.____

    A.
    B.
    C.
    D.
    E.

15. The Grand Army's final estimate is that the cost of expanding the National Home to accommodate the increased number of applicants will be about $61 million.

    15.____

    A.
    B.
    C.
    D.
    E.

16. Just before the national convention, the federal Department of Veterans Affairs announces steep cuts in the benefits package that is currently offered to the widowed spouses and orphans of veterans.

    16.____

    A.
    B.
    C.
    D.

17. After the national convention, the Grand Army of Foreign Wars begins charging a modest   17.____
    "start-up" fee to all families who apply for residence at the national home.

    A.
    B.
    C.
    D.
    E.

Questions 18-25.

DIRECTIONS: Questions 18-25 each provide four factual statements and a conclusion based
               on these statements. After reading the entire question, you will decide
               whether:
               A.   The conclusion is proved by statements 1-4;
               B.   The conclusion is disproved by statements 1-4; or
               C.   The facts are not sufficient to prove or disprove the conclusion.

18. FACTUAL STATEMENTS: 18.____

    1. In the Field Day high jump competition, Martha jumped higher than Frank.
    2. Carl jumped higher than Ignacio.
    3. Ignacio jumped higher than Frank.
    4. Dan jumped higher than Carl.

    CONCLUSION: Frank finished last in the high jump competition.

    A.   The conclusion is proved by statements 1-4.
    B.   The conclusion is disproved by statements 1-4.
    C.   The facts are not sufficient to prove or disprove the conclusion.

19. FACTUAL STATEMENTS: 19.____

    1. The door to the hammer mill chamber is locked if light 6 is red.
    2. The door to the hammer mill chamber is locked only when the mill is operating.
    3. If the mill is not operating, light 6 is blue.
    4. Light 6 is blue.

    CONCLUSION: The door to the hammer mill chamber is locked.

    A.   The conclusion is proved by statements 1-4.
    B.   The conclusion is disproved by statements 1-4.
    C.   The facts are not sufficient to prove or disprove the conclusion.

20. FACTUAL STATEMENTS: 20._____

    1. Ziegfried, the lion tamer at the circus, has demanded ten additional minutes of performance time during each show.
    2. If Ziegfried is allowed his ten additional minutes per show, he will attempt to teach Kimba the tiger to shoot a basketball.
    3. If Kimba learns how to shoot a basketball, then Ziegfried was not given his ten additional minutes.
    4. Ziegfried was given his ten additional minutes.

CONCLUSION: Despite Ziegfried's efforts, Kimba did not learn how to shoot a basketball.

    A.   The conclusion is proved by statements 1-4.
    B.   The conclusion is disproved by statements 1-4.
    C.   The facts are not sufficient to prove or disprove the conclusion.

21. FACTUAL STATEMENTS: 21._____

    1. If Stan goes to counseling, Sara won't divorce him.
    2. If Sara divorces Stan, she'll move back to Texas.
    3. If Sara doesn't divorce Stan, Irene will be disappointed.
    4. Stan goes to counseling.

CONCLUSION: Irene will be disappointed.

    A.   The conclusion is proved by statements 1-4.
    B.   The conclusion is disproved by statements 1-4.
    C.   The facts are not sufficient to prove or disprove the conclusion.

22. FACTUAL STATEMENTS: 22._____

    1. If Delia is promoted to district manager, Claudia will have to be promoted to team leader.
    2. Delia will be promoted to district manager unless she misses her fourth-quarter sales quota.
    3. If Claudia is promoted to team leader, Thomas will be promoted to assistant team leader.
    4. Delia meets her fourth-quarter sales quota.

CONCLUSION: Thomas is promoted to assistant team leader.

    A.   The conclusion is proved by statements 1-4.
    B.   The conclusion is disproved by statements 1-4.
    C.   The facts are not sufficient to prove or disprove the conclusion.

23. FACTUAL STATEMENTS: 23.____

    1. Clone D is identical to Clone B.
    2. Clone B is not identical to Clone A.
    3. Clone D is not identical to Clone C.
    4. Clone E is not identical to the clones that are identical to Clone B.

    CONCLUSION: Clone E is identical to Clone D.

    A. The conclusion is proved by statements 1-4.
    B. The conclusion is disproved by statements 1-4.
    C. The facts are not sufficient to prove or disprove the conclusion.

24. FACTUAL STATEMENTS: 24.____

    1. In the Stafford Tower, each floor is occupied by a single business.
    2. Big G Staffing is on a floor between CyberGraphics and MainEvent.
    3. Gasco is on the floor directly below CyberGraphics and three floors above Treehorn
       Audio.
    4. MainEvent is five floors below EZ Tax and four floors below Treehorn Audio.

    CONCLUSION: EZ Tax is on a floor between Gasco and MainEvent.

    A. The conclusion is proved by statements 1-4.
    B. The conclusion is disproved by statements 1-4.
    C. The facts are not sufficient to prove or disprove the conclusion.

25. FACTUAL STATEMENTS: 25.____

    1. Only county roads lead to Nicodemus.
    2. All the roads from Hill City to Graham County are federal highways.
    3. Some of the roads from Plainville lead to Nicodemus.
    4. Some of the roads running from Hill City lead to Strong City.

    CONCLUSION: Some of the roads from Plainville are county roads.

    A. The conclusion is proved by statements 1-4.
    B. The conclusion is disproved by statements 1-4.
    C. The facts are not sufficient to prove or disprove the conclusion.

KEY (CORRECT ANSWERS)

1.	A		11.	A
2.	A		12.	D
3.	A		13.	E
4.	C		14.	D
5.	A		15.	B
6.	B		16.	B
7.	A		17.	C
8.	A		18.	A
9.	A		19.	B
10.	E		20.	A

21.	A
22.	A
23.	B
24.	A
25.	A

SOLUTIONS TO PROBLEMS

1) (A) Given statement 3, we deduce that James will not be transferred to another department. By statement 2, we can conclude that James will be promoted.

2) (A) Since every player on the softball team wears glasses, these individuals compose some of the people who work at the bank. Although not every person who works at the bank plays softball, those bank employees who do play softball wear glasses.

3) (A) If Henry and June go out to dinner, we conclude that it must be on Tuesday or Thursday, which are the only two days when they have childbirth classes. This implies that if it is not Tuesday or Thursday, then this couple does not go out to dinner.

4) (C) We can only conclude that if a person plays on the field hockey team, then he or she has both bruises and scarred knees. But there are probably a great number of people who have both bruises and scarred knees but do not play on the field hockey team. The given conclusion can neither be proven or disproven.

5) (A) From statement 1, if Jane beats Mathias, then Lance will beat Jane. Using statement 2, we can then conclude that Christine will not win her match against Jane.

6) (B) Statement 1 tells us that no green light can be an indicator of the belt drive status. Thus, the given conclusion must be false.

7) (A) We already know that Ben and Elliot are in the 7th grade. Even though Hannah and Carl are in the same grade, it cannot be the 7th grade because we would then have at least four students in this 7th grade. This would contradict the third statement, which states that either two or three students are in each grade. Since Amy, Dan, and Francine are in different grades, exactly one of them must be in the 7th grade. Thus, Ben, Elliot and exactly one of Amy, Dan, and Francine are the three students in the 7th grade.

8) (A) One man is a teacher, who is Russian. We know that the writer is female and is Russian. Since her husband is an engineer, he cannot be the Russian teacher. Thus, her husband is of German descent, namely Mr. Stern. This means that Mr. Stern's wife is the writer. Note that one couple consists of a male Russian teacher and a female German lawyer. The other couple consists of a male German engineer and a female Russian writer.

9) (A) Since John is more than 10 inches taller than Lisa, his height is at least 46 inches. Also, John is shorter than Henry, so Henry's height must be greater than 46 inches. Thus, Lisa is the only one whose height is less than 36 inches. Therefore, she is the only one who is not allowed on the flume ride.

18) (A) Dan jumped higher than Carl, who jumped higher than Ignacio, who jumped higher than Frank. Since Martha jumped higher than Frank, every person jumped higher than Frank. Thus, Frank finished last.

19) (B) If the light is red, then the door is locked. If the door is locked, then the mill is operating. Reversing the logical sequence of these statements, if the mill is not operating, then the door is not locked, which means that the light is blue. Thus, the given conclusion is disproved.

20) (A) Using the contrapositive of statement 3, if Ziegfried was given his ten additional minutes, then Kimba did not learn how to shoot a basketball. Since statement 4 is factual, the conclusion is proved.

21) (A) From statements 4 and 1, we conclude that Sara doesn't divorce Stan. Then statement 3 reveals that Irene will be disappointed. Thus the conclusion is proved.

22) (A) Statement 2 can be rewritten as "Delia is promoted to district manager or she misses her sales quota." Furthermore, this statement is equivalent to "If Delia makes her sales quota, then she is promoted to district manager." From statement 1, we conclude that Claudia is promoted to team leader. Finally, by statement 3, Thomas is promoted to assistant team leader. The conclusion is proved.

23) (B) By statement 4, Clone E is not identical to any clones identical to clone B. Statement 1 tells us that clones B and D are identical. Therefore, clone E cannot be identical to clone D. The conclusion is disproved.

24) (A) Based on all four statements, CyberGraphics is somewhere below Main Event. Gasco is one floor below CyberGraphics. EZ Tax is two floors below Gasco. Treehorn Audio is one floor below EZ Tax. Main Event is four floors below Treehorn Audio. Thus, EZ Tax is two floors below Gasco and five floors above Main Event. The conclusion is proved.

25) (A) From statement 3, we know that some of the roads from Plainville lead to Nicodemus. But statement 1 tells us that only county roads lead to Nicodemus. Therefore, some of the roads from Plainville must be county roads. The conclusion is proved.

TEST 2

DIRECTIONS: Each question or incomplete statement is followed by several suggested answers or completions. Select the one that BEST answers the question or completes the statement. *PRINT THE LETTER OF THE CORRECT ANSWER IN THE SPACE AT THE RIGHT.*

Questions 1-9.

DIRECTIONS: In questions 1-9, you will read a set of facts and a conclusion drawn from them. The conclusion may be valid or invalid, based on the facts-it's your task to determine the validity of the conclusion.

For each question, select the letter before the statement that BEST expresses the relationship between the given facts and the conclusion that has been drawn from them. Your choices are:
A. The facts prove the conclusion
B. The facts disprove the conclusion; or
C. The facts neither prove nor disprove the conclusion.

1. FACTS: Some employees in the testing department are statisticians. Most of the statisticians who work in the testing department are projection specialists. Tom Wilks works in the testing department.

   CONCLUSION: Tom Wilks is a statistician.

   A. The facts prove the conclusion.
   B. The facts disprove the conclusion.
   C. The facts neither prove nor disprove the conclusion.

1.____

2. FACTS: Ten coins are split among Hank, Lawrence, and Gail. If Lawrence gives his coins to Hank, then Hank will have more coins than Gail. If Gail gives her coins to Lawrence, then Lawrence will have more coins than Hank.

   CONCLUSION: Hank has six coins.

   A. The facts prove the conclusion.
   B. The facts disprove the conclusion.
   C. The facts neither prove nor disprove the conclusion.

2.____

3. FACTS: Nobody loves everybody. Janet loves Ken. Ken loves everybody who loves Janet.

   CONCLUSION: Everybody loves Janet.

   A. The facts prove the conclusion.
   B. The facts disprove the conclusion.
   C. The facts neither prove nor disprove the conclusion.

3.____

4. FACTS: Most of the Torres family lives in East Los Angeles. Many people in East Los   4.____
   Angeles celebrate Cinco de Mayo. Joe is a member of the Torres family.

   CONCLUSION: Joe lives in East Los Angeles.

   A. The facts prove the conclusion.
   B. The facts disprove the conclusion.
   C. The facts neither prove nor disprove the conclusion.

5. FACTS: Five professionals each occupy one story of a five-story office building. Dr.   5.____
   Kane's office is above Dr. Assad's. Dr. Johnson's office is between Dr. Kane's and Dr.
   Conlon's. Dr. Steen's office is between Dr. Conlon's and Dr. Assad's. Dr. Johnson is on
   the fourth story.

   CONCLUSION: Dr. Kane occupies the top story.

   A. The facts prove the conclusion.
   B. The facts disprove the conclusion.
   C. The facts neither prove nor disprove the conclusion.

6. FACTS: To be eligible for membership in the Yukon Society, a person must be able to   6.____
   either tunnel through a snowbank while wearing only a T-shirt and shorts, or hold his
   breath for two minutes under water that is 50° F. Ray can only hold his breath for a
   minute and a half.

   CONCLUSION: Ray can still become a member of the Yukon Society by tunneling
   through a snowbank while wearing a T-shirt and shorts.

   A. The facts prove the conclusion.
   B. The facts disprove the conclusion.
   C. The facts neither prove nor disprove the conclusion.

7. FACTS: A mark is worth five plunks. You can exchange four sharps for a tinplot. It takes   7.____
   eight marks to buy a sharp.

   CONCLUSION: A sharp is the most valuable.

   A. The facts prove the conclusion.
   B. The facts disprove the conclusion.
   C. The facts neither prove nor disprove the conclusion.

8. FACTS: There are gibbons, as well as lemurs, who like to play in the trees at the monkey   8.____
   house. All those who like to play in the trees at the monkey house are fed lettuce and
   bananas.

   CONCLUSION: Lemurs and gibbons are types of monkeys.

   A. The facts prove the conclusion.
   B. The facts disprove the conclusion.
   C. The facts neither prove nor disprove the conclusion.

9. FACTS: None of the Blackfoot tribes is a Salishan Indian tribe. Sal-ishan Indians came   9.____
   from the northern Pacific Coast. All Salishan Indians live east of the Continental Divide.

   CONCLUSION: No Blackfoot tribes live east of the Continental Divide.

   A. The facts prove the conclusion.
   B. The facts disprove the conclusion.
   C. The facts neither prove nor disprove the conclusion.

Questions 10-17.

DIRECTIONS: Questions 10-17 are based on the following reading passage. It is not your
            knowledge of the particular topic that is being tested, but your ability to reason
            based on what you have read. The passage is likely to detail several proposed
            courses of action and factors affecting these proposals. The reading passage
            is followed by a conclusion or outcome based on the facts in the passage, or a
            description of a decision taken regarding the situation. The conclusion is fol-
            lowed by a number of statements that have a possible connection to the con-
            clusion. For each statement, you are to determine whether:

            A. The statement proves the conclusion.
            B. The statement supports the conclusion but does not prove it.
            C. The statement disproves the conclusion.
            D. The statement weakens the conclusion but does not disprove it.
            E. The statement has no relevance to the conclusion.

Remember that the conclusion after the passage is to be accepted as the outcome of
what actually happened, and that you are being asked to evaluate the impact each statement would have had on the conclusion.

PASSAGE:

On August 12, Beverly Willey reported that she was in the elevator late on the previous
evening after leaving her office on the 16th floor of a large office building. In her report,
she states that a man got on the elevator at the 11th floor, pulled her off the elevator,
assaulted her, and stole her purse. Ms. Willey reported that she had seen the man in the
elevators and hallways of the building before. She believes that the man works in the
building. Her description of him is as follows: he is tall, unshaven, with wavy brown hair
and a scar on his left cheek. He walks with a pronounced limp, often dragging his left foot
behind his right.

CONCLUSION: After Beverly Willey makes her report, the police arrest a 43-year-man,
Barton Black, and charge him with her assault.

10. Barton Black is a former Marine who served in Vietnam, where he sustained shrapnel   10.____
    wounds to the left side of his face and suffered nerve damage in his left leg.

    A.
    B.
    C.
    D.
    E.

11. When they arrived at his residence to question him, detectives were greeted at the door   11.____
by Barton Black, who was tall and clean-shaven.

     A.
     B.
     C.
     D.
     E.

12. Barton Black was booked into the county jail several days after Beverly Willey's assault.   12.____

     A.
     B.
     C.
     D.
     E.

13. Upon further investigation, detectives discover that Beverly Willey does not work at the   13.____
office building.

     A.
     B.
     C.
     D.
     E.

14. Upon further investigation, detectives discover that Barton Black does not work at the   14.____
office building.

     A.
     B.
     C.
     D.
     E.

15. In the spring of the following year, Barton Black is convicted of assaulting Beverly Willey   15.____
on August 11.

     A.
     B.
     C.
     D.
     E.

16. During their investigation of the assault, detectives determine that Beverly Willey was   16.____
assaulted on the 12th floor of the office building.

     A.
     B.
     C.
     D.
     E.

17. The day after Beverly Willey's assault, Barton Black fled the area and was never seen   17.____
again.

    A.
    B.
    C.
    D.
    E.

Questions 18-25.

DIRECTIONS: Questions 18-25 each provide four factual statements and a conclusion based on these statements. After reading the entire question, you will decide whether:

    A.   The conclusion is proved by statements 1-4;
    B.   The conclusion is disproved by statements 1-4; or
    C.   The facts are not sufficient to prove or disprove the conclusion.

18. FACTUAL STATEMENTS: 18.____

1. Among five spice jars on the shelf, the sage is to the right of the parsley.
2. The pepper is to the left of the basil.
3. The nutmeg is between the sage and the pepper.
4. The pepper is the second spice from the left.

CONCLUSION: The sage is the farthest to the right.

    A.   The conclusion is proved by statements 1-4.
    B.   The conclusion is disproved by statements 1-4.
    C.   The facts are not sufficient to prove or disprove the conclusion.

19. FACTUAL STATEMENTS: 19.____

1. Gear X rotates in a clockwise direction if Switch C is in the OFF position
2. Gear X will rotate in a counter-clockwise direction if Switch C is ON.
3. If Gear X is rotating in a clockwise direction, then Gear Y will not be rotating at all.
4. Switch C is ON.

CONCLUSION: Gear X is rotating in a counter-clockwise direction.

    A.   The conclusion is proved by statements 1-4.
    B.   The conclusion is disproved by statements 1-4.
    C.   The facts are not sufficient to prove or disprove the conclusion.

20. FACTUAL STATEMENTS: 20._____
   1. Lane will leave for the Toronto meeting today only if Terence, Rourke, and Jackson all file their marketing reports by the end of the work day.
   2. Rourke will file her report on time only if Ganz submits last quarter's data.
   3. If Terence attends the security meeting, he will attend it with Jackson, and they will not file their marketing reports by the end of the work day.
   4. Ganz submits last quarter's data to Rourke.

   CONCLUSION: Lane will leave for the Toronto meeting today.

   A. The conclusion is proved by statements 1-4.
   B. The conclusion is disproved by statements 1-4.
   C. The facts are not sufficient to prove or disprove the conclusion.

21. FACTUAL STATEMENTS: 21._____

   1. Bob is in second place in the Boston Marathon.
   2. Gregory is winning the Boston Marathon.
   3. There are four miles to go in the race, and Bob is gaining on Gregory at the rate of 100 yards every minute.
   4. There are 1760 yards in a mile, and Gregory's usual pace during the Boston Marathon is one mile every six minutes.

   CONCLUSION: Bob wins the Boston Marathon.

   A. The conclusion is proved by statements 1-4.
   B. The conclusion is disproved by statements 1-4.
   C. The facts are not sufficient to prove or disprove the conclusion.

22. FACTUAL STATEMENTS: 22._____

   1. Four brothers are named Earl, John, Gary, and Pete.
   2. Earl and Pete are unmarried.
   3. John is shorter than the youngest of the four.
   4. The oldest brother is married, and is also the tallest.

   CONCLUSION: Gary is the oldest brother.

   A. The conclusion is proved by statements 1-4.
   B. The conclusion is disproved by statements 1-4.
   C. The facts are not sufficient to prove or disprove the conclusion.

23. FACTUAL STATEMENTS: 23._____

   1. Brigade X is ten miles from the demilitarized zone.
   2. If General Woundwort gives the order, Brigade X will advance to the demilitarized zone, but not quickly enough to reach the zone before the conflict begins.
   3. Brigade Y, five miles behind Brigade X, will not advance unless General Woundwort gives the order.
   4. Brigade Y advances.

   CONCLUSION: Brigade X reaches the demilitarized zone before the conflict begins.

A. The conclusion is proved by statements 1-4.
B. The conclusion is disproved by statements 1-4.
C. The facts are not sufficient to prove or disprove the conclusion.

24. FACTUAL STATEMENTS: 24._____

1. Jerry has decided to take a cab from Fullerton to Elverton.
2. Chubby Cab charges $5 plus $3 a mile.
3. Orange Cab charges $7.50 but gives free mileage for the first 5 miles.
4. After the first 5 miles, Orange Cab charges $2.50 a mile.

CONCLUSION: Orange Cab is the cheaper fare from Fullerton to Elverton.

A. The conclusion is proved by statements 1-4.
B. The conclusion is disproved by statements 1-4.
C. The facts are not sufficient to prove or disprove the conclusion.

25. FACTUAL STATEMENTS: 25._____

1. Dan is never in class when his friend Lucy is absent.
2. Lucy is never absent unless her mother is sick.
3. If Lucy is in class, Sergio is in class also
4. Sergio is never in class when Dalton is absent.

CONCLUSION: If Lucy is absent, Dalton may be in class.

A. The conclusion is proved by statements 1-4.
B. The conclusion is disproved by statements 1-4.
C. The facts are not sufficient to prove or disprove the conclusion.

KEY (CORRECT ANSWERS)

1.	C	11.	E
2.	B	12.	B
3.	B	13.	D
4.	C	14.	E
5.	A	15.	A
6.	A	16.	E
7.	B	17.	C
8.	C	18.	B
9.	C	19.	A
10.	B	20.	C

21.	C
22.	A
23.	B
24.	A
25.	B

SOLUTIONS TO PROBLEMS

1) (C) Statement 1 only tells us that some employees who work in the Testing Department are statisticians. This means that we need to allow the possibility that at least one person in this department is not a statistician. Thus, if a person works in the Testing Department, we cannot conclude whether or not this individual is a statistician.

2) (B) If Hank had six coins, then the total of Gails collection and Lawrence's collection would be four. Thus, if Gail gave all her coins to Lawrence, Lawrence would only have four coins. Thus, it would be impossible for Lawrence to have more coins than Hank.

3) (B) Statement 1 tells us that nobody loves everybody. If everybody loved Janet, then Statement 3 would imply that Ken loves everybody. This would contradict statement 1. The conclusion is disproved.

4) (C) Although most of the Torres family lives in East Los Angeles, we can assume that some members of this family do not live in East Los Angeles. Thus, we cannot prove or disprove that Joe, who is a member of the Torres family, lives in East Los Angeles.

5) (A) Since Dr. Johnson is on the 4th floor, either (a) Dr. Kane is on the 5th floor and Dr. Conlon is on the 3rd floor, or (b) Dr. Kane is on the 3rd floor and Dr. Conlon is on the 5th floor. If option (b) were correct, then since Dr. Assad would be on the 1st floor, it would be impossible for Dr. Steen's office to be between Dr. Conlon and Dr. Assad's office. Therefore, Dr. Kane's office must be on the 5th floor. The order of the doctors' offices, from 5th floor down to the 1st floor is: Dr. Kane, Dr. Johnson, Dr. Conlon, Dr. Steen, Dr. Assad.

6) (A) Ray does not satisfy the requirement of holding his breath for two minutes under water, since he can only hold his breath for one minute in that setting. But if he tunnels through a snowbank with just a T-shirt and shorts, he will satisfy the eligibility requirement. Note that the eligibility requirement contains the key word "or." So only one of the two clauses separated by "or" need to be fulfilled.

7) (B) Statement 2 says that four sharps is equivalent to one tinplot. This means that a tinplot is worth more than a sharp. The conclusion is disproved. We note that the order of these items, from most valuable to least valuable are: tinplot, sharp, mark, plunk.

8) (C) We can only conclude that gibbons and lemurs are fed lettuce and bananas. We can neither prove or disprove that these animals are types of monkeys.

9) (C) We know that all Salishan Indians live east of the Continental Divide. But some nonmembers of this tribe of Indians may also live east of the Continental Divide. Since none of the members of the Blackfoot tribe belong to the Salishan Indian tribe, we cannot draw any conclusion about the location of the Blackfoot tribe with respect to the Continental Divide.

18) (B) Since the pepper is second from the left and the nutmeg is between the sage and the pepper, the positions 2, 3, and 4 (from the left) are pepper, nutmeg, sage. By statement 2, the basil must be in position 5, which implies that the parsley is in position 1. Therefore, the basil, not the sage is farthest to the right. The conclusion disproved.

19) (A) Statement 2 assures us that if switch C is ON, then Gear X is rotating in a counterclockwise direction. The conclusion is proved.

20) (C) Based on Statement 4, followed by Statement 2, we conclude that Ganz and Rourke will file their reports on time. Statement 3 reveals that if Terence and Jackson attend the security meeting, they will fail to file their reports on time. We have no further information if Terence and Jackson attended the security meeting, so we are not able to either confirm or deny that their reports were filed on time. This implies that we cannot know for certain that Lane will leave for his meeting in Toronto.

21) (C) Although Bob is in second place behind Gregory, we cannot deduce how far behind Gregory he is running. At Gregory's current pace, he will cover four miles in 24 minutes. If Bob were only 100 yards behind Gregory, he would catch up to Gregory in one minute. But if Bob were very far behind Gregory, for example 5 miles, this is the equivalent of (5)(1760) = 8800 yards. Then Bob would need 8800/100 = 88 minutes to catch up to Gregory. Thus, the given facts are not sufficient to draw a conclusion.

22) (A) Statement 2 tells us that neither Earl nor Pete could be the oldest; also, either John or Gary is married. Statement 4 reveals that the oldest brother is both married and the tallest. By statement 3, John cannot be the tallest. Since John is not the tallest, he is not the oldest. Thus, the oldest brother must be Gary. The conclusion is proved.

23) (B) By statements 3 and 4, General Woundwort must have given the order to advance. Statement 2 then tells us that Brigade X will advance to the demilitarized zone, but not soon enough before the conflict begins. Thus, the conclusion is disproved.

24) (A) If the distance is 5 miles or less, then the cost for the Orange Cab is only $7.50, whereas the cost for the Chubby Cab is $5 + 3x, where x represents the number of miles traveled. For 1 to 5 miles, the cost of the Chubby Cab is between $8 and $20. This means that for a distance of 5 miles, the Orange Cab costs $7.50, whereas the Chubby Cab costs $20. After 5 miles, the cost per mile of the Chubby Cab exceeds the cost per mile of the Orange Cab. Thus, regardless of the actual distance between Fullerton and Elverton, the cost for the Orange Cab will be cheaper than that of the Chubby Cab.

25) (B) It looks like "Dalton" should be replaced by "Dan in the conclusion. Then by statement 1, if Lucy is absent, Dan is never in class. Thus, the conclusion is disproved.

EXAMINATION SECTION
TEST 1

DIRECTIONS: The questions that follow the paragraph below are designed to test your appreciation of correctness and effectiveness of expression in English. The paragraph is presented first in full so that you may read it through for sense. Disregard the errors you find as you will be asked to correct them in the questions that follow. The paragraph is then presented sentence by sentence with portions underlined and numbered. At the end of this material, you will find numbers corresponding to those below the underlined portions, each followed by five alternatives lettered A, B, C, D, and E. In every case, the usage in the alternative lettered A is the same as that in the original paragraph and is followed by four other possible usages. Choose the usage that you consider BEST in each case. *PRINT THE LETTER OF THE CORRECT ANSWER IN THE SPACE AT THE RIGHT.*

The use of the machine produced up to the present time outstanding changes in our modern world. One of the most significant of these changes have been the marked decreases in the length of the working day and the working week. The fourteen-hour day not only has been reduced to one of ten hours but also, in some lines of work, to one of eight or even six. The trend toward a decrease is further evidenced in the longer weekend already given to employees in many business establishments. There seems also to be a trend toward shorter working weeks and longer summer vacations. An important feature of this development is that leisure is no longer the privilege of the wealthy few, - it has become the common right of most people. Using it wisely, leisure promotes health, efficiency and happiness, for there is time for each individual to live their own "more abundant life" and having opportunities for needed recreation.

Recreation, like the name implies, is a process of revitalization. In giving expression to the play instincts of the human race, new vigor and effectiveness are afforded by recreation to the body and to the mind. Of course not all forms of amusement, by no means constitute recreation. Furthermore, an activity that provides recreation for one person may prove exhausting for another. Today, however, play among adults, as well as children, is regarded as a vital necessity of modern life. Play being recognized as an important factor in improving mental and physical health and thereby reducing human misery and poverty.

Among the most important forms of amusement available at the present time are the automobile, the moving picture, the radio, television, and organized sports. The automobile, especially, has been a boon to the American people, since it has been the chief means of them getting out into the open. The motion picture, the radio and television have tremendous opportunities to supply whole-some recreation and to promote cultural advancement. A criticism often leveled against organized sports as a means of recreation is because they make passive spectators of too many people. It has been said "that the American public is afflicted with "spectatoritis," but there is some recreational advantages to be gained even from being a spectator at organized games. Such sports afford a release from the monotony of daily toil, get people outdoors and also provide an exhilaration that is tonic in its effect.

The chief concern, of course, should be to eliminate those forms of amusement that are socially undesirable. There are, however, far too many people who, we know, do not use their leisure to the best advantage. Sometimes leisure leads to idleness, and idleness may lead to demoralization. The value of leisure both to the individual and to society will depend on the uses made of it.

The use of the machine produced up to the
_____
1

1. A. produced   B. produces   1._____
    C. has produced   D. had produced
    E. will have produced

present time many outstanding changes in our modern world. One of the most significant of these changes have been the marked
                  _____
                      2

2. A. have been   B. was   C. were   2._____
    D. has been   E. will be

decreases in the length of the working day and the working week.
The fourteen-hour day not only has been reduced to one of ten hours but also, in some
_____
                    3
lines of work, to one of eight or even six.

3. A. The fourteen-hour day not only has been reduced   3._____
    B. Not only the fourteen-hour day has been reduced
    C. Not the fourteen-hour day only has been reduced
    D. The fourteen-hour day has not only been reduced

The trend toward a decrease is further evidenced in the longer week-end already given
                                                                        _____
                                                                           4

4. A. already   B. all ready   C. allready   4._____
    D. ready   E. all in all

to employees in many business establishments. There seems also to be a trend toward shorter working weeks and longer summer vacations. An important feature of this develop-

ment is that leisure is no longer the privilege of the wealthy few ,-it has become the
                                                                  _____
                                                                     5

common right of most people.

5. A. , - it   B. : it   C. ; it   5._____
    D. ... it   E. omit punctuation

Using it wisely, leisure promotes health, efficiency, and happiness, for there is time for
_____
      6

each individual to live their own "more abundant life" and having opportunities for
                        _____   _____
                           7   8
needed recreation.

6. A. Using it wisely   B. If used wisely   6._____
    C. Having used it wisely   D. Because of its wise use
    E. Because of usefulness

7. A. their   B. his   C. its   D. our   E. your   7.____

8. A. having   B. having had   C. to have   8.____
    D. to have had   E. had

Recreation, like the name implies, is a
                    ―――
                     9

9. A. like   B. since   C. through   D. for   E. as   9.____

process of revitalization. In giving expression to the play instincts of the human race,

new vigor and effectiveness are afforded by recreation to the body and to the mind.
―――
                                10

10. A. new vigor and effectiveness are afforded by recreation to the body and to the mind   10.____
    B. recreation affords new vigor and effectiveness to the body and to the mind
    C. there are afforded new vigor and effectiveness to the body and to the mind
    D. by recreation the body and mind are afforded new vigor and effectiveness
    E. the body and the mind afford new vigor and effectiveness to themselves by rec-
        reation

Of course not all forms of amusement, by no means, constitute recreation. Furthermore, an
                                       ――――――――――
                                           11
activity that provides recreation for one person may prove exhausting for another. Today, however, play among adults, as well as children is regarded as a vital necessity of modern life.

11. A. by no means   B. by those means   11.____
    C. by some means   D. by every means
    E. by any means

Play being recognized as an important factor in improving mental and physical health and
――――――――――――――――
       12
thereby reducing human misery and poverty.

12. A. . Play being recognized as   12.____
    B. , by their recognizing play as
    C. . They recognizing play as
    D. . Recognition of it being
    E. , for play is recognized as

Among the most important forms of amusement available at the present time are the automobile, the moving picture, the radio, television, and organized sports. The automobile, especially, has been a boon to the American people, since it has been the chief means of

 them getting out into the open. The motion picture, the radio and television have tremen-
――――――
  13
dous opportunities to supply wholesome recreation and to promote cultural advancement. A
criticism often leveled against organized

13. A. them   B. their   C. his   13.____
    D. our   E. the people

125

sports as a means of recreation is because they make passive spectators of too many peo-

14

ple.

14.   A.   because   B.   since   C.   as   D.   that   E.   why   14.____

It has been said "that the American public is afflicted with "spectatoritis," but there is some

15   16

recreational advantages to be gained even from being a spectator at organized games.

15.   A.   that   B.   that   C.   that   D.   that   E.   that   15.____

16.   A.   is   B.   was   C.   are   D.   were   E.   will be   16.____

Such sports afford a release from the monotony of daily toil, get people outdoors and also provide an exhilaration that is tonic in its effect. The chief concern, of course, should be to eliminate
those forms of amusement that are socially undesirable. There are, however, far too many peo-

ple who, we know, do not use their leisure

17

to the best advantage. Sometimes leisure leads to idleness, and idleness may lead to demoralization. The value of leisure both to the individual and to society will depend on the uses made
of it.

17.   A.   who   B.   whom   C.   which   17.____
       D.   such as   E.   that which

———

KEY (CORRECT ANSWERS)

1.	C	11.	E
2.	D	12.	E
3.	E	13.	B
4.	A	14.	D
5.	C	15.	E
6.	B	16.	C
7.	B	17.	A
8.	C		
9.	E		
10.	B		

———

TEST 2

DIRECTIONS: The questions that follow the paragraph below are designed to test your appreciation of correctness and effectiveness of expression in English. The paragraph is presented first in full so that you may read it through for sense. Disregard the errors you find, as you will be asked to correct them in the questions that follow. The paragraph is then presented sentence by sentence with portions underlined and numbered. At the end of this material, you will find numbers corresponding to those below the underlined portions, each followed by five alternatives lettered A, B, C, D, and E. In every case, the usage in the alternative lettered A is the same as that in the original paragraph and is followed by four possible usages. Choose the usage you consider BEST in each case. *PRINT THE LETTER OF THE CORRECT ANSWER IN THE SPACE AT THE RIGHT.*

When this war is over, no nation will either be isolated in war or peace. Each will be within trading distance of all the others and will be able to strike them. Every nation will be most as dependent on the rest for the maintainance of peace as is any of our own American states on all the others. The world that we have known was a world made up of individual nations, each of which had the priviledge of doing about as they pleased without being embarassed by outside interference. The world has dissolved before the impact of an invention, the airplane has done to our world what gunpowder did to the feudal world. Whether the coming century will be a period of further tragedy or one of peace and progress depend very largely on the wisdom and skill with which the present generation adjusts their thinking to the problems immediately at hand. Examining the principal movements sweeping through the world, it can be seen that they are being accelerated by the war. There is undoubtedly many of these whose courses will be affected for good or ill by the settlements that will follow the war. The United States will share the responsibility of these settlements with Russia, England and China. The influence of the United States, however, will be great. This country is likely to emerge from the war stronger than any other nation. Having benefitted by the absence of actual hostilities on our own soil, we shall probably be less exhausted than our allies and better able than them to help restore the devastated areas. However many mistakes have been made in our past, the tradition of America, not only the champion of freedom but also fair play, still lives among millions who can see light and hope scarcely nowhere else.

When this war is over, no nation will <u>either be isolated in war or peace.</u>
                                                          1

1. A. either be isolated in war or peace   1.____
    B. be either isolated in war or peace
    C. be isolated in neither war nor peace
    D. be isolated either in war or in peace
    E. be isolated neither in war or peace

<u>Each</u> will be
 2

2. A. Each   B. It   C. Some   2.____
    D. They   E. A nation

within trading distance of all others and will be able to strike them.
                                  3

3.   A.   within trading distance of all the others and will be able to strike them   3.____
     B.   near enough to trade with and strike all the others
     C.   trading and striking the others
     D.   within trading and striking distance of all the others
     E.   able to strike and trade with all the others

Every nation will be most as dependent on
                       4

4.   A. most   B. wholly   C. much   D. mostly   E. almost   4.____

the rest for the maintainance of peace as is
                        5

5.   A. maintainance   B. maintainence   C. maintenence   5.____
     D. maintenance   E. maintanence

any of our own American states on all the others. The world that we have known was a world

made up of individual nations, each
                        6

6.   A. nations, each   B. nations. Each   6.____
     C. nations: each   D. nations; each
     E. nations each

of which had the priviledge of doing about as
                       7

7.   A. priviledge   B. priveledge   C. privelege   7.____
     D. privalege   E. privilege

they pleased without being
  8

8.   A. they   B. it   8.____
     C. they individually   D. he
     E. the nations

embarassed by outside interference. That
     9

9.   A. embarassed   B. embarrassed   C. embaressed   9.____
     D. embarrased   E. embarressed

world has dissolved before the impact of an invention, the airplane has done to our world what

10

gunpowder did to the feudal world. Whether the coming century will be a period of further tragedy or one of peace and

10.   A.   invention, the   B.   invention but the   10.____
      C.   invention: the   D.   invention. The
      E.   invention and the

progress depend very largely on the wisdom and skill with which the present generation

11

11.   A.   depend   B.   will have depended   11.____
      C.   depends   D.   depended
      E.   shall depend

adjusts their thinking to the problems immediately at hand.

12

12.   A.   adjusts their   B.   adjusts there   12.____
      C.   adjusts its   D.   adjust our
      E.   adjust it's

Examining the principal movements sweeping through the world, it can be seen

13

13.   A.   Examining the principal movements sweeping through the world, it can be seen   13.____
      B.   Having examined the principal movements sweeping through the world, it can be
           seen
      C.   Examining the principal movements sweeping through the world can be seen
      D.   Examining the principal movements sweeping through the world, we can see
      E.   It can be seen examining the principal movements sweeping through the world

that they are being accelerated by the war.

14

14.   A.   accelerated   B.   acelerated   C.   accelarated   14.____
      D.   acellerated   E.   acelerrated

There is undoubtedly many of these whose courses will be affected for good or ill by the

15

settlements that will follow the war. The United States will share the responsibility of these
settlements with Russia, England and China. The influence of the United

15.   A.   is   B.   were   C.   was   15.____
      D.   are   E.   might be

States, <u>however,</u> will be great. This country is likely to emerge from the war stronger than
16
any other nation.

16.   A.   , however,   B.   however,   C.   , however   16.____
        D.   however   E.   ; however,

Having <u>benefitted</u> by the absence of actual hostilities on our own soil, we shall probably be
17
less exhausted

17.   A.   benefitted   B.   benifitted   C.   benefited   17.____
        D.   benifited   E.   benafitted

than our allies and better able than <u>them</u> to help restore the devastated areas. However
18
many mistakes have been made in our past, the tradition of America,

18.   A.   them   B.   themselves   C.   they   18.____
        D.   the world   E.   the nations

<u>not only the champion of freedom but also fair play,</u> still lives among millions who can
19

19.   A.   not only the champion of freedom but also fair play,   19.____
        B.   the champion of not only freedom but also of fair play,
        C.   the champion not only of freedom but also of fair play,
        D.   not only the champion but also freedom and fair play,
        E.   not the champion of freedom only, but also fair play,

see light and hope <u>scarcely nowhere else.</u>
20

20.   A.   scarcely nowhere else.   B.   elsewhere.   20.____
        C.   nowheres.   D.   scarcely anywhere else.
        E.   anywhere.

KEY (CORRECT ANSWERS)

1.	D	11.	C
2.	A	12.	C
3.	D	13.	D
4.	E	14.	A
5.	D	15.	D
6.	A	16.	A
7.	E	17.	C
8.	B	18.	C
9.	B	19.	C
10.	D	20.	D

WRITTEN ENGLISH EXPRESSION

EXAMINATION SECTION
TEST 1

DIRECTIONS: The following questions are designed to test your knowledge of grammar, sentence structure, correct usage, and punctuation. In each group, there is one sentence that contains an error. Select the letter of the INCORRECT sentence. *PRINT THE LETTER OF THE CORRECT ANSWER IN THE SPACE AT THE RIGHT.*

1.   A.   All things considered, he did unusually well.   1.____
      B.   The poor boy takes everything too seriously.
      C.   Our club sent two delegates, Ruth and I, to Oswego.
      D.   I like him better than her.
      E.   His eccentricities continually made good newspaper copy.

2.   A.   If we except Benton, no one in the club foresaw the changes.   2.____
      B.   The two-year-old rosebushes are loaded with buds — and beetles!
      C.   Though the pitcher had been broken by the cat, Teena was furious.
      D.   Virginia got the cake recipe off of her grandmother.
      E.   Neither one of the twins was able to get a summer vacation.

3.   A.   "What do you wish?" he asked, "may I help you?"   3.____
      B.   Whose gloves are these?
      C.   Has he drink all the orange juice?
      D.   It was he who spoke to the manager of the store.
      E.   Mary prefers this kind of evening dress.

4.   A.   Charles himself said it before the assembled peers of the realm.   4.____
      B.   The wind stirred the rose petals laying on the floor.
      C.   The storm beat hard on the frozen windowpanes.
      D.   Worn out by the days of exposure and storm, the sailor clung pitifully to the puny raft.
      E.   The day afterward he thought more kindly of the matter.

5.   A.   Between you and me, I think Henry is wrong.   5.____
      B.   This is the more interesting of the two books.
      C.   This is the most carefully written letter of all.
      D.   During the opening course I read not only four plays but also three historical novels.
      E.   This assortment of candies, nuts, and fruits are excellent.

6.   A.   According to your report card, you are not so clever as he.   6.____
      B.   If he had kept his eyes open, he would not have fallen into that trap.
      C.   We were certain that the horse had broken it's leg.
      D.   The troop of scouts and the leader are headed for the North Woods.
      E.   I knew it to be him by the knock at the door.

7. A. Being one of the earliest spring flowers, we welcome the crocus.   7.____
    B. The cold running water became colder as time sped on.
    C. Those boys need not have stood in line for lunch.
    D. Can you, my friend, donate ten dollars to the cause?
    E. Because it's a borrowed umbrella, return it in the morning.

8. A. If Walter would have planted earlier in the spring, the rosebushes would have sur-   8.____
       vived.
    B. The flowers smell overpoweringly sweet.
    C. There are three e's in dependent.
    D. May I be excused at the end of the test?
    E. Carl has three brothers-in-law.

9. A. We have bought neither the lumber nor the tools for the job.   9.____
    B. Jefferson was re-elected despite certain powerful opposition.
    C. The Misses Jackson were invited to the dance.
    D. The letter is neither theirs nor yours.
    E. The retail price for those items are far beyond the wholesale quotations.

10. A. To find peace of mind is to gain treasure beyond price.   10.____
    B. Fred is cheerful, carefree; his brother is morose.
    C. Whoever fails to understand the strategic importance of the Arctic fails to under-
       stand modern geography.
    D. They came promptly at 8 o'clock on August 7, 1978, without prior notification.
    E. Every one tried their best to guess the answer, but no one succeeded.

11. A. Is this hers or theirs?   11.____
    B. Having been recognized, Frank took the floor.
    C. Alex invited Sue; Paul, Marion; and Dan, Helen.
    D. If I were able to do the task, you can be sure that I'd do it.
    E. Stamp collecting, or philately as it is otherwise called is truly an international
       hobby.

12. A. He has proved himself to be reliable.   12.____
    B. The fisherman had arisen before the sun.
    C. By the time the truck arrived, I had put out the blaze.
    D. The doctor with his colleagues were engaged in consultation.
    E. I chose to try out a new method, but in spite of my efforts it failed.

13. A. He has drunk too much iced tea.   13.____
    B. I appreciated him doing that job for me.
    C. The royal family fled, but they were retaken.
    D. The secretary and the treasurer were both present on Friday.
    E. Iago protested his honesty, yet he continued to plot against Desdemona.

14. A. The family were all together at Easter.   14.____
    B. It is altogether too fine a day for us to stay indoors.
    C. However much you dislike him, you should treat him fairly.
    D. The judges were already there when the contestants arrived.
    E. The boy's mother reported that he was alright again after the accident.

15. A. Ham and eggs is a substantial breakfast.   15._____
     B. By the end of the week the pond had frozen.
     C. I should appreciate any assistance you could offer me.
     D. Being that tomorrow is Sunday, we expect to close early.
     E. If he were to win the medal, I for one would be disturbed.

16. A. Give the letter to whoever comes for it.   16._____
     B. He feels bad, but his sister is the one who looks sicker.
     C. He had an unbelievable large capacity for hard physical work.
     D. Earth has nothing more beautiful to offer than the autumn colors of this section of the country.
     E. Happily we all have hopes that the future will soon bring forth fruits of a lasting peace.

17. A. This kind of apples is my favorite.   17._____
     B. Either of the players is capable of performing ably.
     C. Though trying my best to be calm, the choice was not an easy one for me.
     D. The nearest star is not several light years away; it is only 93,000,000 miles away.
     E. There were two things I still wished to do — to see the Lincoln Memorial and to climb up the Washington Monument.

18. A. It is I who is to blame.   18._____
     B. That dress looks very good on Jane.
     C. People often take my brother to be me.
     D. I could but think she had deceived me.
     E. He himself told us that the story was true.

19. A. They all went but Mabel and me.   19._____
     B. Has he ever swum across the river?
     C. We have a dozen other suggestions besides these.
     D. The Jones's are going to visit their friends in Chicago.
     E. The ideal that Arthur and his knights were in quest of was a better world order.

20. A. Would I were able to be there with you!   20._____
     B. Whomever he desires to see should be admitted.
     C. It is not for such as we to follow fashion blindly.
     D. His causing the confusion seemed to affect him not at all.
     E. Please notify all those whom you think should have this information.

21. A. She was not only competent but also friendly in nature.   21._____
     B. Not only must we visualize the play we are reading; we must actually hear it.
     C. The firm was not only acquiring a bad reputation but also indulging in illegal practices.
     D. The bank was not only uncooperative but also was indifferent to new business offered them.
     E. I know that a conscious effort was made not only to guard the material but also to keep it from being used.

22.
   A. How old shall you be on your next birthday?
   B. I am sure that he has been here and did what was expected of him.
   C. Near to the bank of the river, stood, secluded and still, the house of the hermit.
   D. Because of its efficacy in treating many ailments, penicillin has become an important addition to the druggist's stock.
   E. ROBINSON CRUSOE, which is a fairy tale to the child, is a work of social philosophy to the mature thinker.

   22._____

23.
   A. We had no sooner started than it rained.
   B. The fact that the prisoner is a minor will be taken into consideration.
   C. Many parents think more of their older children than of their younger ones.
   D. The boy laid a book, a knife and a fishing line on the table.
   E. John is the tallest of any boy in his class.

   23._____

24.
   A. Although we have been friends for many years, I must admit that May is most inconsiderate.
   B. He is not able to run, not even to walk.
   C. You will bear this pain as you have so many greater ones.
   D. The harder the work, the more studious she became.
   E. Too many "and's" in a sentence produce an immature style.

   24._____

25.
   A. It would be preferable to have you submit questions after, not before, the lecture.
   B. Plan your work; then work your plan.
   C. At last John met his brother, who had been waiting two hours for him.
   D. Should one penalize ones self for not trying?
   E. There are other considerations besides this one.

   25._____

KEY (CORRECT ANSWERS)

1.	C	11.	E
2.	D	12.	D
3.	A	13.	B
4.	B	14.	E
5.	E	15.	D
6.	C	16.	C
7.	A	17.	C
8.	A	18.	A
9.	E	19.	D
10.	E	20.	E

21.	D
22.	B
23.	E
24.	C
25.	D

TEST 2

DIRECTIONS: The following questions are designed to test your knowledge of grammar, sentence structure, correct usage, and punctuation. In each group there is one sentence that contains an error. Select the letter of the INCORRECT sentence. *PRINT THE LETTER OF THE CORRECT ANSWER IN THE SPACE AT THE RIGHT.*

1. A. "Halt!" cried the sentry, "Who goes there?"
   B. "It is in talk alone," said Robert Louis Stevenson, "that we can learn our period and ourselves."
   C. The world will long remember the "culture" of the Nazis.
   D. When duty says, "You must," the youth replies, "I can."
   E. Who said, "Give me liberty or give me death?"

   1.____

2. A. Why are you so quiet, Martha?
   B. Edward Jones, a banker who lives near us, expects to retire very soon.
   C. I picked up the solid-gold chain.
   D. Any boy, who refuses to tell the truth, will be punished.
   E. Yes, honey tastes sweet.

   2.____

3. A. I knew it to be him by the style of his clothes.
   B. No one saw him doing it.
   C. Her going away is a loss to the community.
   D. Mary objected to her being there.
   E. Illness prevented him graduating in June.

   3.____

4. A. Being tired, I stretched out on a grassy knoll.
   B. While we were rowing on the lake, a sudden squall almost capsized the boat.
   C. Entering the room, a strange mark on the floor attracted my attention.
   D. Mounting the curb, the empty car crossed the sidewalk and came to rest against a building.
   E. Sitting down, they watched him demonstrate his skill.

   4.____

5. A. The coming of peace effected a change in her way of life.
   B. Spain is as weak, if not weaker than, she was in 1900.
   C. In regard to that, I am not certain what my attitude will be.
   D. That unfortunate family faces the problem of adjusting itself to a new way of life.
   E. Fred Eastman states in his essay that one of the joys of reading lies in discovering courage.

   5.____

6. A. Not one in a thousand readers take the matter seriously.
   B. Let it lie there.
   C. You are not so tall as he.
   D. The people began to realize how much she had done.
   E. He was able partially to accomplish his purpose.

   6.____

7. A. In the case of members who are absent, a special letter will be sent.
   B. The visitors were all ready to see it.
   C. I like Burns's poem "To a Mountain Daisy."
   D. John told William that he was sure he had seen it.
   E. Both men are Yale alumni.

   7.____

8.   A.   The audience took their seats promptly.   8._____
     B.   Each boy and girl must finish his examination this morning.
     C.   Every person turned their eyes toward the door.
     D.   Everyone has his own opinion.
     E.   The club nominated its officers by secret ballot.

9.   A.   I can do that more easily than you.   9._____
     B.   This kind of weather is more healthful.
     C.   Pick out the really important points.
     D.   Because of his aggressive nature, he only plays the hardest games.
     E.   He pleaded with me to let him go.

10. A.   It is I who am mistaken.   10._____
     B.   Is it John or Susie who stand at the head of the class?
     C.   He is one of those who always do their lessons.
     D.   He is a man on whom I can depend in time of trouble.
     E.   Had he known who it was, he would have come.

11. A.   Somebody has forgotten his umbrella.   11._____
     B.   Please let Joe and me use the car.
     C.   We thought the author to be he.
     D.   Whoever they send will be welcome.
     E.   They thought the intruders were we.

12. A.   If I had known that you were coming, I should have met you.   12._____
     B.   All the girls but her were at the game.
     C.   I expected to have heard the concert before the present time.
     D.   Walter would not have said it if he had thought it would make her unhappy.
     E.   I have always believed that cork is the best material for insulation.

13. A.   Their contributions amounted to the no insignificant sum of ten thousand dollars.   13._____
     B.   None of them was there.
     C.   Ten dollars is the amount I agreed to pay.
     D.   Fewer than one hundred persons assembled.
     E.   Exactly what many others have done and are doing, Frank did.

14. A.   Neither Jane or her sister has arrived.   14._____
     B.   Either Richard or his brother is going to drive.
     C.   Refilling storage batteries is the work of the youngest employee.
     D.   Helen has to lie still for two weeks.
     E.   Mother lay down for an hour yesterday.

15. A.   He is not the man whom you saw entering the house.   15._____
     B.   He asked why I wouldn't come.
     C.   This is the cow whose horns are the longest.
     D.   Helen, this is a man I met on the train one day last February.
     E.   He greeted every foreign representative which came to the conference.

16. A. You, but not I, are invited.   16._____
    B. Guy's technique of service and return is masterly.
    C. Please pass me one of the books that are lying on the table.
    D. Mathematics is my most difficult subject.
    E. Unable to agree on a plan of organization, the class has departed in several directions.

17. A. He spoke to Gertrude and to me of the seriousness of the occasion.   17._____
    B. They seem to have decided to invite everyone except you and I.
    C. Your attitude is insulting to me who am your friend.
    D. He wished to know who our representative was.
    E. You may tell whomsoever you wish.

18. A. My favorite studies were Latin and science.   18._____
    B. The committee made its report.
    C. To get your work done promptly is better than leaving it until the last minute.
    D. That's what he would do if he were governor.
    E. He said that his chosen colors were red and blue.

19. A. Punish whoever disobeys orders.   19._____
    B. Come here, Henry; and sit with me.
    C. Has either of them his notebook?
    D. He talked as if he meant it.
    E. You did well; therefore you should be rewarded.

20. A. Many of us students were called to work.   20._____
    B. He shot the albatross with a crossbow.
    C. A house that is set on a hill is conspicuous.
    D. The wooden beams had raised slowly about a foot and then had settled back into place.
    E. Whom do you want to go with you?

21. A. He does not drive as he should.   21._____
    B. I can't hardly wait for the holidays.
    C. I like it less well than last week's.
    D. You were troubled by his coming.
    E. I don't know but that you are correct.

22. A. He was angry at both of us, her and me.   22._____
    B. When one enters the town, they see big crowds.
    C. They laid the tools on the ground every night.
    D. He is the only one of my friends who has written.
    E. He asked for a raise in wages.

23. A. None came with his excuse.   23._____
    B. Walking down the street, a house comes into view.
    C. "Never!" shouted the boy.
    D. Both are masters of their subject.
    E. His advice was to drive slowly.

24.   A.   There is both beef and lamb on the market.   24.____
       B.   Either beans or beets are enough with potatoes.
       C.   Where does your mother buy bananas?
       D.   Dinners at the new restaurant are excellent.
       E.   Each was rewarded according to his deeds.

25.   A.   Accordingly, we must prepare the food.   25.____
       B.   The work, moreover, must be done today.
       C.   Nevertheless, we must first have dinner.
       D.   I always chose the most liveliest of the ponies.
       E.   At six o'clock tomorrow the job will have been completed.

KEY (CORRECT ANSWERS)

1.	E		11.	C
2.	D		12.	C
3.	E		13.	A
4.	C		14.	A
5.	B		15.	E
6.	A		16.	E
7.	C		17.	B
8.	C		18.	C
9.	D		19.	B
10.	B		20.	D

21.	B
22.	B
23.	B
24.	A
25.	D

TEST 3

DIRECTIONS: In each group of five sentences below, one or more sentences contain an error in usage. Choose the lettered answer which indicates ALL the sentences containing errors in usage. *PRINT THE LETTER OF THE CORRECT ANSWER IN THE SPACE AT THE RIGHT.*

1.
   I. Shortly after the terms of the contract for the new road transpired, an aroused constituency showed its disapproval by voting the senator out of office.
   II. Neither father nor sons work for a living but spend their days in drinking and gambling at the pub.
   III. Like his Italian predecessor, Boccaccio, whose DECAMERON was used as a model, a company of people of various occupations and stations in life, brought together for a pilgrimage, are called upon to relate stories to help relieve the tedium of their journey.
   IV. Sarah hurried into the kitchen and after a half hour emerged with a nauseous brew which she called coffee.
   V. It was to the major that the people applied for redress and by his armed guards that they were driven away.

   A. I   B. III   C. I, II, III
   D. IV, III   E. II, III

1.____

2.
   I. As we approached the castle, which was illuminated suddenly by the full moon breaking through the clouds, we described a rider coming to meet us.
   II. The reason for his loss of interest in boxing, as far as I can see, was due to the pressure of his work and the distance of the local "Y" from his home.
   III. Accompanied by a handsome member of the British legation, Elsie was about to enter the luxuriously furnished salon to meet the countess.
   IV. In spite of all of John's gifts and attentions, little Rosalie, upon being asked to make a choice, said she liked me better than him.
   V. The scar of the clearing for the power line extended for a hundred miles over the mountains, and the great poles with fifty feet between each carried cables from Niagara to Albany.

   A. II, III   B. I, IV, III   C. I, II, IV, III
   D. II, V   E. III, V

2.____

3.
   I. The high wind had blown the roofs off several houses; the water supply had been contaminated by the floods; transportation to the business center had ground to a halt; but the mayor said there was no reason for alarm!
   II. Because there is a need to soften tragic or painful news, we resort to such euphuisms for the simple "to die" as "to pass away," "to go to a better world," or "to join the great majority."
   III. Hardly had the salient on the western shore of the river been obliterated than the one on the eastern bank crossed on a pontoon bridge and in boats of all sorts.
   IV. The distinction between the man who gives in a spirit of charity and him who gives for social recognition is often to be seen in the nature of the gift.
   V. After a few months in office, the new superintendent effected many changes, not all of them for the good, in the administration of the plant.

   A. II, III   B. II, III, IV   C. III, IV
   D. I, II, V   E. I, II, III

3.____

4.   I.   The defendants published an advertisement and notice giving information, directly   4.____
and indirectly, stating where, how, and when, and by what means and what pur-
ports to be the said book can be purchased.

     II.   In common with most Eskimos of her time, she had long spells of silence; and
nature, while endowing her with immense sagacity, had thrust on her a compel-
ling reticence.

    III.   The entire report was read in less than half an hour to the full committee, giving
no time for comment or question, and offered for vote.

    IV.   Students going through this course almost always find themselves becoming
critical of their own writing.

     V.   In his report of 1968, Mr. Jones states that his chief problem is the rapid turnover
of personnel which has prevailed to the moment of writing.

    A.   I, IV   B.   II, III   C.   III, IV, V
    D.   I, IV, V   E.   I, III

5.   I.   The material was destroyed after it had served our purposes, and after portions of   5.____
it had been excluded and portions included in our report.

     II.   We checked our results very carefully, too carefully perhaps, for we spent several
hours on our task.

    III.   We should keep constantly in mind the fact that writing has no purpose save to
meet the needs of the reader.

    IV.   Not even discussed in October, when Lathrop flew in from the Coast, the prob-
lem of expense was settled at the June meeting.

     V.   Whether our facts were right or not, it was not necessary for you to rebuke him in
such a discourteous manner.

    A.   I *only*   B.   I, IV   C.   II, III
    D.   V *only*   E.   I, V

6.   I.   At first the novel was interesting and liked by members of the class; but later the   6.____
long reading assignments dampened the pupils' enthusiasm.

     II.   Donnie had no love or confidence in his mother, who, when abandoned by her
husband, put the boy in an orphanage and seldom went to visit him.

    III.   Built during the Civil War, the house has a delicate air, supported as it is by iron
columns and rimmed by an iron railing.

    IV.   Recently a newspaper editor from the South returned from an eight-week trip
through the Caribbean and made a number of recommendations on what we
should do to counter the lack of accurate information about the United States.

     V.   The need is to be candid about our problems, to be informed on what we are
doing about them, and to resolve them as expeditiously as possible.

    A.   I, II   B.   II, III   C.   III, IV
    D.   I, V   E.   I, III

7.   I.   "Man is flying too fast for a world that is round," he said. "Soon he will catch up with   7.____
himself in a great rear-end collision."

     II.   After the raid on the club, each of the men suspected of accepting racetrack
bets, along with the owner of the club, were held for questioning at police headquarters.

    III.   It seems to me that at the opening performance of the play the audience were of
different opinions about its merit and about its chances for a long run.

IV. Oak from the forests of Vermont and steel from the mills of Pittsburgh are the material of this magnificent modern structure.

V. The machine is subjected to severe strains which it must withstand and at the same time work easily and rapidly.

A. I, II   B. II, III   C. IV, V
D. I, V   E. II, V

8.   I. We don't have to worry about cutting down on expenses; money is no object in this venture.   8.____

II. And now, my dear, let you and I tell our guests of the plans we have for the future.

III. For all his errors of the past, no one can or has said that he did not turn out on this occasion a perfectpiece of work.

IV. Hercule Poirot, when looking for a suspect in the murder case never thought of its being me.

V. During the interpellation the minister refused to answer any questions concerning his predecessor's conduct of the war.

A. I, III   B. I, IV, V   C. II, III, IV
D. III, IV   E. II, III

9.   I. John Steinbeck received the Nobel Prize only a few years ago for his work of the thirties, work, which now, according to some critics, has lost its timeliness and which never had timelessness.   9.____

II. Respect is shown the flag by no matter when it is displayed, whether it be in the window of a private home or on the pole of a public building.

III. When dinner was over, we strolled through the garden and exclaimed at the beauty of the red gladioluses, the pride of the Jenkinses' gardener.

IV. Mrs. Cosgrove's gift of $100,000 to the hospitals is only the latest of the many acts of generosity by which she has before now benefited her fellow men.

V. Am I repeating your question exactly when I say, "How many of you are willing to join me in my attempt to rid America of the traitors who are threatening its freedom"?

A. I, II, III, IV   B. II, IV   C. II, III, IV
D. I, IV, V   E. I, II, IV

10.   I. Slashing the original 73 projects to 20 with little loss of subject matter in the consolidated schedule, a stalemate was avoided and the work of the Council speeded up.   10.____

II. I was particularly struck by the unselfishness of the American school children, many of whom willingly donating their allowances, because they felt that they should help the refugees.

III. As a result of Henry VIII's defiance of the Church of Rome, the ecclesiastical principle of government was substituted by the national.

IV. I wish you had invited me to the concert, for I should have liked particularly to hear Piatigorsky.

V. John will be in the best possible position for getting the most out of his vacation and of making business contacts in new markets.

A. I, II, III, IV   B. I, II, III, V
C. I, II, III   D. III, IV, V
E. I, II, III, IV, V

11.   I.   They took him to be me despite ever so many differences in our appearance and   11.____
despite his addiction to loquacity.

     II.   They may have more money, they may have more possessions, but they are not
any happier than us, as we and they all know.

    III.   Either Betty or Bob must have thought the teacher's remarks were addressed to
him.

    IV.   There was present at today's conference — and at next week's conference the
same group is expected — representatives of many foreign countries, including
Italy, France, England, and Germany.

     V.   The most important criteria in judging the performance of a pianist is not virtuos-
ity but maturity of interpretation.

    A. I, IV   B. II, III, V   C. II, IV, V
    D. I, III   E. I, IV, V

12.   I.   Thoroughly exhausted after we had swum for six hours, we lay breathless on the   12.____
sand and oblivious of anything but our utter fatigue.

     II.   The jury seems in violent disagreement about the culpability of the defendant;
such shouting as we hear from the jury room is most unusual among these halls.

    III.   The difference between the class' average grades for the first week and those for
the eighth week, on alternate forms of the same test, were quite insignificant,
indicating, we thought, that instruction had been ineffective.

    IV.   Each tree and each bush give forth a flaming hue such as we have not seen for
many seasons in these climes.

     V.   We met a man whom we thought we had met many years since, when we lived
in South Africa.

    A. III, IV, V   B. I, II, V   C. III, IV
    D. I, II   E. I, III, IV

13.   I.   That old friend, whom I met again last night after a lapse of many a year, stands   13.____
head and shoulders above any person I have ever known.

     II.   This is one of the finest pictures which have ever been put on canvas, bringing
out rare qualities of tone-color, mature interpretation, and virtuosity in execution.

    III.   Which of them would you prefer to have working for you, considering the inordi-
nate physical and mental demands of the work, him or his brother?

    IV.   Throughout Saturday and Sunday, the townsfolk took scarcely any notice of the
absence of Jed Gorman, believing him to be off on a drunken spree; but on Monday a body was discovered in the river obviously that of the missing handyman.

     V.   Things being so pleasant as they were, we could not fathom the reason for John
leaving so soon after he had started what we considered an excellent job with
unlimited opportunities.

    A. I, V   B. II, III, V   C. II, III
    D. II, IV, V   E. I, IV, V

14.   I.   He is unfailingly polite not only to his superiors and his colleagues but even to   14.____
those who are in subordinate positions, and, in general, to whoever else he thinks
is deserving of kindly consideration.

     II.   Without more ado, he took the books off the radiator, where they had lain quite
neglected for several days and where their bindings were beginning to grow
loose.

III. We can still include a discussion of the lunchroom situation among the topics, for the agenda have not yet been printed and will not be for another hour or two.
IV. We knew who would be at the party and who would take us home, but we didn't know who to expect to meet us at the station upon our arrival.
V. Despite his protestations, we know that the true reason why he was suffering such obvious anguish and failing to do his work was because of marital trouble.

A. I, III, IV   B. II, III, V   C. I, IV, V
D. I, II   E. IV, V

15. I. A difficult stretch of bad road in addition to a long detour which caused a series of minor motor mishaps, have much delayed our visitor's arrival and have created an awkward situation for us all.   15._____
II. To make the campaign effective, there is posted in every building, in full view of all entrants, one notice of the location of the shelter, and a second notice intended to boost morale and win cooperation.
III. One day while leading sheep in the desert and musing upon his people's future, the angel of the Lord appeared to Moses.
IV. Though he plead with the tongue of an angel, he will not ever alter her cold eyes nor trouble her calm fount of speech.
V. Despite continuous and well-advised and well-directed efforts by each of us, neither he nor I am able to improve the situation.

A. I, V   B. III, IV, V   C. I, II, III
D. II, III, IV   E. I, III

16. I. Though business has been brisk of late, this kind of appliances have not sold well at all, despite our continuous and concentrated efforts.   16._____
II. The return trip was a desperate one, with time of the essence; and partly blinded by the unexpected snowstorm, the trip was doubly hazardous.
III. I started on my journey by foot through forest and mountain, after a last warning to be careful about snake bites by my parents — a warning I knew I must heed on that dangerous terrain.
IV. That he was losing to a better man, a man who had worked diligently and a man of impeccable virtue, was a consideration of but small import to him.
V. The precarious state of affairs was aggravated by a new hazard, notwithstanding all our cautions to avoid any change in the situation.

A. I, III, V   B. II, IV   C. IV, V
D. I, II, III   E. II, III

17. I. Who's responsible for the feeding of his cat and its young, I'd like to know, we or they? If we, let's feed them.   17._____
II. The books that had lain on the desk for many weeks were laid in the bookcase, where they lay until picked up by the messenger from the second-handbook shop.
III. You say I merit the award for competence in my duties; but he deserves an award as well as I, for he is as good, without doubt, or even better than I.
IV. The Joneses' car was more luxurious than, but not necessarily as expensive as, the Browns'.
V. Slowly they tiptoed into the living room hoping not to be heard, but we were fully aware of it being they.

A. II, IV   B. I, III, IV   C. I, V
D. I, II, V   E. III, V

18.   I.   I shall lay the rug in the sun, where it has laid many times before; and I shall lie in   18.____
the sun, too, as always I have lain at leisure while the rug has been drying.
     II.   Though he knew a great deal about printing machinery, he thought, mistakenly,
that the new machine could be made to cast type as well as setting it up.
    III.   Knowledge in several major fields with sympathy for varied points of view make
him an excellent choice for student adviser.
    IV.   You will find the girls' equipment in the teachers' lounge where the boy's father
left it at Professor Wills's suggestion.
     V.   I know that the Burnses have worked for the mill for generations, and that the
Smiths have but recently removed from town, but does either of the Norton boys
work here?

A. I, II, III   B. II, III, IV   C. I, IV, V
D. III, V   E. I, II, IV

19.   I.   I can put two and two together as quick as most men; but understanding how he, a   19.____
slow-witted dolt, could achieve so notable a victory over his opponent is one of the
things that puzzle and, forevermore, will puzzle me.
     II.   Besides my two brothers, my sister, and I, there are a cousin and my father's
nephew living at home with us.
    III.   He has lived in the Reno for many years; previously he lived in Chicago for a
short space, after he had come from Los Angeles.
    IV.   Researchers have been baffled for a long time by this statistic, for it contradicts
many of their most highly cherished hypotheses.
     V.   So intense was the heat near the furnace that all the men at work could not carry
on; consequently, production came to a halt.

A. I, II, IV   B. III, V   C. I, III, IV
D. I, II, V   E. II, V

20.   I.   If we can escape from our desks for a brief interval, let's you, Henry, and I put in an   20.____
appearance at the party.
     II.   If you persevere in your ambitions, you are likely to achieve at least a modicum
of success; if you malinger, you are liable to court failure.
    III.   You may find conditions here congenial, but since I neither like the work nor the
salary, it is to no avail for you to attempt to persuade me to stay.
    IV.   He has never deigned to take a drink with us, his office colleagues, though we
know him now for over fifteen years; and he takes an occasional drink, we know,
at home and at his golf club.
     V.   Though the results of your investigation are at variance with the hypothesis we
advanced, I believe you have interpreted these data in the only ways that have
scientific validity.

A. I, II, IV   B. I, II   C. IV, V
D. II, III, V   E. I, III, IV

21.　I.　He can't hardly hear anything unless the room is completely quiet.
　　II.　His attitude seemed perfectly alright to me.
　　III.　One can't be too careful, can one?
　　IV.　He is one of those people who believe in the perfectability of man.
　　V.　His uneasiness is reflected in his unwillingness to compromise on even the smallest point.

　　A.　II, III, V　　　B.　I, III　　　C.　I, IV, V
　　D.　I, II, IV　　　E.　III, IV

22.　I.　"Have you found what you were looking for?" he asked.
　　II.　"I have never," she insisted, "Seen such careless disregard for the rights of oters."
　　III.　"I found this ticket on the step," he said. "Did you lose it?"
　　IV.　"In one way I'd like to enter the contest," said Anne; "in another way I'm not too eager."
　　V.　Did he say, "I'm coming?"

　　A.　I, III, IV　　　B.　II, V　　　C.　III, V
　　D.　II, IV　　　E.　I, II, IV

23.　I.　Were I the owner of the dog, I'd keep him muzzled.
　　II.　In the tennis match Don was paired with Bill; Ed, with Al.
　　III.　He was given an excellent trade-in allowance on his old car.
　　IV.　Why doesn't this window raise?
　　V.　The prow of the vessel had almost completely sank by the time the rescuers arrived on the scene.

　　A.　I, II, V　　　B.　I, IV, V　　　C.　I, II, III
　　D.　II, V　　　E.　IV, V

24.　I.　Turning the pages rapidly, his glance fell upon a peculiarly worded advertisement.
　　II.　Turning the pages rapidly, his eyes noticed a peculiarly worded advertisement.
　　III.　Turning the pages rapidly, he noticed a peculiarly worded advertisement.
　　IV.　Turning the pages rapidly made him more attentive to the unusual.
　　V.　Turning the pages rapidly does not guarantee rapid comprehension.

　　A.　III, IV, V　　　B.　I, II, IV　　　C.　III, V
　　D.　I, II　　　E.　I, II, III

25.　I.　They told us how they had suffered.
　　II.　It is interesting (a) to the student, (b) to the parent, and (c) to the teacher.
　　III.　There were blue, green and red banners.
　　IV.　"Will you help", he asked?
　　V.　In addition to reproducibility, an attitude scale must meet various other requirements characteristic of scale analysis procedures.

　　A.　I, II　　　B.　II, III　　　C.　I only
　　D.　IV only　　　E.　IV, V

KEY (CORRECT ANSWERS)

1.	C	11.	C
2.	D	12.	C
3.	A	13.	D
4.	E	14.	E
5.	A	15.	C
6.	A	16.	D
7.	E	17.	C
8.	A	18.	A
9.	B	19.	E
10.	B	20.	A

21.	D
22.	B
23.	E
24.	D
25.	D

PREPARING WRITTEN MATERIAL

EXAMINATION SECTION
TEST 1

DIRECTIONS : Each of the sentences in the tests that follow may be classified under one of the following four categories:

    A. *Incorrect* because of faulty grammar or sentence structure
    B. *Incorrect* because of faulty punctuation
    C. *Incorrect* because of faulty capitalization
    D. *Correct*

       Examine each sentence carefully to determine under which of the above four options it is best classified. Then, in the space on the right, print the capital letter preceding the option which is the *BEST* of the four suggested above.
       (Each incorrect sentence contains but one type of error. Consider a sentence to be correct if it contains none of the types of errors mentioned, even though there may be other correct ways of expressing the same thought.)

1. This fact, together with those brought out at the previous meeting, prove that the schedule is satisfactory to the employees.   1.____

2. Like many employees in scientific fields, the work of bookkeepers and accountants requires accuracy and neatness.   2.____

3. "What can I do for you," the secretary asked as she motioned to the visitor to take a seat.   3.____

4. Our representative, Mr. Charles will call on you next week to determine whether or not your claim has merit.   4.____

5. We expect you to return in the spring; please do not disappoint us.   5.____

6. Any supervisor, who disregards the just complaints of his subordinates, is remiss in the performance of his duty.   6.____

7. Because she took less than an hour for lunch is no reason for permitting her to leave before five o'clock.   7.____

8. "Miss Smith," said the supervisor, "Please arrange a meeting of the staff for two o'clock on Monday."   8.____

9. A private company's vacation and sick leave allowance usually differs considerably from a public agency.   9.____

10. Therefore, in order to increase the efficiency of operations in the department, a report on the recommended changes in procedures was presented to the departmental committee in charge of the program.   10.____

11. We told him to assign the work to whoever was available.   11.____

12. Since John was the most efficient of any other employee in the bureau, he received the highest service rating.   12.____

13. Only those members of the national organization who resided in the middle West   13.____
attended the conference in Chicago.

14. The question of whether the office manager has as yet attained, or indeed can ever hope   14.____
to secure professional status is one which has been discussed for years.

15. No one knew who to blame for the error which, we later discovered, resulted in a consid-   15.____
erable loss of time.

KEY (CORRECT ANSWERS)

1.	A	6.	B
2.	A	7.	A
3.	B	8.	C
4.	B	9.	A
5.	D	10.	D

11. D
12. A
13. C
14. B
15. A

TEST 2

DIRECTIONS : Each of the sentences in the tests that follow may be classified under one of
the following four categories:

      A. *Incorrect* because of faulty grammar or sentence structure
      B. *Incorrect* because of faulty punctuation
      C. *Incorrect* because of faulty capitalization
      D. *Correct*

1. The National alliance of Businessmen is trying to persuade private businesses to hire youth in the summertime.　1._____

2. The supervisor who is on vacation, is in charge of processing vouchers.　2._____

3. The activity of the committee at its conferences is always stimulating.　3._____

4. After checking the addresses again, the letters went to the mailroom.　4._____

5. The director, as well as the employees, are interested in sharing the dividends.　5._____

KEY (CORRECT ANSWERS)

1. C
2. B
3. D
4. A
5. A

———

TEST 3

DIRECTIONS: In each of the following groups of sentences, one of the four sentences is faulty in grammar, punctuation, or capitalization. Select the incorrect sentence in each case.

1.   A.   Sailing down the bay was a thrilling experience for me.
     B.   He was not consulted about your joining the club.
     C.   This story is different than the one I told you yesterday.
     D.   There is no doubt about his being the best player.

1.____

2.   A.   He maintains there is but one road to world peace.
     B.   It is common knowledge that a child sees much he is not supposed to see.
     C.   Much of the bitterness might have been avoided if arbitration had been resorted to earlier in the meeting.
     D.   The man decided it would be advisable to marry a girl somewhat younger than him.

2.____

3.   A.   In this book, the incident I liked least is where the hero tries to put out the forest fire.
     B.   Learning a foreign language will undoubtedly give a person a better understanding of his mother tongue.
     C.   His actions made us wonder what he planned to do next.
     D.   Because of the war, we were unable to travel during the summer vacation.

3.____

4.   A.   The class had no sooner become interested in the lesson than the dismissal bell rang.
     B.   There is little agreement about the kind of world to be planned at the peace conference.
     C.   "Today," said the teacher, "we shall read 'The Wind in the Willows.' I am sure you'll like it.
     D.   The terms of the legal settlement of the family quarrel handicapped both sides for many years.

4.____

5.   A.   I was so suprised that I was not able to say a word.
     B.   She is taller than any other member of the class.
     C.   It would be much more preferable if you were never seen in his company.
     D.   We had no choice but to excuse her for being late.

5.____

———————

KEY (CORRECT ANSWERS)

1. C
2. D
3. A
4. C
5. C

———

TEST 4

DIRECTIONS: In each of the following groups of sentences, one of the four sentences is faulty in grammar, punctuation, or capitalization. Select the incorrect sentence in each case.

1. A. Please send me these data at the earliest opportunity.
    B. The loss of their material proved to be a severe handicap.
    C. My principal objection to this plan is that it is impracticable.
    D. The doll had laid in the rain for an hour and was ruined.

    1.____

2. A. The garden scissors, left out all night in the rain, were in a badly rusted condition.
    B. The girls felt bad about the misunderstanding which had arisen.
    C. Sitting near the campfire, the old man told John and I about many exciting adventures he had had.
    D. Neither of us is in a position to undertake a task of that magnitude.

    2.____

3. A. The general concluded that one of the three roads would lead to the besieged city.
    B. The children didn't, as a rule, do hardly anything beyond what they were told to do.
    C. The reason the girl gave for her negligence was that she had acted on the spur of the moment.
    D. The daffodils and tulips look beautiful in that blue vase.

    3.____

4. A. If I was ten years older, I should be interested in this work.
    B. Give the prize to whoever has drawn the best picture.
    C. When you have finished reading the book, take it back to the library.
    D. My drawing is as good as or better than yours.

    4.____

5. A. He asked me whether the substance was animal or vegetable.
    B. An apple which is unripe should not be eaten by a child.
    C. That was an insult to me who am your friend.
    D. Some spy must of reported the matter to the enemy.

    5.____

6. A. Limited time makes quoting the entire message impossible.
    B. Who did she say was going?
    C. The girls in your class have dressed more dolls this year than we.
    D. There was such a large amount of books on the floor that I couldn't find a place for my rocking chair.

    6.____

7. A. What with his sleeplessness and his ill health, he was unable to assume any responsibility for the success of the meeting.
    B. If I had been born in February, I should be celebrating my birthday soon.
    C. In order to prevent breakage, she placed a sheet of paper between each of the plates when she packed them.
    D. After the spring shower, the violets smelled very sweet.

    7.____

8. A. He had laid the book down very reluctantly before the end of the lesson.
    B. The dog, I am sorry to say, had lain on the bed all night.
    C. The cloth was first lain on a flat surface; then it was pressed with a hot iron.
    D. While we were in Florida, we lay in the sun until we were noticeably tanned.

    8.____

9. A. If John was in New York during the recent holiday season, I have no doubt he spent most of his time with his parents.
   B. How could he enjoy the television program; the dog was barking and the baby was crying.
   C. When the problem was explained to the class, he must have been asleep.
   D. She wished that her new dress were finished so that she could go to the party.

9.____

10. A. The engine not only furnishes power but light and heat as well.
    B. You're aware that we've forgotten whose guilt was established, aren't you?
    C. Everybody knows that the woman made many sacrifices for her children.
    D. A man with his dog and gun is a familiar sight in this neighborhood.

10.____

KEY (CORRECT ANSWERS)

1.	D	6.	D
2.	C	7.	B
3.	B	8.	C
4.	A	9.	B
5.	D	10.	A

TEST 5

DIRECTIONS: Each of Questions 1 to 15 consists of a sentence which may be classified appropriately under one of the following four categories:
- A. *Incorrect* because of faulty grammar
- B. *Incorrect* because of faulty punctuation
- C. *Incorrect* because of faulty spelling
- D. *Correct*

Examine each sentence carefully. Then, print, in the space on the right, the letter preceding the category which is the best of the four suggested above.

(Note: Each incorrect sentence contains only one type of error. Consider a sentence correct if it contains no errors, although there may be other correct ways of writing the sentence.)

1. Of the two employees, the one in our office is the most efficient.   1.____

2. No one can apply or even understand, the new rules and regulations.   2.____

3. A large amount of supplies were stored in the empty office.   3.____

4. If an employee is occassionally asked to work overtime, he should do so willingly.   4.____

5. It is true that the new procedures are difficult to use but, we are certain that you will learn them quickly.   5.____

6. The office manager said that he did not know who would be given a large allotment under the new plan.   6.____

7. It was at the supervisor's request that the clerk agreed to postpone his vacation.   7.____

8. We do not believe that it is necessary for both he and the clerk to attend the conference.   8.____

9. All employees, who display perseverance, will be given adequate recognition.   9.____

10. He regrets that some of us employees are dissatisfied with our new assignments.   10.____

11. "Do you think that the raise was merited," asked the supervisor?   11.____

12. The new manual of procedure is a valuable supplament to our rules and regulations.   12.____

13. The typist admitted that she had attempted to pursuade the other employees to assist her in her work.   13.____

14. The supervisor asked that all amendments to the regulations be handled by you and I.   14.____

15. The custodian seen the boy who broke the window.   15.____

KEY (CORRECT ANSWERS)

1.	A	6.	D
2.	B	7.	D
3.	A	8.	A
4.	C	9.	B
5.	B	10.	D

11.	B
12.	C
13.	C
14.	A
15.	A

———

REPORT WRITING

EXAMINATION SECTION
TEST 1

DIRECTIONS: Each question or incomplete statement is followed by several suggested answers or completions. Select the one that *BEST* answers the question or completes the statement. *PRINT THE LETTER OF THE CORRECT ANSWER IN THE SPACE AT THE RIGHT.*

1. Following are six steps that should be taken in the course of report preparation: 1._____
   I.   Outlining the material for presentation in the report
   II.   Analyzing and interpreting the facts
   III. Analyzing the problem
   IV.   Reaching conclusions
   V.   Writing, revising, and rewriting the final copy
   VI.   Collecting data

   According to the principles of good report writing, the CORRECT order in which these steps should be taken is:

   A. VI, III, II, I, IV, V   B. III, VI, II, IV, I, V
   C. III, VI, II, I, IV, V   D. VI, II, III, IV, I, V

2. Following are three statements concerning written reports: 2._____
   I.   Clarity is generally more essential in oral reports than in written reports.
   II.   Short sentences composed of simple words are generally preferred to complex sentences and difficult words.
   III. Abbreviations may be used whenever they are customary and will not distract the attention of the reader

   Which of the following choices correctly classifies the above statements in to whose which are valid and those which are not valid?

   A. I and II are valid, but III is not valid.
   B. I is valid, but II and III are not valid.
   C. II and III are valid, but I is not valid.
   D. III is valid, but I and II are not valid.

3. In order to produce a report written in a style that is both understandable and effective,   3._____
   an investigator should apply the principles of unit, coherence, and emphasis. The one of the following which is the BEST example of the principle of coherence is

   A. interlinking sentences so that thoughts flow smoothly
   B. having each sentence express a single idea to facilitate comprehension
   C. arranging important points in prominent positions so they are not overlooked
   D. developing the main idea fully to insure complete consideration

4. Assume that a supervisor is preparing a report recommending that a standard work pro-   4._____
   cedure be changed. Of the following, the MOST important information that he should include in this report is

   A. a complete description of the present procedure
   B. the details and advantages of the recommended procedure

A. the type and amount of retraining needed
B. the percentage of men who favor the change

5. When you include in your report on an inspection some information which you have obtained from other individuals, it is *MOST* important that

   A. this information have no bearing on the work these other people are performing
   B. you do not report as fact the opinions of other individuals
   C. you keep the source of the information confidential
   D. you do not tell the other individuals that their statements will be included in your report.

6. Before turning in a report of an investigation of an accident, you discover some additional information you did not know about when you wrote the report.
   Whether or not you re-write your report to include this additional information should depend *MAINLY* on the

   A. source of this additional information
   B. established policy covering the subject matter of the report
   C. length of the report and the time it would take you to re-write it
   D. bearing this additional information will have on the conclusions in the report

7. The *most desirable FIRST* step in the planning of a written report is to

   A. ascertain what necessary information is readily available in the files
   B. outline the methods you will employ to get the necessary information
   C. determine the objectives and uses of the report
   D. estimate the time and cost required to complete the report

8. In writing a report, the practice of taking up the *least* important points *first* and the *most* important points *last* is a

   A. *good* technique since the final points made in a report will make the greatest impression on the reader
   B. *good* technique since the material is presented in a more logical manner and will lead directly to the conclusions
   C. *poor* technique since the reader's time is wasted by having to review irrelevant information before finishing the report
   D. *poor* technique since it may cause the reader to lose interest in the report and arrive at incorrect conclusions about the report

9. Which one of the following serves as the *BEST* guideline for you to follow for effective written reports? Keep sentences

   A. *short* and limit sentences to *one* thought
   B. *short* and use *as many* thoughts as possible
   C. *long* and limit sentences to *one* thought
   D. *long* and use *as many* thoughts as possible

10. One method by which a supervisor might prepare written reports to management is to begin with the conclusions, results, or summary, and to follow this with the supporting data.
    The *BEST* reason why management may *prefer* this form of report is that

5.____

6.____

7.____

8.____

9.____

10.____

A. management lacks the specific training to understand the data
B. the data completely supports the conclusions
C. time is saved by getting to the conclusions of the report first
D. the data contains all the information that is required for making the conclusions

11. When making written reports, it is MOST important that they be   11.____

A. well-worded   B. accurate as to the facts
B. brief   D. submitted immediately

12. Of the following, the *MOST* important reason for a supervisor to prepare good written   12.____
reports is that

A. a supervisor is rated on the quality of his reports
B. decisions are often made on the basis of the reports
C. such reports take less time for superiors to review
D. such reports demonstrate efficiency of department operations

13. Of the following, the *BEST* test of a good report is whether it   13.____

A. provides the information needed
B. shows the good sense of the writer
C. is prepared according to a proper format
D. is grammatical and neat

14. When a supervisor writes a report, he can *BEST* show that he has an understanding of   14____
the subject of the report by

A. including necessary facts and omitting nonessential details
B. using statistical data
C. giving his conclusions but not the data on which they are based
D. using a technical vocabulary

15. Suppose you and another supervisor on the same level are assigned to work together on   15.____
a report. You disagree strongly with one of the recommendations the other supervisor
wants to   include in the report but you cannot change his views.
Of the following, it would be BEST that

A. you refuse to accept responsibility for the report
B. you ask that someone else be assigned to this project to replace you
C. each of you state his own ideas about this recommendation in the report
D. you give in to the other supervisor's opinion for the sake of harmony

16. Standardized forms are often provided for submitting reports.   16.____
Of the following, the *MOST* important advantage of using standardized forms for
reports is that

A. they take less time to prepare than individually written reports
B. the person making the report can omit information he considers unimportant
C. the responsibility for preparing these reports can be turned over to subordinates
D. necessary information is less likely to be omitted

17. A report which may *BEST* be classed as a *periodic* report is one which   17. ____

    A. requires the same type of information at regular intervals
    B. contains detailed information which is to be retained in permanent records
    C. is prepared whenever a special situation occurs
    D. lists information in graphic form

18. In the writing of reports or letters, the ideas presented in a paragraph are usually of   18. ____
unequal importance and require varying degrees of emphasis.
All of the following are methods of placing extra stress on an idea *EXCEPT*

    A. repeating it in a number of forms
    B. placing it in the middle of the paragraph
    C. placing it either at the beginning or at the end of the paragraph
    D. underlining it

Questions 19-25.

DIRECTIONS: Questions 19 to 25 concern the subject of report writing and are based on the information and incidents described in the paragraph below. (In answering these questions, assume that the facts and incidents in the paragraph are true.)

On December 15, at 8 a.m., seven Laborers reported to Foreman Joseph Meehan in the Greenbranch Yard in Queens. Meehan instructed the men to load some 50-pound boxes of books on a truck for delivery to an agency building in Brooklyn. Meehan told the men that, because the boxes were rather heavy, two men should work together, helping each other lift and load each box. Since Michael Harper, one of the Laborers, was without a partner, Meehan helped him with the boxes for a while. When Meehan was called to the telephone in a nearby building, however, Harper decided to lift a box himself. He appeared able to lift the box, but, as he got the box halfway up, he cried out that he had a sharp pain in his back. Another Laborer, Jorge Ortiz, who was passing by, ran over to help Harper put the box down. Harper suddenly dropped the box, which fell on Ortiz' right foot. By this time Meehan had come out of the building. He immediately helped get the box off Ortiz' foot and had both men lie down. Meehan covered the men with blankets and called an ambulance, which arrived a half hour later. At the hospital, the doctor said that the X-ray results showed that Ortiz' right foot was broken in three places.

19. What would be the *BEST* term to use in a report describing the injury of Jorge Ortiz?   19. ____

    A. Strain   B. Fracture   C. Hernia   D. Hemorrhage

20. Which of the following would be the MOST accurate summary for the Foreman to put in   20. ____
his report of the incident?

    A. Ortiz attempted to help Harper carry a box which was too heavy for one person, but Harper dropped it before Ortiz got there.
    B. Ortiz tried to help Harper carry a box but Harper got a pain in his back and accidentally dropped the box on Ortiz' foot.
    C. Harper refused to follow Meehan's orders and lifted a box too heavy for him; he deliberately dropped it when Ortiz tried to help him carry it.
    D. Harper lifted a box and felt a pain in his back; Ortiz tried to help Harper put the box down but Harper accidentally dropped it on Ortiz' foot.

21. One of the Laborers at the scene of the accident was asked his version of the incident.   21. ___
Which information obtained from this witness would be *LEAST* important for
including in the accident report?

    A. His opinion as to the cause of the accident
    B. How much of the accident he saw
    C. His personal opinion of the victims
    D. His name and address

22. What should be the *MAIN* objective of writing a report about the incident described in the   22.___
above paragraph? To

    A. describe the important elements in the accident situation
    B. recommend that such Laborers as Ortiz be advised not to interfere in
       another's work unless given specific instructions
    C. analyze the problems occurring when there are not enough workers to perform
       a certain task
    D. illustrate the hazards involved in performing routine everyday tasks

23. Which of the following is information *missing* from the passage above but which *should*   23. ___
be included in a report of the incident? The

    A. name of the Laborer's immediate supervisor
    B. contents of the boxes
    C. time at which the accident occurred
    D. object or action that caused the injury to Ortiz' foot

24. According to the description of the incident, the accident occurred *because*   24. ___

    A. Ortiz attempted to help Harper who resisted his help
    B. Harper failed to follow instructions given him by Meehan
    C. Meehan was not supervising his men as closely as he should have
    D. Harper was not strong enough to carry the box once he lifted it

25. Which of the following is *MOST* important for a foreman to *avoid* when writing up an offi-   25.___
cial accident report?

    A. Using technical language to describe equipment involved in the accident
    B. Putting in details which might later be judged unnecessary
    C. Giving an opinion as to conditions that contributed to the accident
    D. Recommending discipline for employees who, in his opinion, caused the accident

———————

KEY (CORRECT ANSWERS)

1.	B		11.	B
2.	C		12.	B
3.	A		13.	A
4.	B		14.	A
5.	B		15.	C
6.	D		16.	D
7.	C		17.	A
8.	D		18.	B
9.	A		19.	B
10.	C		20.	D

21. C
22. A
23. C
24. B
25. D

TEST 2

DIRECTIONS: Each question or incomplete statement is followed by several suggested answers or completions. Select the one that *BEST* answers the question or completes the statement. *PRINT THE LETTER OF THE CORRECT ANSWER IN THE SPACE AT THE RIGHT.*

1. Lieutenant X is preparing a report to submit to his commanding officer in order to get approval of a plan of operation he has developed.
   The report starts off with the statement of the problem and continues with the details of the problem. It contains factual information gathered with the help of field and operational personnel. It contains a final conclusion and recommendation for action. The recommendation is supplemented by comments from other precinct staff members on how the recommendations will affect their areas of responsibility. The report also includes directives and general orders ready for the commanding officer's signature. In addition, it has two statements of objections presented by two precinct staff members.
   Which one of the following, if any, is *either* an item that Lieutenant X should have included in his report and which is not mentioned above, *or* is an item which Lieutenant X improperly did include in his report?

   A. Considerations of alternative courses of action and their consequences should have been covered in the report.
   B. The additions containing documented objections to the recommended course of action should not have been included as part of the report.
   C. A statement on the qualifications of Lieutenant X, which would support his expertness in the field under consideration, should have been included in the report.
   D. The directives and general orders should not have been prepared and included in the report until the commanding officer had approved the recommendations.
   E. None of the above, since Lieutenant X's report was both proper and complete.

1. ___

2. During a visit to a section, the district supervisor criticizes the method being used by the assistant foreman to prepare a certain report and orders him to modify the method. This change ordered by the district supervisor is in direct conflict with the specific orders of the foreman. In this situation, it would be *BEST* for the assistant foreman to

   A. change the method and tell the foreman about the change at the first opportunity
   B. change the method and rely on the district supervisor to notify the foreman
   C. report the matter to the foreman and delay the preparation of the report
   D. ask the district supervisor to discuss the matter with the foreman but use the old method for the time being

2. ___

3. A department officer should realize that the *most usual* reason for writing a report is to

   A. give orders and follow up their execution
   B. establish a permanent record
   C. raise questions
   D. supply information

3. ___

4. A very important report which is being prepared by a department officer will soon be due on the desk of the district supervisor. No typing help is available at this time for the officer. For the officer to write out this report in longhand in such a situation would be

4. ___

A. *bad;* such a report would not make the impression a typed report would
B. *good;* it is important to get the report in on time
C. *bad;* the district supervisor should not be required to read longhand reports
D. *good;* it would call attention to the difficult conditions under which this section must work

5. In a well-written report, the length of each paragraph in the report should be   5.____

    A. varied according to the content
    B. not over 300 words
    C. pretty nearly the same
    D. gradually longer as the report is developed and written

6. A clerk in the headquarters office complains to you about the way in which you are filling   6.____
out a certain report. It would be *BEST* for you to

    A. tell the clerk that you are following official procedures in filling out the report
    B. ask to be referred to the clerk's superior
    C. ask the clerk exactly what is wrong with the way in which you are filling out the report
    D. tell the clerk that you are following the directions of the district supervisor

7. The use of an outline to help in writing a report is   7.____

    A. *desirable* in order to insure good organization and coverage
    B. *necessary* so it can be used as an introduction to the report itself
    C. *undesirable* since it acts as a straight jacket and may result in an unbalanced report
    D. *desirable* if you know your immediate supervisor reads reports with extreme care and attention

8. It is advisable that a department officer do his paper work and report writing as soon as   8.____
he has completed an inspection *MAINLY* because

    A. there are usually deadlines to be met
    B. it insures a steady work-flow
    C. he may not have time for this later
    D. the facts are then freshest in his mind

9. Before you turn in a report you have written of an investigation that you have made, you   9.____
discover some additional information you didn't know about before. Whether or not you
re-write your report to include this additional information should depend *MAINLY* on the

    A. amount of time remaining before the report is due
    B. established policy of the department covering the subject matter of the report
    C. bearing this information will have on the conclusions of the report
    D. number of people who will eventually review the report

10. When a supervisory officer submits a periodic report to the district supervisor, he should   10.____
realize that the *CHIEF* importance of such a report is that it

    A. is the principal method of checking on the efficiency of the supervisor and his sub-ordinates
    B. is something to which frequent reference will be made

    C.   eliminates the need for any personal follow-up or inspection by higher echelons
    D.   permits the district supervisor to exercise his functions of direction, supervision, and control better

11. Conclusions and recommendations are usually better placed at the *end* rather than at the *beginning* of a report because 11.____

    A.   the person preparing the report may decide to change some of the conclusions and recommendations before he reaches the end of the report
    B.   they are the most important part of the report
    C.   they can be judged better by the person to whom the report is sent after he reads the facts and investigations which come earlier in the report
    D.   they can be referred to quickly when needed without reading the rest of the report

12. The use of the same method of record-keeping and reporting by *all* agency sections is 12.____

    A.   *desirable, MAINLY* because it saves time in section operations
    B.   *undesirable, MAINLY* because it kills the initiative of the individual section foreman
    C.   *desirable, MAINLY* because it will be easier for the administrator to evaluate and compare section operations
    D.   *undesirable, MAINLY* because operations vary from section to section and uniform record-keeping and reporting is not appropriate

13. The *GREATEST* benefit the section officer will have from keeping complete and accurate records and reports of section operations is that   ____

    A.   he will find it easier to run his section efficiently
    B.   he will need less equipment
    C.   he will need less manpower
    D.   the section will run smoothly when he is out

14. You have prepared a report to your superior and are ready to send it forward. But on re-reading it, you think some parts are not clearly expressed and your superior may have difficulty getting your point.
Of the following, it would be *BEST* for you to 14.____

    A.   give the report to one of your men to read, and if he has no trouble understanding it send it through
    B.   forward the report and call your superior the next day to ask whether it was all right
    C.   forward the report as is; higher echelons should be able to understand any report prepared by a section officer
    D.   do the report over, re-writing the sections you are in doubt about

15. The *BEST* of the following statements concerning reports is that 15.____

    A.   a carelessly written report may give the reader an impression of inaccuracy
    B.   correct grammar and English are unimportant if the main facts are given
    C.   every man should be required to submit a daily work report
    D.   the longer and more wordy a report is, the better it will read

16. In writing a report, the question of whether or not to include certain material could be determined *BEST* by considering the   16.____

    A. amount of space the material will occupy in the report
    B. amount of time to be spent in gathering the material
    C. date of the material
    D. value of the material to the superior who will read the report

17. Suppose you are submitting a fairly long report to your superior. The *one* of the following sections that should come *FIRST* in this report is a   17.____

    A. description of how you gathered material
    B. discussion of possible objections to your recommendations
    C. plan of how your recommendations can be put into practice
    D. statement of the problem dealt with

Questions 18-20.

DIRECTIONS: A foreman is asked to write a report on the incident described in the following passage. Answer Questions 18 through 20 based on the following information.

On March 10, Henry Moore, a laborer, was in the process of transferring some equipment from the machine shop to the third floor. He was using a dolly to perform this task and, as he was wheeling the material through the machine shop, laborer Bob Greene called to him. As Henry turned to respond to Bob, he jammed the dolly into Larry Mantell's leg, knocking Larry down in the process and causing the heavy drill that Larry was holding to fall on Larry's foot. Larry started rubbing his foot and then, infuriated, jumped up and punched Henry in the jaw. The force of the blow drove Henry's head back against the wall. Henry did not fight back; he appeared to be dazed. An ambulance was called to take Henry to the hospital, and the ambulance attendant told the foreman that it appeared likely that Henry had suffered a concussion. Larry's injuries consisted of some bruises, but he refused medical attention.

18. An adequate report of the above incident should give as minimum information the names of the persons involved, the names of the witnesses, the date and the time that each event took place, *and* the   18.____

    A. names of the ambulance attendants
    B. names of all the employees working in the machine shop
    C. location where the accident occurred
    D. nature of the previous safety training each employee had been given

19. The *only* one of the following which is *NOT* a fact is   19.__

    A. Bob called to Henry
    B. Larry suffered a concussion
    C. Larry rubbed his foot
    D. the incident took place in the machine shop

20. Which of the following would be, the MOST accurate summary of the incident for the foreman to put in his report of the accident?   20. ___

    A. Larry Mantell punched Henry Moore because a drill fell on his foot and he was angry. Then Henry fell and suffered a concussion.
    B. Henry Moore accidentally jammed a dolly into Larry Mantell's foot, knocking Larry down. Larry punched Henry, pushing him into the wall and causing him to bang his head against the wall.
    C. Bob Greene called Henry Moore. A dolly then jammed into Larry Mantell and knocked him down. Larry punched Henry who tripped and suffered some bruises. An ambulance was called.
    D. A drill fell on Larry Mantell's foot. Larry jumped up suddenly and punched Henry Moore and pushed him into the wall. Henry may have suffered a concussion as a result of falling.

Questions 21-25.

DIRECTIONS: Answer Questions 21 through 25 *only* on the basis of the information provided in the following passage.

A written report is a communication of information from one person to another. It is an account of some matter especially investigated, however routine that matter may be. The ultimate basis of any good written report is facts, which become known through observation and verification. Good written reports may seem to be no more than general ideas and opinions. However, in such cases, the facts leading to these opinions were gathered, verified, and reported earlier, and the opinions are dependent upon these facts. Good style, proper form and emphasis cannot make a good written report out of unreliable information and bad judgment; but, on the other hand, solid investigation and brilliant thinking are not likely to become very useful until they are effectively communicated to others. If a person's work calls for written reports, then his work is often no better than his written reports.

21. Based on the information in the passage, it can be concluded that opinions expressed in a report should be   21. ___

    A. based on facts which are gathered and reported
    B. emphasized repeatedly when they result from a special investigation
    C. kept to a minimum
    D. separated from the body of the report

22. In the above passage, the one of the following which is mentioned as a way of establishing facts is   22. ___

    A. authority   B. communication
    C. reporting   D. verification

23. According to the passage, the characteristic shared by *all* written reports is that they are   23. ___

    A. accounts of routine matters
    B. transmissions of information
    C. reliable and logical
    D. written in proper form

24. Which of the following conclusions can *logically* be drawn from the information given in   24. ____
the passage?

    A. Brilliant thinking can make up for unreliable information in a report.
    B. One method of judging an individual's work is the quality of the written reports
       he is required to submit.
    C. Proper form and emphasis can make a good report out of unreliable information.
    D. Good written reports that seem to be no more than general ideas should be
       rewritten.

25. Which of the following suggested titles would be *MOST* appropriate for this passage?   25. ____

    A. Gathering and Organizing Facts
    B. Techniques of Observation
    C. Nature and Purpose of Reports
    D. Reports and Opinions: Differences and Similarities

KEY (CORRECT ANSWERS)

1.	A		11.	C
2.	A		12.	C
3.	D		13.	A
4.	B		14.	D
5.	A		15.	A
6.	C		16.	D
7.	A		17.	D
8.	D		18.	C
9.	C		19.	B
10.	D		20.	B

21.	A
22.	D
23.	B
24.	B
25.	C

TEST 3

DIRECTIONS: The following is an accident report similar to those used in departments for reporting accidents. Answer Questions 1 to 5 using *only* the information given in this report.

ACCIDENT REPORT

FROM *John Doe* TITLE *Sanitation Man*	DATE OF REPORT *June 23*
DATE OF ACCIDENT *June 22* time 3 ~~AM~~ PM PLACE *1489 Third Avenue*	CITY *Metropolitan*
VEHICLE NO. *1*	VEHICLE NO. *2*
OPERATOR John Doe, *Sanitation Man* TITLE	OPERATOR *Richard Roe*
VEHICLE CODE NO. *14-238*	ADDRESS *498 High Street*
LICENSE NO. *0123456*	OWNER *Henry Roe* ADDRESS *786 E. 83 St*	LIC NUMBER *5N1492*

DESCRIPTION OF ACCIDENT *Light green Chevrolet sedan while trying to pass drove in to rear side of Sanitation truck which had stopped to collect garbage. No one was injured but there was property damage.*

NATURE OF DAMAGE TO PRIVATE VEHICLE *Right front fender crushed, bumper bent.*

DAMAGE TO CITY VEHICLE *Front of left rear fender pushed in. Paint scraped.*

NAME OF WITNESS *Frank Brown*	ADRESS *48 Kingsway*
John Doe **Signature of person making this report**	BADGE NO. *428*

1. Of the following, the one which has been omitted from this accident report is the   1. ___

    A.   location of the accident
    B.   drivers of the vehicles involved
    C.   traffic situation at the time of the accident
    D.   owners of the vehicles involved

2. The address of the driver of Vehicle No. 1 is not required because he   2. ___

    A.   is employed by the department
    B.   is not the owner of the vehicle
    C.   reported the accident
    D.   was injured in the accident

3. The report indicates that the driver of Vehicle No. 2 was *probably*   3.____

    A.   passing on the wrong side of the truck
    B.   not wearing his glasses
    C.   not injured in the accident
    D.   driving while intoxicated

4. The number of people *specifically* referred to in this report is   4.____

    A. 3   B. 4   C. 5   D. 6

5. The license number of Vehicle No. 1 is   5.____

    A. 428   B. 5N1492   C. 14-238   D. 0123456

6. In a report of unlawful entry into department premises, it is *LEAST* important to include   6.____
   the

    A.   estimated value of the property missing
    B.   general description of the premises
    C.   means used to get into the premises
    D.   time and date of entry

7. In a report of an accident, it is *LEAST* important to include the   7.____

    A.   name of the insurance company of the person injured in the accident
    B.   probable cause of the accident
    C.   time and place of the accident
    D.   names and addresses of all witnesses of the accident

8. Of the following, the one which is_____ *NOT* required in the preparation of a weekly
   functional expense report is the

    A.   hourly distribution of the time by proper heading in accordance with the actual work
        performed
    B.   signatures of officers not involved in the preparation of the report
    C.   time records of the men who appear on the payroll of the respective locations
    D.   time records of men working in other districts assigned to this location

KEY (CORRECT ANSWERS)

1.	C	5.	D
2.	A	6.	B
3.	C	7.	A
4.	B	8.	B

PHILOSOPHY, PRINCIPLES, PRACTICES AND TECHNICS
OF
SUPERVISION, ADMINISTRATION, MANAGEMENT AND ORGANIZATION

TABLE OF CONTENTS

TABLE OF CONTENTS (CONTINUED)

PHILOSOPHY, PRINCIPLES, PRACTICES, AND TECHNICS
OF
SUPERVISION, ADMINISTRATION, MANAGEMENT AND ORGANIZATION

I. MEANING OF SUPERVISION

The extension of the democratic philosophy has been accompanied by an extension in the scope of supervision. Modern leaders and supervisors no longer think of supervision in the narrow sense of being confined chiefly to visiting employees, supplying materials, or rating the staff. They regard supervision as being intimately related to all the concerned agencies of society, they speak of the supervisor's function in terms of "growth", rather than the "improvement," of employees.

This modern concept of supervision may be defined as follows:

Supervision is leadership and the development of leadership within groups which are cooperatively engaged in inspection, research, training, guidance and evaluation.

II. THE OLD AND THE NEW SUPERVISION

TRADITIONAL
1. Inspection
2. Focused on the employee
3. Visitation
4. Random and haphazard
5. Imposed and authoritarian
6. One person usually

MODERN
1. Study and analysis
2. Focused on aims, materials, methods, supervisors, employees, environment
3. Demonstrations, intervisitation, workshops, directed reading, bulletins, etc.
4. Definitely organized and planned (scientific)
5. Cooperative and democratic
6. Many persons involved (creative)

III THE EIGHT (8) BASIC PRINCIPLES OF THE NEW SUPERVISION

1. *PRINCIPLE OF RESPONSIBILITY*
   Authority to act and responsibility for acting must be joined.
   a. If you give responsibility, give authority.
   b. Define employee duties clearly.
   c. Protect employees from criticism by others.
   d. Recognize the rights as well as obligations of employees.
   e. Achieve the aims of a democratic society insofar as it is possible within the area of your work.
   f. Establish a situation favorable to training and learning.
   g. Accept ultimate responsibility for everything done in your section, unit, office, division, department.
   h. Good administration and good supervision are inseparable.

2. PRINCIPLE OF AUTHORITY
The success of the supervisor is measured by the extent to which the power of authority is not used.
- a. Exercise simplicity and informality in supervision.
- b. Use the simplest machinery of supervision.
- c. If it is good for the organization as a whole, it is probably justified.
- d. Seldom be arbitrary or authoritative.
- e. Do not base your work on the power of position or of personality.
- f. Permit and encourage the free expression of opinions.

3. PRINCIPLE OF SELF-GROWTH
The success of the supervisor is measured by the extent to which, and the speed with which, he is no longer needed.
- a. Base criticism on principles, not on specifics.
- b. Point out higher activities to employees.
- c. Train for self-thinking by employees, to meet new situations.
- d. Stimulate initiative, self-reliance and individual responsibility.
- e. Concentrate on stimulating the growth of employees rather than on removing defects.

4. PRINCIPLE OF INDIVIDUAL WORTH
Respect for the individual is a paramount consideration in supervision.
- a. Be human and sympathetic in dealing with employees.
- b. Don't nag about things to be done.
- c. Recognize the individual differences among employees and seek opportunities to permit best expression of each personality.

5. PRINCIPLE OF CREATIVE LEADERSHIP
The best supervision is that which is not apparent to the employee.
- a. Stimulate, don't drive employees to creative action.
- b. Emphasize doing good things.
- c. Encourage employees to do what they do best.
- d. Do not be too greatly concerned with details of subject or method.
- e. Do not be concerned exclusively with immediate problems and activities.
- f. Reveal higher activities and make them both desired and maximally possible.
- g. Determine procedures in the light of each situation but see that these are derived from a sound basic philosophy.
- h. Aid, inspire and lead so as to liberate the creative spirit latent in all good employees.

6. PRINCIPLE OF SUCCESS AND FAILURE
There are no unsuccessful employees, only unsuccessful supervisors who have failed to give proper leadership.
- a. Adapt suggestions to the capacities, attitudes, and prejudices of employees.
- b. Be gradual, be progressive, be persistent.
- c. Help the employee find the general principle; have the employee apply his own problem to the general principle.
- d. Give adequate appreciation for good work and honest effort.
- e. Anticipate employee difficulties and help to prevent them.
- f. Encourage employees to do the desirable things they will do anyway.
- g. Judge your supervision by the results it secures.

7. *PRINCIPLE OF SCIENCE*
Successful supervision is scientific, objective, and experimental. It is based on facts, not on prejudices.

     a. Be cumulative in results.
     b. Never divorce your suggestions from the goals of training.
     c. Don't be impatient of results.
     d. Keep all matters on a professional, not a personal level.
     e. Do not be concerned exclusively with immediate problems and activities.
     f. Use objective means of determining achievement and rating where possible.

8. *PRINCIPLE OF COOPERATION*
Supervision is a cooperative enterprise between supervisor and employee.

     a. Begin with conditions as they are.
     b. Ask opinions of all involved when formulating policies.
     c. Organization is as good as its weakest link.
     d. Let employees help to determine policies and department programs.
     e. Be approachable and accessible - physically and mentally.
     f. Develop pleasant social relationships.

IV. WHAT IS ADMINISTRATION?

Administration is concerned with providing the environment, the material facilities, and the operational procedures that will promote the maximum growth and development of supervisors and employees. (Organization is an aspect, and a concomitant, of administration.)

There is no sharp line of demarcation between supervision and administration; these functions are intimately interrelated and, often, overlapping. They are complementary activities.

1. *PRACTICES COMMONLY CLASSED AS "SUPERVISORY"*
     a. Conducting employees conferences
     b. Visiting sections, units, offices, divisions, departments
     c. Arranging for demonstrations
     d. Examining plans
     e. Suggesting professional reading
     f. Interpreting bulletins
     g. Recommending in-service training courses
     h. Encouraging experimentation
     i. Appraising employee morale
     j. Providing for intervisitation

2. *PRACTICES COMMONLY CLASSIFIED AS "ADMINISTRATIVE"*
     a. Management of the office
     b. Arrangement of schedules for extra duties
     c. Assignment of rooms or areas
     d. Distribution of supplies
     e. Keeping records and reports
     f. Care of audio-visual materials
     g. Keeping inventory records
     h. Checking record cards and books
     i. Programming special activities
     j. Checking on the attendance and punctuality of employees

3. *PRACTICES COMMONLY CLASSIFIED AS BOTH "SUPERVISORY" AND "ADMINISTRATIVE"*
   a. Program construction
   b. Testing or evaluating outcomes
   c. Personnel accounting
   d. Ordering instructional materials

V. RESPONSIBILITIES OF THE SUPERVISOR

A person employed in a supervisory capacity must constantly be able to improve his own efficiency and ability. He represents the employer to the employees and only continuous self-examination can make him a capable supervisor.

Leadership and training are the supervisor's responsibility. An efficient working unit is one in which the employees work with the supervisor. It is his job to bring out the best in his employees. He must always be relaxed, courteous and calm in his association with his employees. Their feelings are important, and a harsh attitude does not develop the most efficient employees.

VI. COMPETENCIES OF THE SUPERVISOR

1. Complete knowledge of the duties and responsibilities of his position.
2. To be able to organize a job, plan ahead and carry through.
3. To have self-confidence and initiative.
4. To be able to handle the unexpected situation and make quick decisions.
5. To be able to properly train subordinates in the positions they are best suited for.
6. To be able to keep good human relations among his subordinates.
7. To be able to keep good human relations between his subordinates and himself and to earn their respect and trust.

VII. THE PROFESSIONAL SUPERVISOR-EMPLOYEE RELATIONSHIP

There are two kinds of efficiency: one kind is only apparent and is produced in organizations through the exercise of mere discipline; this is but a simulation of the second, or true, efficiency which springs from spontaneous cooperation. If you are a manager, no matter how great or small your responsibility, it is your job, in the final analysis, to create and develop this involuntary cooperation among the people whom you supervise. For, no matter how powerful a combination of money, machines, and materials a company may have, this is a dead and sterile thing without a team of willing, thinking and articulate people to guide it.

The following 21 points are presented as indicative of the exemplary basic relationship that should exist between supervisor and employee:

1. Each person wants to be liked and respected by his fellow employee and wants to be treated with consideration and respect by his superior.
2. The most competent employee will make an error. However, in a unit where good relations exist between the supervisor and his employees, tenseness and fear do not exist. Thus, errors are not hidden or covered up and the efficiency of a unit is not impaired.
3. Subordinates resent rules, regulations, or orders that are unreasonable or unexplained.
4. Subordinates are quick to resent unfairness, harshness, injustices and favoritism.
5. An employee will accept responsibility if he knows that he will be complimented for a job well done, and not too harshly chastised for failure; that his supervisor will check the cause of the failure, and, if it was the supervisor's fault, he will assume the blame therefore. If it was the employee's fault, his supervisor will explain the correct method or means of handling the responsibility.

6. An employee wants to receive credit for a suggestion he has made, that is used. If a suggestion cannot be used, the employee is entitled to an explanation. The supervisor should not say "no" and close the subject.
7. Fear and worry slow up a worker's ability. Poor working environment can impair his physical and mental health. A good supervisor avoids forceful methods, threats and arguments to get a job done.
8. A forceful supervisor is able to train his employees individually and as a team, and is able to motivate them in the proper channels.
9. A mature supervisor is able to properly evaluate his subordinates and to keep them happy and satisfied.
10. A sensitive supervisor will never patronize his subordinates.
11. A worthy supervisor will respect his employees' confidences.
12. Definite and clear-cut responsibilities should be assigned to each executive.
13. Responsibility should always be coupled with corresponding authority.
14. No change should be made in the scope or responsibilities of a position without a definite understanding to that effect on the part of all persons concerned.
15. No executive or employee, occupying a single position in the organization, should be subject to definite orders from more than one source.
16. Orders should never be given to subordinates over the head of a responsible executive. Rather than do this, the officer in question should be supplanted.
17. Criticisms of subordinates should, whoever possible, be made privately, and in no case should a subordinate be criticized in the presence of executives or employees of equal or lower rank.
18. No dispute or difference between executives or employees as to authority or responsibilities should be considered too trivial for prompt and careful adjudication.
19. Promotions, wage changes, and disciplinary action should always be approved by the executive immediately superior to the one directly responsible.
20. No executive or employee should ever be required, or expected, to be at the same time an assistant to, and critic of, another.
21. Any executive whose work is subject to regular inspection should, whever practicable, be given the assistance and facilities necessary to enable him to maintain an independent check of the quality of his work.

VIII. MINI-TEXT IN SUPERVISION, ADMINISTRATION, MANAGEMENT, AND ORGANIZATION

A. BRIEF HIGHLIGHTS

Listed concisely and sequentially are major headings and important data in the field for quick recall and review.

1. LEVELS OF MANAGEMENT

Any organization of some size has several levels of management. In terms of a ladder the levels are:

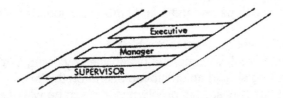

The first level is very important because it is the beginning point of management leadership.

2. WHAT THE SUPERVISOR MUST LEARN
A supervisor must learn to:
- (1) Deal with people and their differences
- (2) Get the job done through people
- (3) Recognize the problems when they exist
- (4) Overcome obstacles to good performance
- (5) Evaluate the performance of people
- (6) Check his own performance in terms of accomplishment

3. A DEFINITION OF SUPERVISOR
The term supervisor means any individual having authority, in the interests of the employer, to hire, transfer, suspend, lay-off, recall, promote, discharge, assign, reward, or discipline other employees or responsibility to direct them, or to adjust their grievances, or effectively to recommend such action, if, in connection with the foregoing, exercise of such authority is not of a merely routine or clerical nature but requires the use of independent judgment.

4. ELEMENTS OF THE TEAM CONCEPT
What is involved in teamwork? The component parts are:

(1) Members	(3) Goals	(5) Cooperation
(2) A leader	(4) Plans	(6) Spirit

5. PRINCIPLES OF ORGANIZATION
- (1) A team member must know what his job is.
- (2) Be sure that the nature and scope of a job are understood.
- (3) Authority and responsibility should be carefully spelled out.
- (4) A supervisor should be permitted to make the maximum number of decisions affecting his employees.
- (5) Employees should report to only one supervisor.
- (6) A supervisor should direct only as many employees as he can handle effectively.
- (7) An organization plan should be flexible.
- (8) Inspection and performance of work should be separate.
- (9) Organizational problems should receive immediate attention.
- (10) Assign work in line with ability and experience.

6. THE FOUR IMPORTANT PARTS OF EVERY JOB
- (1) Inherent in every job is the *accountability* for results.
- (2) A second set of factors in every job is *responsibilities*.
- (3) Along with duties and responsibilities one must have the *authority* to act within certain limits without obtaining permission to proceed.
- (4) No job exists in a vacuum. The supervisor is surrounded by key *relationships*.

7. PRINCIPLES OF DELEGATION
Where work is delegated for the first time, the supervisor should think in terms of these questions:
- (1) Who is best qualified to do this?
- (2) Can an employee improve his abilities by doing this?
- (3) How long should an employee spend on this?
- (4) Are there any special problems for which he will need guidance?
- (5) How broad a delegation can I make?

8. PRINCIPLES OF EFFECTIVE COMMUNICATIONS
  (1) Determine the media
  (2) To whom directed?
  (3) Identification and source authority
  (4) Is communication understood?

9. PRINCIPLES OF WORK IMPROVEMENT
  (1) Most people usually do only the work which is assigned to them
  (2) Workers are likely to fit assigned work into the time available to perform it
  (3) A good workload usually stimulates output
  (4) People usually do their best work when they know that results will be reviewed or inspected
  (5) Employees usually feel that someone else is responsible for conditions of work, workplace layout, job methods, type of tools/equipment, and other such factors
  (6) Employees are usually defensive about their job security
  (7) Employees have natural resistance to change
  (8) Employees can support or destroy a supervisor
  (9) A supervisor usually earns the respect of his people through his personal example of diligence and efficiency

10. AREAS OF JOB IMPROVEMENT
  The areas of job improvement are quite numerous, but the most common ones which a supervisor can identify and utilize are:

  (1) Departmental layout
  (2) Flow of work
  (3) Workplace layout
  (4) Utilization of manpower
  (5) Work methods
  (6) Materials handling
  (7) Utilization
  (8) Motion economy

11. SEVEN KEY POINTS IN MAKING IMPROVEMENTS
  (1) Select the job to be improved
  (2) Study how it is being done now
  (3) Question the present method
  (4) Determine actions to be taken
  (5) Chart proposed method
  (6) Get approval and apply
  (7) Solicit worker participation

12. CORRECTIVE TECHNIQUES OF JOB IMPROVEMENT

Specific Problems	General Improvement	Corrective Techniques
(1) Size of workload	(1) Departmental layout	(1) Study with scale model
(2) Inability to meet schedules	(2) Flow of work	(2) Flow chart study
(3) Strain and fatigue	(3) Work plan layout	(3) Motion analysis
(4) Improper use of men and skills	(4) Utilization of manpower	(4) Comparison of units produced to standard allowance
(5) Waste, poor quality, unsafe conditions	(5) Work methods	(5) Methods analysis
(6) Bottleneck conditions that hinder output	(6) Materials handling	(6) Flow chart & equipment study
(7) Poor utilization of equipment and machine	(7) Utilization of equipment	(7) Down time vs. running time
(8) Efficiency and productivity of labor	(8) Motion economy	(8) Motion analysis

13. A *PLANNING CHECKLIST*

(1) Objectives	(6) Resources	(11) Safety
(2) Controls	(7) Manpower	(12) Money
(3) Delegations	(8) Equipment	(13) Work
(4) Communications	(9) Supplies and materials	(14) Timing of improvements
(5) Resources	(10) Utilization of time	

14. *FIVE CHARACTERISTICS OF GOOD DIRECTIONS*

In order to get results, directions must be:

(1) Possible of accomplishment	(3) Related to mission	(5) Unmistakably clear
(2) Agreeable with worker interests	(4) Planned and complete	

15. *TYPES OF DIRECTIONS*

(1) Demands or direct orders	(3) Suggestion or implication
(2) Requests	(4) Volunteering

16. *CONTROLS*

A typical listing of the overall areas in which the supervisor should establish controls might be:

(1) Manpower	(3) Quality of work	(5) Time	(7) Money
(2) Materials	(4) Quantity of work	(6) Space	(8) Methods

17. *ORIENTING THE NEW EMPLOYEE*

(1) Prepare for him	(3) Orientation for the job
(2) Welcome the new employee	(4) Follow-up

18. *CHECKLIST FOR ORIENTING NEW EMPLOYEES*

                    Yes No

(1) Do your appreciate the feelings of new employees when they first report for work?

(2) Are you aware of the fact that the new employee must make a big adjustment to his job?

(3) Have you given him good reasons for liking the job and the organization?

(4) Have you prepared for his first day on the job?

(5) Did you welcome him cordially and make him feel needed?

(6) Did you establish rapport with him so that he feels free to talk and discuss matters with you?

(7) Did you explain his job to him and his relationship to you?

(8) Does he know that his work will be evaluated periodically on a basis that is fair and objective?

(9) Did you introduce him to his fellow workers in such a way that they are likely to accept him?

(10) Does he know what employee benefits he will receive?

(11) Does he understand the importance of being on the job and what to do if he must leave his duty station?

(12) Has he been impressed with the importance of accident prevention and safe practice?

(13) Does he generally know his way around the department?

(14) Is he under the guidance of a sponsor who will teach the right ways of doing things?

(15) Do you plan to follow-up so that he will continue to adjust successfully to his job?

19. PRINCIPLES OF LEARNING
      (1) Motivation   (2) Demonstration or explanation   (3) Practice

20. CAUSES OF POOR PERFORMANCE
(1) Improper training for job	(6) Lack of standards of
(2) Wrong tools	performance
(3) Inadequate directions	(7) Wrong work habits
(4) Lack of supervisory follow-up	(8) Low morale
(5) Poor communications	(9) Other

21. FOUR MAJOR STEPS IN ON-THE-JOB INSTRUCTION
(1) Prepare the worker	(3) Tryout performance
(2) Present the operation	(4) Follow-up

22. EMPLOYEES WANT FIVE THINGS
      (1) Security (2) Opportunity (3) Recognition (4) Inclusion (5) Expression

23. SOME DON'TS IN REGARD TO PRAISE
      (1) Don't praise a person for something he hasn't done
      (2) Don't praise a person unless you can be sincere
      (3) Don't be sparing in praise just because your superior withholds it from you
      (4) Don't let too much time elapse between good performance and recognition of it

24. HOW TO GAIN YOUR WORKERS' CONFIDENCE
Methods of developing confidence include such things as:
      (1) Knowing the interests, habits, hobbies of employees
      (2) Admitting your own inadequacies
      (3) Sharing and telling of confidence in others
      (4) Supporting people when they are in trouble
      (5) Delegating matters that can be well handled
      (6) Being frank and straightforward about problems and working conditions
      (7) Encouraging others to bring their problems to you
      (8) Taking action on problems which impede worker progress

25. SOURCES OF EMPLOYEE PROBLEMS
On-the-job causes might be such things as:
      (1) A feeling that favoritism is exercised in assignments
      (2) Assignment of overtime
      (3) An undue amount of supervision
      (4) Changing methods or systems
      (5) Stealing of ideas or trade secrets
      (6) Lack of interest in job
      (7) Threat of reduction in force
      (8) Ignorance or lack of communications
      (9) Poor equipment
    (10) Lack of knowing how supervisor feels toward employee
    (11) Shift assignments

Off-the-job problems might have to do with:
      (1) Health   (2) Finances   (3) Housing   (4) Family

26. THE SUPERVISOR'S KEY TO DISCIPLINE

There are several key points about discipline which the supervisor should keep in mind:

(1) Job discipline is one of the disciplines of life and is directed by the supervisor.
(2) It is more important to correct an employee fault than to fix blame for it.
(3) Employee performance is affected by problems both on the job and off.
(4) Sudden or abrupt changes in behavior can be indications of important employee problems.
(5) Problems should be dealt with as soon as possible after they are identified.
(6) The attitude of the supervisor may have more to do with solving problems than the techniques of problem solving.
(7) Correction of employee behavior should be resorted to only after the supervisor is sure that training or counseling will not be helpful.
(8) Be sure to document your disciplinary actions.
(9) Make sure that you are disciplining on the basis of facts rather than personal feelings.
(10) Take each disciplinary step in order, being careful not to make snap judgments, or decisions based on impatience.

27. FIVE IMPORTANT PROCESSES OF MANAGEMENT

(1) Planning   (2) Organizing   (3) Scheduling
(4) Controlling   (5) Motivating

28. WHEN THE SUPERVISOR FAILS TO PLAN

(1) Supervisor creates impression of not knowing his job
(2) May lead to excessive overtime
(3) Job runs itself -- supervisor lacks control
(4) Deadlines and appointments missed
(5) Parts of the work go undone
(6) Work interrupted by emergencies
(7) Sets a bad example
(8) Uneven workload creates peaks and valleys
(9) Too much time on minor details at expense of more important tasks

29. FOURTEEN GENERAL PRINCIPLES OF MANAGEMENT

(1) Division of work
(2) Authority and responsibility
(3) Discipline
(4) Unity of command
(5) Unity of direction
(6) Subordination of individual interest to general interest
(7) Remuneration of personnel
(8) Centralization
(9) Scalar chain
(10) Order
(11) Equity
(12) Stability of tenure of personnel
(13) Initiative
(14) Esprit de corps

30. CHANGE

Bringing about change is perhaps attempted more often, and yet less well understood, than anything else the supervisor does. How do people generally react to change? (People tend to resist change that is imposed upon them by other individuals or circumstances.

Change is characteristic of every situation. It is a part of every real endeavor where the efforts of people are concerned.

A. Why do people resist change?
    People may resist change because of:
        (1) Fear of the unknown
        (2) Implied criticism
        (3) Unpleasant experiences in the past
        (4) Fear of loss of status
        (5) Threat to the ego
        (6) Fear of loss of economic stability

B. How can we best overcome the resistance to change?
    In initiating change, take these steps:
        (1) Get ready to sell
        (2) Identify sources of help
        (3) Anticipate objections
        (4) Sell benefits
        (5) Listen in depth
        (6) Follow up

B. BRIEF TOPICAL SUMMARIES

I. WHO/WHAT IS THE SUPERVISOR?

1. The supervisor is often called the "highest level employee and the lowest level manager."
2. A supervisor is a member of both management and the work group. He acts as a bridge between the two.
3. Most problems in supervision are in the area of human relations, or people problems.
4. Employees expect: Respect, opportunity to learn and to advance, and a sense of belonging, and so forth.
5. Supervisors are responsible for directing people and organizing work. Planning is of paramount importance.
6. A position description is a set of duties and responsibilities inherent to a given position.
7. It is important to keep the position description up-to-date and to provide each employee with his own copy.

II. THE SOCIOLOGY OF WORK

1. People are alike in many ways; however, each individual is unique.
2. The supervisor is challenged in getting to know employee differences. Acquiring skills in evaluating individuals is an asset.
3. Maintaining meaningful working relationships in the organization is of great importance.
4. The supervisor has an obligation to help individuals to develop to their fullest potential.
5. Job rotation on a planned basis helps to build versatility and to maintain interest and enthusiasm in work groups.
6. Cross training (job rotation) provides backup skills.
7. The supervisor can help reduce tension by maintaining a sense of humor, providing guidance to employees, and by making reasonable and timely decisions. Employees respond favorably to working under reasonably predictable circumstances.
8. Change is characteristic of all managerial behavior. The supervisor must adjust to changes in procedures, new methods, technological changes, and to a number of new and sometimes challenging situations.
9. To overcome the natural tendency for people to resist change, the supervisor should become more skillful in initiating change.

III. PRINCIPLES AND PRACTICES OF SUPERVISION

1. Employees should be required to answer to only one superior.
2. A supervisor can effectively direct only a limited number of employees, depending upon the complexity, variety, and proximity of the jobs involved.
3. The organizational chart presents the organization in graphic form. It reflects lines of authority and responsibility as well as interrelationships of units within the organization.
4. Distribution of work can be improved through an analysis using the "Work Distribution Chart."
5. The "Work Distribution Chart" reflects the division of work within a unit in understandable form.
6. When related tasks are given to an employee, he has a better chance of increasing his skills through training.
7. The individual who is given the responsibility for tasks must also be given the appropriate authority to insure adequate results.
8. The supervisor should delegate repetitive, routine work. Preparation of recurring reports, maintaining leave and attendance records are some examples.
9. Good discipline is essential to good task performance. Discipline is reflected in the actions of employees on the job in the absence of supervision.
10. Disciplinary action may have to be taken when the positive aspects of discipline have failed. Reprimand, warning, and suspension are examples of disciplinary action.
11. If a situation calls for a reprimand, be sure it is deserved and remember it is to be done in private.

IV. DYNAMIC LEADERSHIP

1. A style is a personal method or manner of exerting influence.
2. Authoritarian leaders often see themselves as the source of power and authority.
3. The democratic leader often perceives the group as the source of authority and power.
4. Supervisors tend to do better when using the pattern of leadership that is most natural for them.
5. Social scientists suggest that the effective supervisor use the leadership style that best fits the problem or circumstances involved.
6. All four styles -- telling, selling, consulting, joining -- have their place. Using one does not preclude using the other at another time.
7. The theory X point of view assumes that the average person dislikes work, will avoid it whenever possible, and must be coerced to achieve organizational objectives.
8. The theory Y point of view assumes that the average person considers work to be as natural as play, and, when the individual is committed, he requires little supervision or direction to accomplish desired objectives.
9. The leader's basic assumptions concerning human behavior and human nature affect his actions, decisions, and other managerial practices.
10. Dissatisfaction among employees is often present, but difficult to isolate. The supervisor should seek to weaken dissatisfaction by keeping promises, being sincere and considerate, keeping employees informed, and so forth.
11. Constructive suggestions should be encouraged during the natural progress of the work.

V. PROCESSES FOR SOLVING PROBLEMS

1. People find their daily tasks more meaningful and satisfying when they can improve them.
2. The causes of problems, or the key factors, are often hidden in the background. Ability to solve problems often involves the ability to isolate them from their backgrounds. There is some substance to the cliché that some persons "can't see the forest for the trees."
3. New procedures are often developed from old ones. Problems should be broken down into manageable parts. New ideas can be adapted from old ones.

4. People think differently in problem-solving situations. Using a logical, patterned approach is often useful. One approach found to be useful includes these steps:

(a) Define the problem	(d) Weigh and decide
(b) Establish objectives	(e) Take action
(c) Get the facts	(f) Evaluate action

VI. TRAINING FOR RESULTS

1. Participants respond best when they feel training is important to them.
2. The supervisor has responsibility for the training and development of those who report to him.
3. When training is delegated to others, great care must be exercised to insure the trainer has knowledge, aptitude, and interest for his work as a trainer.
4. Training (learning) of some type goes on continually. The most successful supervisor makes certain the learning contributes in a productive manner to operational goals.
5. New employees are particularly susceptible to training. Older employees facing new job situations require specific training, as well as having need for development and growth opportunities.
6. Training needs require continuous monitoring.
7. The training officer of an agency is a professional with a responsibility to assist supervisors in solving training problems.
8. Many of the self-development steps important to the supervisor's own growth are equally important to the development of peers and subordinates. Knowledge of these is important when the supervisor consults with others on development and growth opportunities.

VII. HEALTH, SAFETY, AND ACCIDENT PREVENTION

1. Management-minded supervisors take appropriate measures to assist employees in maintaining health and in assuring safe practices in the work environment.
2. Effective safety training and practices help to avoid injury and accidents.
3. Safety should be a management goal. All infractions of safety which are observed should be corrected without exception.
4. Employees' safety attitude, training and instruction, provision of safe tools and equipment, supervision, and leadership are considered highly important factors which contribute to safety and which can be influenced directly by supervisors.
5. When accidents do occur they should be investigated promptly for very important reasons, including the fact that information which is gained can be used to prevent accidents in the future.

VIII. EQUAL EMPLOYMENT OPPORTUNITY

1. The supervisor should endeavor to treat all employees fairly, without regard to religion, race, sex, or national origin.
2. Groups tend to reflect the attitude of the leader. Prejudice can be detected even in very subtle form. Supervisors must strive to create a feeling of mutual respect and confidence in every employee.
3. Complete utilization of all human resources is a national goal. Equitable consideration should be accorded women in the work force, minority-group members, the physically and mentally handicapped, and the older employee. The important question is: "Who can do the job?"
4. Training opportunities, recognition for performance, overtime assignments, promotional opportunities, and all other personnel actions are to be handled on an equitable basis.

IX. IMPROVING COMMUNICATIONS

1. Communications is achieving understanding between the sender and the receiver of a message. It also means sharing information -- the creation of understanding.
2. Communication is basic to all human activity. Words are means of conveying meanings; however, real meanings are in people.
3. There are very practical differences in the effectiveness of one-way, impersonal, and two-way communications. Words spoken face-to-face are better understood. Telephone conversations are effective, but lack the rapport of person-to-person exchanges. The whole person communicates.
4. Cooperation and communication in an organization go hand in hand. When there is a mutual respect between people, spelling out rules and procedures for communicating is unnecessary.
5. There are several barriers to effective communications. These include failure to listen with respect and understanding, lack of skill in feedback, and misinterpreting the meanings of words used by the speaker. It is also common practice to listen to what we want to hear, and tune out things we do not want to hear.
6. Communication is management's chief problem. The supervisor should accept the challenge to communicate more effectively and to improve interagency and intra-agency communications.
7. The supervisor may often plan for and conduct meetings. The planning phase is critical and may determine the success or the failure of a meeting.
8. Speaking before groups usually requires extra effort. Stage fright may never disappear completely, but it can be controlled.

X. SELF-DEVELOPMENT

1. Every employee is responsible for his own self-development.
2. Toastmaster and toastmistress clubs offer opportunities to improve skills in oral communications.
3. Planning for one's own self-development is of vital importance. Supervisors know their own strengths and limitations better than anyone else.
4. Many opportunities are open to aid the supervisor in his developmental efforts, including job assignments; training opportunities, both governmental and non-governmental -- to include universities and professional conferences and seminars.
5. Programmed instruction offers a means of studying at one's own rate.
6. Where difficulties may arise from a supervisor's being away from his work for training, he may participate in televised home study or correspondence courses to meet his self-develop- ment needs.

XI. TEACHING AND TRAINING

A. The Teaching Process

Teaching is encouraging and guiding the learning activities of students toward established goals. In most cases this process consists in five steps: preparation, presentation, summarization, evaluation, and application.

1. Preparation

Preparation is twofold in nature; that of the supervisor and the employee.

Preparation by the supervisor is absolutely essential to success. He must know what, when, where, how, and whom he will teach. Some of the factors that should be considered are:

(1) The objectives	(5) Employee interest
(2) The materials needed	(6) Training aids
(3) The methods to be used	(7) Evaluation
(4) Employee participation	(8) Summarization

Employee preparation consists in preparing the employee to receive the material. Probably the most important single factor in the preparation of the employee is arousing and maintaining his interest. He must know the objectives of the training, why he is there, how the material can be used, and its importance to him.

2. Presentation

In presentation, have a carefully designed plan and follow it.
The plan should be accurate and complete, yet flexible enough to meet situations as they arise. The method of presentation will be determined by the particular situation and objectives.

3. Summary

A summary should be made at the end of every training unit and program. In addition, there may be internal summaries depending on the nature of the material being taught. The important thing is that the trainee must always be able to understand how each part of the new material relates to the whole.

4. Application

The supervisor must arrange work so the employee will be given a chance to apply new knowledge or skills while the material is still clear in his mind and interest is high. The trainee does not really know whether he has learned the material until he has been given a chance to apply it. If the material is not applied, it loses most of its value.

5. Evaluation

The purpose of all training is to promote learning. To determine whether the training has been a success or failure, the supervisor must evaluate this learning.
In the broadest sense evaluation includes all the devices, methods, skills, and techniques used by the supervisor to keep him self and the employees informed as to their progress toward the objectives they are pursuing. The extent to which the employee has mastered the knowledge, skills, and abilities, or changed his attitudes, as determined by the program objectives, is the extent to which instruction has succeeded or failed.
Evaluation should not be confined to the end of the lesson, day, or program but should be used continuously. We shall note later the way this relates to the rest of the teaching process.

B. Teaching Methods

A teaching method is a pattern of identifiable student and instructor activity used in presenting training material.
All supervisors are faced with the problem of deciding which method should be used at a given time.
As with all methods, there are certain advantages and disadvantages to each method.

1. Lecture

The lecture is direct oral presentation of material by the supervisor. The present trend is to place less emphasis on the trainer's activity and more on that of the trainee.

2. Discussion

Teaching by discussion or conference involves using questions and other techniques to arouse interest and focus attention upon certain areas, and by doing so creating a learning situation. This can be one of the most valuable methods because it gives the employees 'an opportunity to express their ideas and pool their knowledge.

3. Demonstration

The demonstration is used to teach how something works or how to do something. It can be used to show a principle or what the results of a series of actions will be. A well-staged demonstration is particularly effective because it shows proper methods of performance in a realistic manner.

4. Performance

Performance is one of the most fundamental of all learning techniques or teaching methods. The trainee may be able to tell how a specific operation should be performed but he cannot be sure he knows how to perform the operation until he has done so.

5. Which Method to Use

Moreover, there are other methods and techniques of teaching. It is difficult to use any method without other methods entering into it. In any learning situation a combination of methods is usually more effective than anyone method alone.

Finally, evaluation must be integrated into the other aspects of the teaching-learning process.

It must be used in the motivation of the trainees; it must be used to assist in developing understanding during the training; and it must be related to employee application of the results of training.

This is distinctly the role of the supervisor.